About the Author

John Searancke is restaurant reviewer for the Tenerife newspaper *Island Connections*. Born in 1943 at Derby Royal Infirmary, a war baby, he lived his early life in Ashby-de la-Zouch and was sent away to be educated at Kings Mead Preparatory School, Seaford and afterwards at Rugby School. Later commissioned into the Territorial Army, he has been variously an hotel and restaurant owner, director and chairman of a marketing consortium, and latterly a partner with his wife in a commercial legal services company. He has enjoyed working in England and Switzerland and now lives with his wife Sally in northern Tenerife. This is his first book.

www.johnsearancke.com

DOG DAYS IN THE FORTUNATE ISLANDS

A New Life in Hidden Tenerife

John Searancke

Cover design by John Harding
www.johnharding.net

Matador
9 Priory Business Park
Kibworth Beauchamp
Leicestershire LE8 0RX, UK
Tel: (+44) 116 279 2299
Fax: (+44) 116 279 2277
Email: books@troubador.co.uk
Web: www.troubador.co.uk/matador

ISBN 978-1783063-413

British Library Cataloguing in Publication Data.
A catalogue record for this book is available from the British Library.

Typeset in Aldine by Troubador Publishing Ltd
Printed and bound in the UK by TJ International, Padstow, Cornwall

Matador is an imprint of Troubador Publishing Ltd

MIX
Paper from
responsible sources
FSC
www.fsc.org   FSC® C013056

For
Marcus, Tina, Josh & Sam
& my wife Sally
With Love

Contents

Acknowledgements

There are a number of people whom I must thank for their efforts in supporting me through to the production of my final manuscript and beyond. When I first put finger to keyboard, I really did not realise that I knew nothing, absolutely nothing, about the writing and construction of a book. I was about to enter a different world.

Most importantly, I must thank my wife, Sally, who has read each draft, made suggestions and generally supported me through the process, mostly without complaint! Whilst I have enjoyed the process, it must have been a serious trial for her.

My editor, Jennifer Barclay, has been tireless in slicing huge swathes of useless verbiage from the finished product. She has not only shaped my book, she has improved and honed my writing and presentation, let alone my punctuation. Her skill has been greatly to my benefit, and, simply put, I could not have done all this without her. How lucky I am to have met her.

I am grateful to all the people at Troubador Publishing who have worked to bring the manuscript forward to become the finished article. Their help and advice along the way has been invaluable. The publisher, Jeremy Thompson, took my manuscript home with him and read it in his garden, before enthusiastically giving me the green light.

I cannot leave out our dear friend Peter Morgan. He has unwittingly provided me with the basis for some wonderful stories, and joined us on many of our adventures, not least by taking Freddie into his house and treating him as if he were his own. I can never repay him for that.

My thanks also go to John Harding, my talented brother-in-law, who so ably interpreted my wishes for the front cover of this book.

And lastly, I must thank Sheila Collis, Editor of *Island Connections*, for her support and encouragement, and for helping me to promote this book throughout the Canary Islands.

My heartfelt thanks go out to you all.

The great majority of events in this book are true, although I have occasionally changed some names to protect anonymity. My characters have been inspired by real people, my friends, and I hope that they will excuse me if I have inadvertently exaggerated anything in my storytelling. If I have made mistakes, particularly in relation to Spanish laws or protocols, then they are mine, and I hope that I may be forgiven. This is my first book, so please, if you can, look on my work with tolerance and kindness. I still have so much to learn.

1

Arrivals

I peered out through the cabin window as the plane eased down below 20,000 feet, nearly four and a half hours almost due south from our starting point, ever rainy Manchester.

I could clearly see one of my favourite sights, one that I had yet to tire of seeing; that stunning volcano, El Teide. It formed an almost perfect cone, jutting out above a circle of clouds which looked just like pink candy floss in the evening light as the earth slowly tilted on its axis and the sun began to sink below the horizon. And topping the cone was the usual dusting of winter snow. Truly, it was a sight for sore eyes.

We were cruising at what seemed like a snail's pace along the northern side of the island, the captain no doubt twiddling his knobs and dials, and talking with the control tower at the airport further along the coast. By craning my neck, I could just see down to my new home town. But all too soon, the jagged green contoured cliffs passed from view behind puffy balls of cloud.

In almost the blink of an eye we had passed by my hidden Tenerife, the countryside all lush and verdant, with the banana plantations seen from high above, formed up like serried ranks of green soldiers marching downwards from the high valleys towards the sea, descending, in strict battalion formation, from one terrace to the next. All too soon, my view altered again back to rock and crag, and then to a semi-desert landscape, with the occasional wizened and spindly cactus reaching for the sky, hoping to be the first to attract any drop of rain. Here was the best known region of Tenerife, favoured by the mass of package tourists who, for the most part, would only see the wall to wall hotels and beaches of the holiday resorts so beloved by the majority of the visitors to this island.

A bumpy landing in a light, feathery cross-wind prompted some of the passengers to offer up a slow hand-clap as if to suggest they could have done the job a great deal better. Bearing in mind how much the majority of them had enjoyed the bar facilities on board the flight, it was an unlikely thought.

Doors were cranked open and the first blast of hot air, heavily laden with the smell of dry earth, dust, aviation kerosene and all those complex and heady scents that are the essence of Spain blew in through the cabin. While people pushed and shoved to get down the steps, tempers frayed. I sniffed deeply and sat back in my seat, savouring the moment. I was home!

I was the advance guard for my family: Sally, my wife, and Freddie, our dog. Today was the culmination of months of military style planning to ensure that we would all arrive safely in our new home to start a new life, well off the beaten track in northern Tenerife.

Bienvenidos a Tenerife, la isla de la eterna primavera!
Welcome to Tenerife, the island of eternal spring!

Our dear friend Peter was at Tenerife's Reina Sofia southern airport to meet me.

Laden down with two large suitcases and as much other stuff as I could secrete around my person without the authorities believing me to be the reincarnation of the original Michelin man, I must have looked a strange sight as I waddled out towards him, into the arrivals area.

Bags soon stowed away in the back of his car, we drove out of the airport and on to the *autopista*, heading north. It should be just under an hour's run back to base. For the first half hour we had the sea on our right, today with a gusting wind whipping up the *palomas blancas*, little white crested waves. Inland to our left was dry and barren land, nothing growing, nothing much of interest other than the occasional petrol station to interrupt the monotony. After half an hour or so we reached the island capital, Santa Cruz de Tenerife, and turned off up the hill which would take us to the other side of the island. I was always being told by the locals that this bit of *autopista* was the steepest of anywhere in Europe, and I was very ready to believe it. Small cars with even smaller engines resorted to using the crawler lane, their indicators blinking their desperation to reach the top before they expired in a cloud of steam as their radiators gave up the unequal struggle.

As we crested the hill and passed by Los Rodeos, the northern airport, it was as though we were entering another country. Instead of featureless and barren land interspersed with wilting palm trees and spindly cacti, we suddenly had a profusion of bushy, healthy palms, greenery along the sides of the road, shrubs like oleander, hibiscus and bougainvillea bursting into bloom all over the place, and the start of the vines. We were fast approaching vineyard country as the road dropped away. It was only about 15 kilometres now to our home town, and, although I had never tried it because I am a foreigner here and a mite scared of the Spanish gun toting police, I reckoned that I could easily coast all the way back down to Puerto de la Cruz.

Back at the apartment, all was as it should be, since my last visit. Peter had thoughtfully brought me a "welcome pack" of bread, milk, fruit and other staples. After a light meal and a glass of wine I collapsed into bed. Travelling can be so tiring, even though one has seemingly done so little.

There were just two days for me to sort everything out at this end before our dog, Freddie, would be boarding a plane at Manchester Airport to set off into the unknown to join me. Peter and I would again be at the airport in the south, this time going to the cargo area to greet Freddie on his arrival. My heart was in my mouth worrying how he would make the journey safely.

It had all started with my dream; that age old dream of retiring to live in the sun. In that, I and my wife Sally were no different from probably millions of others. But a dream such as that is usually destined to remain just that, a pipedream, unless one can come up with a plan to bring the dream to reality.

Tenerife, well known of old as the most fortunate of The Fortunate Islands, more generally nowadays called The Canaries, still suffered from a rather downmarket image when we first visited together. We had originally gone there together to stay with an old friend. The south seemed infertile and dreary to us; but if you loved a healthy dose of concrete mixed into your holiday menu, then it was assuredly the place for you.

Many years ago, when I was a young man, I had been to Playa de Las Americas – a new and, if you like, artificial resort in the south of Tenerife – for a holiday. The south of the island had not yet been fully developed but there was an acceptable beach, a number of high rise hotels that seemed to be proliferating almost of their own accord, and row upon row of bars. And of course, there was guaranteed sunshine, so important to English people living under grey skies and sporting spotty skins, just like me I suppose. All the talk then was that Richard Burton and Elizabeth Taylor had bought a property in this part of the island, but I never found out if it was true; it was probably a good bit of PR issued by the local *Ayuntamiento* (Town Hall). It was all great fun, but without doubt everyone's expectations all those years ago would have been that much lower.

When Sally and I went years later, the south of Tenerife had spread out to become a vast concrete jungle, a huge built-up metropolis where one small village merged into the next, with an explosion of English type bars serving double egg and chips with pints of lager. It was transitorily inhabited by people of lobster-like hue, often sporting almost completely tattooed bodies. Despite the building of some huge hotels, most looking almost akin to the Acropolis in Greece, with huge fake Doric columns bolted on to their fronts, it all still had a slightly unfortunate image. Cranes towered like giant Praying Mantises over ever spreading rashes of new concrete boxes creeping inland up the hillsides. But it remained extremely popular for package holidays because of the almost guaranteed sunshine, so who can blame people for going there?

The north, however, was green, with banana plantations tumbling down the hillsides, flowers in abundance round every corner, and with a typically local, Spanish way of life. We loved it so much that after that holiday we decided to buy a place, an apartment as a bolthole to get away from the pressures of work. The more we visited, the more we fell in love with the north of the island.

The north and the south of the island are clearly separated by the large volcano El Teide, the highest peak in the whole of Spain, which sits right in the centre of the island, rising majestically to over twelve thousand feet. Being the height that he is (because this volcano is definitely masculine), he creates two entirely differing micro-climates.

While the south is always arid and uncultivated except for the newly created golf courses, sprouting like oases in a desert, and the seemingly never ending ocean of poly tunnels made from flapping opaque plastic that supply the UK in winter with our famous and tasty Canary tomatoes and other (un)seasonable vegetables, the north, our hidden Tenerife, could not be more different.

It's a land of rugged beauty, a region of surging, changing, flowing landscapes, melding quickly between ancient pine forests, hillside vineyards sweeping down the ancient terraces carved out by the indigenous Guanche population of old, then upwards to volcanic formations in prehistoric mountain ranges. Our coastline displays scenery breathtaking in its beauty and savagery, the rainbow of colours from beaches, cliffs, valleys and mountains all offering some of the most spectacular views to be had on earth. The water is unpolluted and clear, and the aquamarine blue of the Atlantic Ocean contrasts boldly with the white surf crashing onto the popular surfing beaches or the rocky foreshore.

It is true that here in the north we enjoy just a little less sunshine, because the cloud formations generated by El Teide tend to hang around until a breeze arrives to waft them away. Those clouds bring us welcome rain and that is why the settlers, from those original Guanches to the mainland Spanish *Conquistadores* and later British settlers, chose to make their homes up here. What small amount of rain that we do enjoy (and enjoy it we most certainly do!) makes our hillsides and valleys into a panorama of different shades of green, from the pale green of fields of lettuce through the deeper hues of the banana plantations, then the vineyards, and on to the solid darker greens of leeks and potato fields. Apart from some of the older, steeper terraces that no mechanical rotovator can nowadays reach economically, everywhere is under cultivation where there is the slightest scrap of soil covering the rock, and every roadside verge is carpeted with wild flowers that seem to bloom all through the year.

It has been said that our micro-climate in the north is that of eternal spring, and that's not far from the truth. I think that only once in the last 60 years has the temperature in "winter" time dropped below 15 degrees at night. During the day, we normally enjoy the low to middle 20s, rising in summer to the early 30s. Very exceptionally, about three times a year, when Africa decides to have a grumble, the hot *La Calima* wind will blow, lifting temperatures to 40 degrees. *La Calima,* raising a dust storm originating deep in the Sahara desert, is driven by the prevailing winds over towards the Canary Islands, and drops what seems to us like most of the aforesaid Sahara onto every surface it can find. We batten down the hatches and ride it out. Afterwards, when it has abated, we open our doors and windows to find our green garden chairs have gone brown, as has every other surface. Cars left out have turned a uniform shade of sepia. It must do wonders for the profits of the local car wash.

2

Taking the Plunge

We decided to look for a place to buy in Puerto de la Cruz. This is the main town in the north excluding the capital, Santa Cruz, which is actually on the other side of the island. Puerto, as the name implies, is the old port to the inland town of La Orotava, and was originally built for trade, shipping bananas and other produce. Now it is a lovely. old fashioned, laid back town, with a slightly faded elegance, and fortunately still more Spanish than tourist, but catering for the more discerning tourist clientele who seek more than just a sun bed and a nightclub.

There is a small collection of tourist hotels down by the Martianez beach, but the town also has attractive, palm fringed streets, some of them now pedestrianised, a number of leafy, shady squares, a small harbour for the dwindling fishing fleet, and a world class lido. There is much talk of revitalisation by the creation of a marina, and we have learned that some funds for this are now in place. When it comes about it will halve the size of the car park by the harbour, which I am reliably informed is still the largest open air free car park in Europe. But it will also bring tourist boat leisure traffic, as well as, we hope, a stop on the inter-island ferry routes.

I originally thought we would end up buying a typical Canary property, long and narrow, dark and cool, with perhaps a balcony upstairs, and a flat roof above for the drying of our laundry in the Atlantic breezes. Garage space we reckoned to be vital – we had seen so many cars with their paintwork faded or bubbled due to the intense summer heat.

Our first port of call had been to set up an arrangement with a friendly bank. What could sound friendlier than a bank rejoicing in the name of Solbank? It is a subsidiary of one of the largest banks in Spain, dealing specifically with those seeking to move to the Canary Islands to live, for business or retirement. We marched in there clutching a letter of introduction from our bankers in England. Everyone was amiable and helpful and in no time at all we had Spanish bank accounts and letters of credit.

That sorted, it was time to do the rounds of those whom we might call estate agents, although they offered a different type of service to those back in England. We ended up going to half a dozen to see what they had on their books at a price we could afford. Our specification was for something typically Canarian, but with a garage or secure, covered, off road parking. A small garden area would be a bonus for Freddie.

Some of the agents we visited either had nothing suitable on their books, or expressed profound lack of interest in our quest. Some could not even be bothered to raise their corpulent frames from the comfort of their reclining leather chairs in their air conditioned offices.

Then we were pointed towards one particular agent, a lady who had lived in Tenerife for many years, and who showed us a number of different properties, some old, some newer, but none of them matching our stated criteria. We ended up feeling pretty depressed, and trying hard not to show it, by the end of the third day. We had looked at probably 20 opportunities and had not liked any of them. Fair enough we thought, what we were looking for just was not on the market at that moment. We could afford to wait, and come back on another visit in a few months.

"Well, I do have just one more property to show you," said Collette.

"Oh, no thanks, Collette, you have been wonderful, but it's been a hard three days and we are both knackered and possibly a bit tetchy too, by now! But thanks for all your efforts."

"Just come and have a look at this last one on my list. I know it's not what you have asked for, but I have got some idea now of what pleases you and what doesn't, over these last few days. I can drive you there within ten minutes."

"OK, you win. Let's go."

We drew up at this large complex, seemingly brand new. Our hearts sank in unison. We did not need to say anything as one glance between us was enough.

But we were there now, and had to put a brave face on it; so off we went to give it the once over.

We were shown up from a very smart, cool, underground garage into a lift and thence to a brand new ground floor apartment. It was painted throughout in the most delicate and tasteful shade of pale yellow, with white coving and ceilings. All the floors were light beige coloured marble, giving a spacious, upmarket feel to the place. Everything clearly had been constructed to a very high standard.

"You are the first to see this apartment. It was only released by the developer at the beginning of this week, and I have an exclusive on it."

"Oh yeah?" I mumbled as an aside. Where have we heard that one before? But strangely, it turned out to be true.

We walked around, and were taken through to the back terrace. It looked out over lovely gardens which had already been landscaped. Semi-mature bushes and palm trees were dotted around everywhere. Somebody had invested an awful lot of money on this building.

Collette could see that she had finally captured our interest.

"But this is nothing like the specification that we have asked for!" I cried.

"No," came the swift riposte, "but I think it would really suit you both. I have been taking on board everything that you have said over the last three days about the other properties that I have shown you. Do you quite like it, then?" she asked again.

"Weeeell…"

"OK. I also have another one, so come next door. I have the key for that one as well."

She had got our measure, and was reeling us in like a salmon on a line. We went next door. It was half as large again! It had an extra bathroom, both bedrooms were larger and there was a full sized kitchen, a separate storage room, a utility room, and so on. It was right on the end of the block, and so came with two terraces, one very large (again, double the size of the others) and a small garden round the side.

And from both terraces there were views of El Teide!

"How much is this one, then?" I asked, careful to keep my enquiry noncommittal.

"Well, it is just a little bit above your budget. But what do you think of it? Could you be happy here?"

This last question was eased across to us as we went out into the gardens and looked down towards the huge, free form swimming pool.

We were secretly bowled over, but trying hard to keep straight faces. Indeed, the price was more than we wanted to pay. But the extra money (which we could at that time ill afford) gave us half as much space again, with much better facilities. Was that all it would cost for so much more space? It was far and away the best place that we had seen so far, by a country mile. It came with a ten year developer guarantee, and the vital underground garage space.

We looked at each other, and the look said it all. There was no need for us to speak. Between us, we knew that we should go for it.

"Well," I said to Collette, "there is a lot to discuss. It is very different to what we had in mind. We will have to think about it overnight. As you know, we are going back to England tomorrow evening. I'll call you in a day or so after we get home."

"Don't leave it too long. It's the best apartment in the whole building, and it will be snapped up."

What did I say about being reeled in? Smart lady, that Collette.

By just after lunchtime the next day we felt that we had held back sufficiently not to seem too enthusiastic, and we called her.

"Can we go back and have another quick peek at that place again? Do a few measurements? We can just find the time before we have to leave for the airport."

Collette collected us and we walked back in and it felt really good. We were still playing it cool, but I am sure that Collette had realised that she had a purchase on her hands.

"I'll definitely ring you in a day or two, one way or the other." I said, shaking her by the hand, after we had taken a good mooch round. "Can I take an option on it, just for a few days?"

"I'm sorry, no. As I told you, this place will sell very quickly."

So, the next day I called her back, and that, as they say, was that. Mission accomplished. We are still in love with the place eight years later. Whilst a number of the apartments in our building were bought as holiday apartments or just bought and locked up as investments, the majority are owned by families who live and work locally. As such, *siesta* here is strictly observed, and the whole place goes silent between 2 and 4 p.m. No lawnmower or drill is permitted to break the peace and quiet.

Our thought all those years ago was that it was only going to be a holiday home; indeed it should be available to be let out as an extra source of income in between our own visits, to service the mounting outgoings.

Sally, being Sally, then furnished it all so nicely and tastefully that she flatly refused to let it out.

Estate agents in the Canaries are a different type of animal and fulfil very different needs. For example, you would find it really hard to get any one of them to put a sales price on your property, preferring you to name your own requirement instead. It can lead to some strange anomalies and there are always oddly priced homes on sale everywhere. On the upside, they do deal on your behalf with part of the legal side of the transaction, liaising with your bank and also the notary public for the legal approval to the sale and the registration of the property.

There is an almost impenetrable fog surrounding the various taxes that must be paid when you buy a property. The rate of these taxes varies dependent upon whether you purchase a new property or a re-sale property. There is then an on-going tax on your property value (which we might know as the rates) and a number of others too, including an annual Wealth Tax. All of these were a nightmare of bureaucracy for us new members of Tenerife society and it is fair to say that, had it not been for a few guiding hands that steered us from one requirement to the next, we would have found it very hard work to get things done at the right time, with the right people. We were also very lucky to have been introduced to Paul Montague, a well-known financial adviser on the island, a partner in a major European practice. He helped us enormously, proving once again the old adage: *it's not what you know, it's who you know.*

When we first purchased the apartment, just as a holiday home, we learned that we must obtain an NIE Certificate from the police, which would give us a certain Spanish residency and quasi-legal status. Your NIE is also your tax identification number, affirming your legitimacy to be in Spain as more than just a casual holidaymaker.

In order to obtain our NIE numbers we had to collect forms

from the main central police station and take them away to be filled in with such information as our address here in Tenerife, reasons for being here, ages, nationalities and marital status and from where we originated. All in all, not too arduous, and we managed to complete them successfully.

The difficult part was getting the forms accepted and stamped by the authorities. So, it was back to the police station. Outside in the street there were lines of people queuing. We went to the front and explained to the bored officer in charge that we were humble foreigners, wanting to get our NIE forms stamped. We were summarily dismissed and directed back out into the street and told to join the end of the queue.

It was so hot out there, no shade at all. We baked in the sun for what seemed like hours, and the queue hardly seemed to move. But eventually we were shunted into a large, airless waiting room and called forward to sit before a gorgon of a woman whom we had seen through the glass partition handling previous customers. She had not learned the advantages of smiling, nor possessed any people skills whatsoever. In her job, perhaps she did not need them.

We sat down in front of her desk. She continued to shuffle papers and did not look up at us.

I coughed politely. It elicited no response.

Behind her desk was a magnificent aerial photograph of Santiago de Compostela on the Peninsula, as the mainland of Spain is called by Canarians. Perhaps it might be a clue?

"That is a truly stunning photograph of Santiago." I opened the batting.

She looked up at me, looked across to the picture, and then smiled beatifically.

"Yes, *señor*, indeed it is. I was born there and grew up there. Do you know the city?"

The ice was broken, and I haltingly asked a few questions about the city, and what had brought her to Tenerife. As usual, the answer was a husband. In no time at all our forms were stamped and we were sent on our way with cheery good wishes. Now all that was needed was to register them at the Town Hall, the tongue twisting *Ayuntamiento*.

3

Peter & the Poodles

Soon after we had bought our place in Tenerife, but before we had moved here permanently with Freddie, we were having a short break away from work and rain back in England, and were invited by our friend Peter to accompany him on an afternoon out. It turned out to be an afternoon never to be forgotten; and, for that matter, it lasted well past the afternoon.

Peter has lived in Tenerife for about 17 years, originally hailing from the West Country, where he owned a coaching inn type hotel which he had bought and improved until it became one of the best on Dartmoor. It was a toss-up as to whether he or his hotel was more famous across three counties.

He is now owned by his two big black standard poodles, Millie and her daughter Poppy (more usually known as Nipper for obvious reasons), and his life has become entirely subsumed to their wishes. His life revolves around them, and indeed, they are his life. About the size of small Shetland ponies, and famous in his village, they cause quite a stir when he walks them to the square to meet with us for coffee.

Peter has recently knocked on the door of 70, and passed through successfully. After 17 years, he knows a lot of people over here, and he has worked hard at it. But he does not appear to have managed to shed his old life completely. Everything that he says is always related back to his roots. When he opens up his computer in the morning, lo and behold, the first thing to be automatically displayed is the weather forecast for that day in the West Country.

When he phones us, the usual opening is along the lines of: "Do you know, it's only four degrees back in Newton Abbot."

"Well, yes, Peter, but neither of us is in Newton Abbot today, are we?"

"I know, but isn't it really amazing that whilst we are sitting out on our terraces here, they are shivering in their boots back in Devon?"

"Isn't that why we live out here instead, Peter?" What more can I say?

He always gets the last word, though. "It's so windy back there that it's flattening the palm trees on the promenade at Torquay!"

Conversations are ever peppered with the goings on back in deepest Devon. Who has been doing what, with or to whom, who has been where, and everything you may conceive in between. Never having met any of his friends from back there, we nevertheless feel that we know them so well by now. He is still a walking advertisement for tourism to Devon. And yet he just loves Tenerife. And we both love him dearly.

Peter has a sister back in Devon, a farmer of a smallholding, keeping a variety of animals. She is one of the nicest people we know, and we enjoy her company greatly when she comes over on her annual visit to stay with Peter. We will sit with a cold bottle of wine and she will regale us with stories of life down on the farm. We hear about her horses (one sadly has just died of old age), her llamas (presented to her when the owners gave up on them for being too much trouble), her small flock of sheep (off to market, some of them, and then into her big freezers, later to be sold at the farm gate), her pigs (which annually grace the charity pig-out that she runs for the local village), her ducks, her hens and so many more. What a menagerie for us to keep up to date with!

Meanwhile, Peter is simply the most generous person that we know, and I take my hat off to him. We count ourselves lucky to have him as a friend.

We discovered that he had recently given his sister a present of a mature olive tree. Whilst on one of her holidays to Tenerife, she had been admiring the large olive trees that you see over here. I imagine that the conversation may have gone somewhat along the following lines:

"Peter! Just look at that olive tree! Isn't it just fantastic!"

"Well, my dear, yes it is, but why so excited about an olive tree?"

"Oh, you know. It's probably silly, but I've always wanted one of my own."

"Mmmm. But on a farm in deepest Devon?"

"Yes, I suppose that I am being silly."

Cut to a month or so later, when a large lorry tried to back into her farmyard, carrying an immense, fully grown olive tree that had probably started its journey in Greece. As I said, Peter is the most generous of people.

The two poodles, Millie and Poppy, are a bit lacking in the training and intelligence department. What they keep between their ears continues to mystify us all. But they do have the loveliest of natures. Peter, we learnt, liked to take them in his van-with-windows up into the hills for a good run each week. He would park in the woods on the lower slopes, often in a public picnic area, and the dogs would rocket around until exhausted. All in all, good fun was had by all three of them.

The phone rang one lunchtime. It was Peter.

"I am taking the dogs out a bit later on when it gets cooler. Would you like to come? We can go up into the hills and you will see a bit of Tenerife that perhaps you have not yet seen. Oh, and I have another dog staying with me at the moment, Tia, she is so sweet. Come round and we can all pack in together."

"Great! Sounds fun. We'd love to come along."

Off we went to his house to meet up with them all. Three humans, two immense poodles and a medium sized dog; all packed like sardines into his small van-with-windows.

Peter bowled along, the van beginning to wheeze as it attempted the steep gradients towards the mountains, and, quite a distance up into the foothills, we dived off without warning to the right along a completely unmade track. I started thinking about tyres and the inevitable damage that must be caused by travelling over such a rough and sharp surface. However, my thoughts moved on rather quickly to the entire underneath of the vehicle, because it was taking the most terrible pounding from almost man-sized boulders casually strewn across our path, perchance by giants of old. You couldn't hear anyone speak for the din of rock pounding on the chassis. The dogs went into what I assumed was a catatonic trance. Sally blanched.

"No problem. Don't worry at all." shouted Peter through the din, while rather unnervingly facing almost backwards to chat to us. "We've been up here before, lots of times. Well, perhaps not quite so far up, though." he added as an afterthought.

Higher and higher we went, past clearings and fire breaks, and eventually the track widened and we popped out into an open area in which lay the vestigial remains of a picnic area, possibly last camped in by Neanderthal man.

We pulled to a halt, and everyone tumbled out, gasping for breath. It certainly was much cooler right up there, and that was very welcome after the game of sardines enacted out over the last hour. We stretched our legs. The poodles did the same, more literally, by flying off over the nearest horizon.

"No problem," says Peter. "They'll be back in a bit when they have let off steam."

We wandered about, admiring the scenery. El Teide definitely looked a lot closer from where we stood. And the snow on top of it was having a definite effect on the temperature.

"How long does this steam-letting-off generally take?" I eventually asked.

"Oh, anything up to half an hour or so."

And so we waited, and waited. We wandered to and fro, feeling the chill in the air, raising goose pimples on our arms.

Tia, easily the oldest of us in doggy terms, tired of it all first. She went and lay down by the van.

"Will they really be coming back?" asked Sally. "I'm getting a bit chilly now because I have no coat."

"Me too," said I.

Peter was still playing it cool and trying to look unconcerned.

"Well, they know the way, so perhaps they have set off back down the mountain and will meet us at the bottom."

Eh? Those dogs were bonkers. We all knew that. They had a problem finding each other when they were standing side by side.

We had started calling out for them a while ago and it had made us all hoarse by now, and Peter was getting just a tad less cool about it all. His decision was that we move off downhill because the light was fading fast, and pick up the trail lower down. Just how did you pick up the trail of two black poodles in the dark on an unknown mountainside?

About halfway back down, we came to a halt at a junction in the track next to a crumbling refuge hut, which looked a bit like an old stone built bus shelter would look like, back in civilization. We pulled up by it and got out of the van, but could now hardly see anything in the dark because the clouds had come down and it was very misty too. Elderly Tia and Sally (a little younger) huddled together in the refuge. Peter decided to set off down to the main road without us in case his dogs had fetched up there. We were to remain and stand on the track, shouting to attract the pesky poodles.

We watched the glow of the tail lights fading away downhill into the murk. It was not a comforting sight.

It was getting damned cold. The mist had really settled. We were actually worried by then about Tia, because she was shaking. It was totally silent except for my calls. Time ticked on by.

Suddenly, there was a roaring noise, and a white Land Rover with the park ranger logo emblazoned on the side came hurtling down the hill out of the gloom, headlights cutting a fuzzy swathe through the swirling mist. It slowed marginally as the driver gave a cheery wave to us huddled there in that refuge, and then proceeded merrily on his way down the other fork in the track, the headlights and exhaust note quickly swallowed up in the darkness. Did the stupid bloke think we were stuck there just for fun?!

In the dark and thick mist, it had all looked like a ghostly apparition. We were totally stuck where we were. We had nowhere to go, and we could not leave anyway.

About half an hour later, a black poodle, grinning unconcernedly, popped her head round the side of the refuge. We screamed and shouted at her, and, then there came the other one, ambling down the track, grinning from ear to ear, I could swear. So I did, extremely rudely.

Tia was too cold to even greet them. We were too cold to properly scold them. Our mobile phone did not work because of lack of signal. All we could do was wait, and wait.

It seemed like hours before Peter got tired of staking out the main road down below and thought of us again. We finally saw headlights lurching up the track, and we were all reunited.

We could not wait to get home for a large brandy and a hot bath. Sally and I went back to our apartment, but all we could think about was what would have been our reaction should one of those dogs have been Freddie?

Never again!

Those were grand times that we had in Tenerife after we had bought the apartment. It seems that we had a particular story to tell from each visit to the island. It was all cementing our decision to eventually settle there and put down roots.

Like ourselves, Peter likes exploring. Why sit in a tourist restaurant for an average meal when you can discover somewhere new and exciting off the beaten track? We often chose a place up in the hills, unknown to tourists where the food is better, and half the price to boot. One evening, he picked us up and drove us to a place that he, and later we, just called "Chicken & Chips."

Out of Puerto we went, snaking up the valley, taking the road towards Santa Ursula. Halfway along the main street of that town Peter started accelerating. We held on tight to each other as he suddenly swerved off the main road and careered up a narrow side street as fast as he could go. This, we saw, was to combat the extremely steep hill that faced us. How cars got up there and parked outside the houses seemed to us to be a miracle. The road was mostly only wide enough for one at a time, so if you were unfortunate and met someone coming down, you might have to display the long forgotten driving test requirement of the (dreaded) hill start. Not that the English authorities would have allowed a road to be constructed at such a steep angle. It was not a place for the uninitiated or the faint hearted.

"Where on earth are we going, Peter?" I said.

"Nearly there now, just a bit further up this hill."

And almost immediately from Sally came, "Peter, I can see headlights coming down towards us." She was a nervous back seat passenger.

Peter kept on grinding down through the gears. No lower one was now possible in his gearbox.

"Peter, I know that car is coming towards us, but we can't afford to stop, can we? You will never get going again. Surely he will brake to let us past?"

"And if he doesn't?"

"Oh, shut up then and keep going!!"

Eventually we pulled up at the very top of the hill. The procedure then was to turn the car around in the lane hardly wider than the car, so as not to have to do it after the intake of wine would make it well-nigh impossible without altering the superstructure of the vehicle. We tottered out of his van, with the front wheels firmly turned into the kerb to prevent the car avalanching down to the town far below, and we wedged a large rock against one too, just to be on the safe side. A number of such rocks seemed to have been thoughtfully placed there by the management.

We were really high up in the valley, and the views were stupendous in the clear evening light. We could see right down the coast, the waves foaming in white lines as they broke on the base of the cliff edges. The sea gave off a silvery pewter sheen in the early moonlight. Such views of our hidden Tenerife would never be seen by most tourists.

We entered the place. I did not really know what to call it. You couldn't use one of the more regular names, such as restaurant or bistro. It was just a large room on the side of a tumbledown old house, in the corner of which was an immense brazier with a rudimentary extractor hood over it. Regardless of the extractor, it was throwing out a fierce heat into the room. The room might have originally been painted white, but the smoke being chucked out from the brazier and the associated heat had turned everything almost yellow. Around the walls hung, quite randomly, a number of old agricultural implements, probably well over a hundred years old. I seem to remember the odd picture too, faded and at a bit of an angle. It was that sort of place.

There was a huge wooden hay fork, perfectly carved and shaped, with three long tines. Was it just for show, or were the Guanche inhabitants of old really giants?

We chose to sit in the corner furthest away from the maximum heat. The table was covered in plastic oilcloth, the pattern long faded to almost nothing by continuous usage. An extremely elderly lady, lacking the majority of her teeth, came over and stood by the table. Clad all in black, she asked our wishes. We in turn asked for a menu. There was no menu, but we could see pieces of chicken on the brazier, and also vast slabs of pork. We could not understand her (was the problem the lack of teeth, the local dialect or our poor Spanish?). So we ordered the chicken by pointing to it, and it soon arrived, piled high on a platter, with a mountain of really good chips. Half a chicken each, it was absolutely delicious, basted with herbs and some gentle spices, all a mix secretly handed down, no doubt, through the generations.

Drink was something else. Whether you wanted red or white wine, it would be as cold as from a Swiss mountain stream, the container it came in glistening with condensation. This wasn't wine in proper bottles with corks. This was local village wine, grown on their own doorstep, and kept in a huge keg or *garrafón*. Our container for the wine that night was an old litre Grolsch lager bottle. On a later night, we were demoted to a bottle looking suspiciously like an old bedpan or something similar that would have been equally at home in a hospital. But the flavour was good!

How we got back down to the main road, or even back home, was something that was better being everlastingly shrouded in mystery.

But we kept on going back there. The chicken was so delicious, and the prices were so cheap. That man on the brazier, probably her husband, did the best chicken anywhere, ever. Perhaps the basic flavour was enhanced by all the drops of sweat that seemed to leave his brow in rivulets.

We had been going there quite regularly for about five years, but on the last occasion, we crunched to a stop outside, and the place was closed, shrouded in darkness. Had we come on a closure night? No, surely not? It was the weekend, and their normal closure day was a Monday. Perhaps they were away on holiday?

A couple of locals were sitting on the front step of the house next door, chatting away in a cloud of pungent cigarette smoke.

"It's closed next door." You could tell that our Spanish was not yet really up to speed.

"You have come to eat there?" said one of them.

"Yes, we have been many times before. Why is it closed?"

"Ah, the lady of the house has died." (She who had served us, with the lack of teeth.) "Without her, nobody wished to continue. The family is desolate."

We spent a moment or two commiserating with them and mumbled some appropriate words, then, with the usual difficulty in such a tight space, we turned the car around for the roller coaster ride back down the hill.

So sad, and we still talk about that extraordinary place many years later.

4

The Point of No Return

Hard at the grindstone back in England, a couple of years after we had first bought the apartment, we were just returned from one of our M6 commutes to Manchester when an old friend and ex-colleague from a previous business, Duncan, called for a chat, the result of which would form the springboard to alter our futures.

"Hi, John. How are you both? What are you doing for the weekend in three weeks' time?" He knew it was no use asking unless he gave us a lot of prior warning.

"Why?" said I a bit guardedly, not wishing to be pushed into anything that I might later regret.

"Oh, stop being such bores, the pair of you. You're always working. How about coming with us to the Great Yorkshire Show? Lewis and Patricia are going to come along, and with the six of us, it will be like old times. We thought that we would stay at Ascot House Hotel in Harrogate for two or three nights. I've provisionally reserved three rooms for us all. Are you on?"

It sounded a good idea to both of us, and having consulted our diaries, we called him straight back.

"Yes, count us in. Will you confirm our hotel booking when you do yours?"

"Will do, and Lewis and Patricia send their love, and we are all looking forward to getting together again."

The annual Great Yorkshire Show was a huge event, not just for the people of Yorkshire. It was going to be held just outside the town of Harrogate, and hundreds of thousands of people would pour through the gates during the week that it was on.

The six of us arranged to meet at the hotel three weeks hence. Freddie went to visit his friends at the local kennels, where he was always made a great fuss of. He always enjoyed going, and never once displayed the slightest nervousness that he might be being returned whence he had originally come. He was the favourite boarder, we were told.

Where can one go for afternoon tea in Harrogate other than Betty's Tearooms? They are assuredly famous the world over, and the place is always packed. We lived in hope of getting a table, and fortunately people got up at the same time as we arrived and we all got seated together. We tried not to gorge ourselves too much on the renowned cakes as there would be a special dinner that evening. Our four friends seemed to have a bit of an agenda going, however, and we were the targets. Both couples were retired from their hotels, one from Glasgow and the other from a little town in Northumberland. We were regaled with stories of the wonderful lives that they led now that they were no longer shackled to their businesses.

One couple had bought property in Florida, and went out there for part of the year to avoid the harshness of the northern winter. The others had moved out of the city to the seaside a little further south, he having taken on a directorship of a football club. It all seemed like hard work to me, but the message was coming across, loud and clear.

Retirement!

It was about time that we did something about this retirement business. Neither of us was getting any younger, although I teased Sally that she still had a bit of mileage in her yet.

The next day turned out bright, clear and warm. We could not have picked a better day for the visit. We got a lift to the showground and were soon walking round the exhibits. There were companies selling every type of agricultural machinery that you could think of. The price of tractors seemed to be stratospheric, and I realised that you could buy a new Bentley for the price of some of them. There was every sort of animal that you can imagine, cows, bulls, horses, goats, sheep, and they were all being groomed to the "nth" degree for the show ring.

Over a cold beer, it was time for Duncan to bend my ear again.

"Do you have a plan for your retirement? I know that the new business is doing well, but surely you must be thinking of letting go fairly soon?"

"Well, it's a bit difficult. It took a while to get it all going to this level, and it seems a shame to let it go when it is now doing so well."

Lewis chimed in. "Yes, but none of us are getting any younger, and retirement is really suiting us".

I suspected that Sally would be receiving something similar from Joan and Patricia.

The three girls went off the next day for a pampering afternoon at some local spa that was clearly going to cost an arm and a leg, while we chaps went off for half a day to the Royal Armouries in Leeds, and had a wonderful time looking round all the medieval exhibits there. Sally reported back that her ear was bent in no uncertain fashion.

Actually, Sally and I had been lately discussing how we could have an easier time of it without parting with the business. Perhaps they were right and we really should be thinking of selling and retiring?

"You always seem to be popping off to Tenerife for short breaks, so how about going for longer? Who would want to be in England in winter nowadays?" said Patricia, over dinner that night. She had a good point. We did love our time in Tenerife, where we could sit in the sun and recharge our batteries to be ready for the next onslaught. We found ourselves going there more and more often. So how about making it permanent?

In truth, we were burnt out, we knew it and they knew it, and we had to find a way of putting our feet up for good. Our time with those four friends was to prove the catalyst for the big push to permanent retirement.

And the incessantly rainy weather of Lancashire had continued to take its toll on our health and happiness. A lovely county is Lancashire, but it seems to have a monopoly on the world supply of endless precipitation. Of all the places that I have lived, Lancashire is by far the wettest. I dreamed of moving permanently to the sunny climes of Tenerife.

Was the time right? Could we find a buyer? How much could we ask? How on earth could I fund a retirement when there would be no regular income coming in to support us? It was a frightening prospect in the dire economic climate that prevailed.

Before I met Sally, I had enjoyed a chequered life, always self-employed as I could never reconcile myself to working for someone else and therefore not being in charge of my own destiny. Latterly I'd owned and operated an hotel in Sussex for a number of years with a one and then two AA Rosette restaurant. When you have two AA Rosettes awarded year on year, customers expect a pretty high level of quality and expertise. I'd sold it whilst it was all on a high and took a few months off, but it was not long before I got itchy feet once again. Life still held a few challenges, I hoped.

The sale of my hotel roughly coincided with my divorce from my first wife and, as a result of the financial implications of the latter, I found that instead of continuing to drive my beloved Porsche, I had now become the proud owner of a ten year old Toyota, the engine of which had clearly passed its optimum in terms of life cycle, and which leaked through the sunroof. It never let me down though, and I had it for a couple of years, but I could not wait until something better was affordable. I am sure that there were many so-called friends having a laugh at me behind closed doors.

It was therefore time to pick myself up and start all over again. I needed a job that was going to help me achieve the lifestyle that I had lost. When my father died, he had not left me one brass farthing, just a load of problems, and I had had to make my own way in life since I left school. Now, I felt that I was going to have to go through the same sort of process all over again in order to rebuild a business and get back a life. I was now much older, with more experience of life, but the corollary of that was that, being older, all things would be that much more difficult.

I took great comfort from both my son Marcus and Sally to help me through this very difficult period and I could not have asked for more. But a well-paid job was paramount, and that right soon.

Sally had been the Financial Director of an SME and my friends kept telling me that I could sell anything to anyone, so between us we decided to go the route of buying a franchise where the initial hard work had been done for us. We eventually bought a franchise with a large national legal services company. Our patch was to be Greater Manchester. I think that it was the largest area that our franchisor had ever handed out. They wanted to split the area into three franchises, but either through luck or skilled negotiation, we held out for the lot.

We went back to the schoolroom to learn our new business. The weeks spent at the Head Office down in Sussex were filled with all aspects of training for us to be able to service our new clients properly whilst earning a reasonable living out of the process. Figures for likely income were bandied about, though we had long ago learned to take such things with the proverbial pinch of salt. But if we earned half of what they said, we would have a good business on our hands.

At the end of it all came the inevitable series of examinations. I had never been good at exams, struggling to six O Levels and two A Levels. But we got all the ticks in the right boxes at the end, and went home happy. Those exams had been pretty heavy duty, and I knew that there would be more of the same to come as we continued to grow into our new business. CPD (Continuous Professional Development) would become part of our lives, with a high number of minimum hours being required for on-going training each and every year.

It was now time to go into action. Full of energy, we set off into the great unknown. Little did I realise that both of us would be travelling down that motorway to Manchester most days thereafter, as we sought to establish a profitable client base.

We grew through word of mouth and soon the letterbox each day would be opened to reveal a pile of incoming business. I was soon also organising, supporting and training other franchisees in the north of England, all for the benefit of the mother ship, but with only a little extra reward.

After some four years, it was getting too much for just the two of us. Was it time to let our franchise go and branch out for ourselves? It would mean jettisoning our original investment, but we had comprehensively learned our business and were paying more in royalties each year back to our franchisor than a lot of people would have been earning as a salary. And so the die was cast. We parted with our franchisor on good terms and so our own brand was born, freed from the shackles of a franchise. There was soon more business, more work, more profit. But less time off. It was all going too well.

That's when we'd flown to Tenerife for a holiday, discovered the unspoilt northern part of the island, and fell for it. But now, the pull of the north of the island was growing ever stronger. Maybe, as our friends had said, it was time to let go of the business and make the big leap?

It was nearly time for my 65th birthday.

People have told me that they dreaded this milestone in their lives. Perhaps they saw it more as a millstone than a milestone. I was approaching it as just another birthday. Marcus, Tina, Josh and Sam were coming up from Hove to stay with us for the weekend, and that was good enough for me. Sally was going all out to ensure that it would be a time to be remembered.

I had no idea that anything particularly special had been planned until an enormous white stretched limousine glided to a halt at the bottom of the driveway. The grandchildren were glued to the bay window in the drawing room. The driver (or should I call him the chauffeur?) walked up the drive, and rang the bell.

"Good evening, sir. My name is John, and your wife has booked our service for the next three hours. Are you all ready to accompany me? I have chilled champagne waiting on board."

Looking at the car, champagne was just what I needed. I was still in shock. So were Marcus and Co. There was already a cluster of neighbours gathered on the pavement, wondering what all the fuss was about. Not that stretched limos were a rarity; we were only ten miles south of Blackpool, after all, probably their spiritual home.

With the six of us piled inside, there was still a lot of room to spare. It was all grey leather, with a cocktail cabinet, a television, the full works. Champagne and soft drinks were passed around, and off we went. It was a very strange feeling at first to see the front end of the car going round the corner before we had reached it in the back seat.

"Where are we going on this magical mystery tour?" I asked of John.

"To Blackpool, sir," was his reply. We were going to Blackpool? But if it was to Blackpool we were to go, then I was determined to milk it for all it was worth.

The pace was slow and stately. I could probably have cycled faster. But no matter, the grandchildren had a window down and took to it like ducks to water. They waved to passers-by, and incredibly, everyone smiled and waved back. I decided to join in, much to the mortification of Marcus. There was much fun to be had from all this.

In time we arrived at South Shore. The car pulled up. We were told by John that it was a photo opportunity. All the people on stag and hen nights liked to be photographed here. We alighted to see a huge glitter ball on a pole the height of a lamp post, slowly revolving in the early evening sunshine. No, surely not? I was hustled into position with everyone else, and we were all recorded for posterity by the ever smiling John.

And then it was off once again to yet another photo opportunity, helped by the issue of another bottle of champagne. At the back of my mind was a small niggle about what I was to be cooking for dinner that evening, until it dawned on me that we were all going to Portofino restaurant in Lytham.

We cruised up and down Blackpool seafront, admiring the view and the locals, as they all seemed to be admiring us. We were but one of many stretched limousines out that night, but no matter, I saw only the one, with my family all around me. What more could I ask? Simple pleasures are often the best. It had been the perfect gift from Sally.

If we were going to move to Tenerife permanently, we felt that we needed to obtain family approval for moving so far away from our loved ones.

Sally floated our ideas past her elderly parents who lived in Poulton le Fylde, a village near to Blackpool. They were most supportive, knowing full well that she had a life to lead, and that she would, without doubt, get back to England to see them on a regular basis.

For my part, I had only my son, Marcus, and his immediate

family to consider. The discussion was held, and his answer came back to me straight away.

"Go for it!"

This was typical of Marcus, and he added that he would no doubt see more of me when I lived over 2,000 miles away than when I lived in Lancashire. We would have more quality time together, at least a week or more per visit, rather than the current snatched weekends between the increasing workload of our current business. I did like that thinking of his.

The dream was nearly in the bag. Now it was time to flesh out our plan to turn it into reality.

We had budgets to prepare, a house to sell, a business to sell, cars to sell, and a myriad of other ties to be cut. Accountants and solicitors would need to be drafted in. Estate agents would need to be retained. All of this would need to be co-ordinated into one great plan, and a batting order would need to be agreed, and hopefully stuck to.

The plan was going to be a five year one for various reasons. To demonstrate to the powers that be that we were correctly distancing ourselves from the clutches of the UK tax regime, we would need to follow the strict guidelines, and the guideline period was co-incidentally a minimum of five years away from the UK (excluding timed and documented visits back). No problem for us! I, for one, would be happy to sit on a sunny terrace for a lot longer than that.

When we first decided to move to Tenerife, like many others in a similar position, we cobbled together some "pros" and "cons." Looking back on it all now, our thoughts didn't really make it on to a formalized document. A bottle of claret had helped no end in producing some sort of a list, which, if I remember correctly, went, in no particular order of importance, on the "pro" side, something like this:

- Less rain than in Lancashire
- Big savings on Spanish taxes, fuel, food and wine
- No central heating would be required

- A swimming pool on site for daily exercise
- Proximity to cafés, restaurants, food shops etc.
- Tax savings back in the UK from becoming officially non-resident
- The atmosphere of living in a Spanish community
- More flexible pension arrangements
- A healthier and warmer climate
- More foreign travel opportunities in retirement

On the "con" side, we were a bit stumped to get further than lack of Spanish language and distance from remaining family. These were easily disposed of, the first by the rhetorical question of "How difficult can that be?" and the latter by referring to the easyJet timetable. That bottle of claret clearly had quite a lot of in-built benefits.

And so, with that, we retired to bed. Would that reality should prove to be so easy!

We would be in for some rude awakenings and disasters along the way.

5

Freddie

I can't really remember being without a dog in the family. First there had been Max, a Dalmatian, and then Brandy, a Labrador. After I finished my schooling away at Rugby, along came Becket, a Cairn terrier who introduced me to the pleasures of cleaning vomit from the vinyl seats of my Ford Anglia when I collected him from a farm near Stratford upon Avon and took him back to my home in Ashby de la Zouch. That one journey cured him of car sickness and he then travelled with me everywhere. Later came Midge and her daughter Moss, both Border terriers, and now, and finally, there is Freddie.

Freddie is truly a one off. We love him to bits.

He is quite a bit larger than a Jack Russell, and chunkier too, with an undocked tail, and rippling muscles. His tail forms an almost perfect circle so that, as he walks, the end bounces along his spine. He is white, with a black head and ears, and two large black spots, some 4 inches wide, on his back. There is clearly some Staffie ancestry in him too. He is really a big softie, though he is equipped with the jaws and teeth to win any argument. He came to us courtesy of the local branch of the RSPCA situated between Lytham and Blackpool, where he had been taken in at a very few weeks old when found walking the streets of Blackpool, abandoned to his fate.

How could anyone be so cruel to an animal at so young an age?

We had already seen so many deserving dogs at that RSPCA sanctuary, and it was with heavy hearts that we presented ourselves for the third time at their door, still on the search for our perfect doggie companion. Freddie was brought through to the reception area by one of the kennel maids (he was still too young to be put on display in one of the cages) and he sealed the deal by immediately piddling on my new shoes. It was love at first sight on both sides. I sat on the floor and he washed my face as I tried to wash my shoes. We hugged and knew it would be for life. He was too young to be taken away there and then, and so the RSPCA told us to come back in three weeks. I told them that we were definite purchasers and offered a deposit, which they declined, telling me that he would be offered on the day of release on a first come, first served, basis. What a strange way to go about things.

In the meantime, we were to be investigated as to our suitability and *bona fides*!

It seemed that the RSPCA was not prepared to accept the fact that I had had dogs all my life, and wanted to check out the facts, and see if our home was suitable for this little refugee. A lovely lady visited us and took a cup of tea with us before a cursory glance around the house and garden. We had seen her many times before, walking past our front gate with her own dog Jamie towards the sea front, which was only about a hundred yards away. We felt that we knew her already, and we got the nod.

Release date for Freddie (that was his RSPCA given name, and we could not better it, it so suited his character) was to be on a Saturday at 11 a.m. I was there, shivering in the cold January weather (have you been to Blackpool in the winter?) at 8 a.m. to be on the safe side. I had been alerted to the fact that there was another potential purchaser for Freddie.

But at 11 a.m., teeth chattering in the cold, I was still the only person on the site except for the kennel maids. I paid the required £75 which included a neutering fee, and promised to have that done. Freddie was mine. I conveniently forgot to tell him about the future neutering so as not to spoil a lovely day for either of us.

He is the only dog I have had that has never become accustomed to car journeys. We started with sickness and continued with sickness. Over many years, I had graduated from those vinyl seats in my old (and still remembered with much love) Ford Anglia to leather ones in a 911. Freddie grudgingly accepted any journey with a severe hang-dog expression, and often actual sickness. Regardless of that, he never wanted to be left behind.

Freddie was famous on the seafront at Lytham, where most of the locals with dogs either had black Labradors or similar status-like dogs. Freddie was a "character" dog because nobody could pigeonhole him. Some people were far too grand to own an RSPCA foundling of mixed breed. He made friends with everyone, canine and human, and particularly so with William and Richard. William was a Dalmatian whilst Richard was his human owner. I think that William was actually the fourth in an unbroken line of Dalmatians that Richard had owned. Freddie (half the size) adored William and just the mention of his name when we arrived on the seafront was enough to send him streaking for the horizon, quartering the dunes in his search for his best chum. The same went for Holly, another great friend, a Doberman this time. Anything smaller was just ignored.

Freddie was seven when we talked about whether he would be able to cope, to acclimatise, and enjoy a completely different lifestyle. There would be no more hurtling along through the Lytham dunes playing with his doggy friends. Richard hinted that he would have taken him in, but how could we have left him behind?

Of course, Freddie had to come with us to Tenerife. It was a given.

It all had to be planned so carefully. How was he to travel? We quickly decided to let the plane take the strain, and our vet helped out by recommending a company at Manchester Airport that specialised in pet transport, which she had used satisfactorily in the past for other customers. When we asked the owner of the kennels that Freddie infrequently patronised, they came up with the same name too. We took that to be a good omen for his welfare.

So we paid a visit next time we were in the area and met a kindly lady who sorted it all out for us, including the provision of a large travel box acceptable to the airlines. Between us we settled on Monarch, partly because of the sensible flight timings, and partly because they were clearly dog friendly.

That travel box was to become a part of our daily routine in order to get Freddie used to it, so that he would not be terrified on the actual day. We placed it near to his bed in the kitchen. We propped its front gate open and put an old item of clothing inside that smelt of me. He sniffed it and then wanted no further part of it. Between meals, cunningly placed food morsels were totally ignored. His main meals were scoffed like lightning and he reversed out before we could close the door. Things did improve slowly, but never to anyone's entire satisfaction. Certainly, not to his.

Whilst we were busy with that travel box, others were busy organising a European Pet Passport for us. At the time, this was a rather new-fangled document, not at all easy to understand. Once it had been issued, Freddie could travel hither and thither within Europe without any quarantine restrictions. Spain was a party to the regulations, so we should have a clear entry procedure.

Without this formal document, it was impossible to take a dog out of the country, and even more difficult to bring one back in if the full set of stamps was missing. Our local vet set the wheels in motion. As usual there was a lot of legislation, most of it less than clear. We ended up ringing DEFRA, the experts in this area, to obtain absolute clarification of each next step in the process.

The biggest hit was to be the rabies jab. The UK was still rabies free but I believe that France was not. With the tunnel now connecting the one to the other, it could only be a matter of time before one of those Frenchies, foaming at the mouth, slipped under the wire.

Freddie's first rabies jab did not "take", by which I mean the dose that had been injected into him had not worked sufficiently well to afford him the level of protection required by officialdom. That appeared to be not unusual. There was a waiting period, and then it had to be done all over again, with a further waiting period, before the all clear could be given. Fortunately, we had left just enough time for the first failure, otherwise I don't know what we would have done.

After all that, there was the requirement for a full health check. Anyway, we did not want to be taking our dog until he was in tip top condition. Freddie passed everything with flying colours and received his passport.

Now we were all cleared for departure.

It had been a hectic few months. No sooner had we had taken the final decision to relocate abroad than the UK property market went into free-fall, and with it, the value of our home. We had thought our lovely Victorian property, built in 1890, overlooking the seafront in Lytham, would be snapped up. But our signboard was suddenly one of hundreds popping up all over the town. No road, lane or avenue was now complete without the confetti of this street furniture.

A hasty rethink brought us to the rental market, and we went back to our estate agent. He introduced us to specialists in this market, and we soon had their board up.

No sooner up than down! They found us a business family wanting to move locally. Papers were exchanged, money was deposited, and that was that. We were so lucky.

During that time, our joint business venture had also been sold. The commercial legal services company, now some ten years old, attracted a lot of interest in the specialised marketplace in which we did our complicated business. A trust corporation, a building society, an offshoot of a national bank and a couple of large nationally known financial adviser practices were amongst a number of early interested parties.

A three month work-out period with the new owners soon passed and at last we were free.

Our move to Tenerife was complicated by those 2,000 miles of water in between the starting point and the final destination. We got quotes from all of the big international carriers that would be prepared to deliver to the Canaries and who advertised world-wide removals, no load too big or too small. We put a number of them to the test. They all wanted a ridiculous amount of money, and strangely could not offer a specific delivery date. We had also been put in touch with a small removals company on Tenerife with the grand name of Worldwide, and the young lady there, Lynne, was both friendly and efficient. If we could estimate how many boxes that would need to be moved, she could quote exactly for a complete door to door service.

The agent specified to uplift our goods turned out to have a depot in Skipton, an hour or so's drive away. We would have to go and fetch the boxes for ourselves, unless we could wait until the next time that they happened to have had a lorry in our area. For some reason or other, we had mentioned in passing to our contact in Tenerife that we were going to be away that weekend down in Hove, at the other end of the country, on a family visit.

"Hove? Where exactly is Hove, actually?" she asked.

"It's near Brighton. Do you have a UK map there? Can you see it?"

"Ha! Yes! We have a Britannia agent in Newhaven. That looks close by. You could collect boxes from them if you wish?"

It was a bit inconvenient, but no matter if it would push things forward. And so it was all arranged. On the Saturday morning, bright and early, we motored over to Newhaven from Hove, found the depot, and the kind people there loaded us up with the required number, all flat packed, adding in a few extra for good measure, together with a huge carton of wrapping paper, and waved us on our way. They would take no money, saying we had been inconvenienced, and it was all part of their service.

There was a bonus to all of this. We knew that Newhaven had a small fish market. We made a detour to the quayside, to find that a catch of lemon soles had been landed a couple of hours beforehand. We bought enough for all the family, for little money, and so had a wonderful feast for dinner that evening.

Back home in Lytham, Sally was very much in charge of all the packing. The pile of cartons grew and grew, until at long last the collection day arrived. Britannia was with us at the appointed time, smiling men disgorging from a huge pantechnicon, and in due course they took it all away. We would not see it again until we met it at our front door in Tenerife once Sally, Freddie and I had taken up our permanent residence in Tenerife.

Ideally, we decided, there needed to be one of us in the UK to wave Freddie off (actually to go through and sign all of the final and complicated paperwork) and one of us in Tenerife to give him a really big welcome after his journey (and also to do the necessary Spanish incoming paperwork).

Sally drew the short straw for taking Freddie to the airport at Manchester at the crack of dawn. Neither she nor Freddie was much good at that time of day. A combination of an hour and a half in the car and the very early start in the pouring rain at 4 a.m. left her fully aware of Freddie's lack of enthusiasm.

At the airport, paperwork completed by the shipper and the airline, at last he could be coaxed into his travel box, and was taken away on a fork lift truck to be x-rayed. What an indignity! Sally could see the outrage on his face as he and his box trundled along about eight feet in the air. Eventually he was boarded onto the plane and, we hope, settled down to an uninterrupted flight.

But we shall never know, shall we, what went on for those four and a half hours?

Meanwhile, in Tenerife, I was travelling down to the airport in the south with Peter to meet and greet Freddie on his arrival. We were there good and early, and saw his flight coming in to land. After what seemed an eternity, with me hopping from one foot to the other in my anxiety, along came a small tractor towing a very large trailer, the sole item on which was Freddie's box, with him peering morosely out of it. There were reams of importation paperwork to be completed and stamped, before Freddie was signed off and could be released to us.

After a drink of water, he tottered to our car and had to be lifted in, so pleased to see friendly faces and no doubt to hear a friendly language too. However, we were scarcely off the airport boundary before he demanded to stretch his legs, with a Guinness Book of Records length piddle.

All in all, it was an expensive exercise to bring him to Tenerife. But worth every penny to have him with us.

A few days later, it was Sally's turn to board the plane at Manchester with a one way ticket. At last, Tenerife here we all come!

6

On the Road

Although rental cars are cheap over here, we must have spent a fortune with one particular company, using them each time we came over for our snatched breaks. When we decided to move permanently, I had originally thought to bring my M3 to the island because it was extremely low mileage. I was put off by Sally who said that she would be uncomfortable driving a right hand drive car over here, and to be fair to her some of the minor roads would have played havoc with the suspension. So the car was sold on, into a private collection.

It was time to buy.

You would think that it is as easy to buy a car in Tenerife as it is to buy one back in England. How wrong could one be! The system in Tenerife is completely different from start to finish.

I made a quick solo trip out from England on a car buying expedition. We had looked cursorily on a previous holiday visit, and there seemed to be a singular lack of decent used cars to be found. On this latest trip I found out just why.

It had been the wrong time of the year!

It seems that there is a car buying "window" on the island when most transactions are done, and when there is a lot of stock to be had. At other times of the year there is little or nothing. I went into the local Citroen dealer and they had one, yes one, new car in their showroom. The local Toyota dealer had no used cars in stock at all. How did they stay in business?

After a lot of thought, we knew what we wanted in terms of size and specification, but the ranges of manufacturer's products were not necessarily the same as those sold in the UK. I traipsed round dealerships trying to get a handle on prices versus specifications, and all the various delivery options. We eventually settled on a new people carrier, a SEAT Altea XL diesel with the largest engine and the family option pack. SEAT, for anyone who may be interested, stands for *Sociedad Espanola de Automoviles de Turismo*.

The car was a decent size, had a big enough VW engine to pull us and all our kit around, plenty of space for the shopping, was built to VW standards and, most importantly, had enough room in the back for Freddie, with only a low jump being required for him to hop in.

The purchase process started as you might expect, with a visit to the showroom. It is never a given, is it, that a salesperson will rush up and offer their services? In our chosen SEAT dealership, all heads remained down and tapping on computers continued, almost as though the customer presented an unwelcome intrusion.

"Harrumph!" I grunted eventually.

"Oh, good afternoon. I didn't see you there. How can I help you?" How on earth can someone say that they haven't noticed anyone pottering about in their showroom for upwards of ten minutes?

"I'm interested in buying a new car."

"Oh? Yes, yes. Good. And who are you exactly? I have to know."

"Here is my card. I am newly arrived to live here on the island, so I need to buy a car."

"What do you want it for?"

"Why do you need to know?" I really must keep cool.

"Do you have the right to purchase a car?"

"Eh?" I was getting a little bit irritated now.

"Have you got permission in writing from the Town Hall to buy a car?"

"No. I have not. Why do I have to get permission? From whom, exactly, and why?"

"But from the Town Hall, of course!" This was said as though I were a complete idiot.

"Yes, you said that. But why? And how would I go about that?"

"If you do not have the proper written permission from your local Town Hall, the Traffic Department in the capital, Santa Cruz de Tenerife, will not issue us with the necessary approval document to enable us to sell you this car."

"Eh?"

"Do you not know that in order to buy a car you must have a stamped certificate? Without that certificate we cannot sell you the car, and you will be unable to matriculate it."

"Sorry, what does matriculate mean?"

"It means to register it in the motor registry at the *Trafico* department in Santa Cruz and then for them to authorise the provision of number plates for the car."

Only when I had sorted my way through this sort of minefield would I actually be allowed to finally commit to the purchase. Only when I had all the paperwork back, stamped a million times by every official that could be found, could I apply for the matriculation number, and that would take some more paperwork too. Spaniards just love paperwork and stamps. The more stamps and signatures that you can acquire on a form, the better that form will serve you for the future.

There is always a ream of paperwork and the need for stamps from various unheard of departments. Generally, you might have to go to the capital, Santa Cruz, on the other side of the island a number of times to get it all done. When you think it's all over, they find another reason to get you to go back – of course, another infernal stamp is missing, although on the last visit you had been told that everything was now finally in order.

Once we moved over to the island on a permanent basis, the next step was to integrate further into the formidable Spanish system by applying for a *Residencia* certificate, also from the Town Hall. This would start to open the door to accessing local health care, enable us to qualify for discounts on internal Spanish flights and inter-island ferries, and all sorts of things in between. For so many things of a formal nature, the *Residencia* certificate had to be shown. We were soon to find that we should never go out without having a whole battery of forms to hand (usually it is the originals that are required, but we use colour photocopies, and have had no problems). It was to be a major step along the route, strewn with pitfalls for the unwary, to becoming legal locals.

All cars, we discovered, whether new or used, cost more over in Tenerife than their equivalent back in England. Was it due reasonably enough to transportation costs, or was England a cheap destination for car purchase?

Thank heavens, though, we purchased a new car from a franchised main dealer. If we had bought second hand, we would have had to have obtain extra paperwork to ensure that there were no outstanding debts on the vehicle, such as hire purchase or local or speeding fines, as they move on with the car! You should never buy a car second hand without employing a specialist agent (known as a *gestor*) to check on any outstanding fines. It is not unusual to discover thousands of euros in back taxes unpaid, and you will be liable for them unless you are fortunate enough to persuade the previous owner to cough up.

Wading through it all took a few weeks before the keys were finally handed over. When we got home we discovered a TV screen fitted above the rear seats in a drop down overhead unit that we had neither asked for nor paid for.

Car tax can be really inventive in Spain. There is no national set scale of charges, so you pay, if you want to, the rate set by the administrative area in which you live and where the car is registered. As we live in Puerto de la Cruz, where the Town Hall seems to be permanently short of money, we paid €85 a year as the equivalent of a road fund licence in the UK. Not bad by UK standards for a people carrier, but if we had lived three miles further out of town in the next municipal area, Los Realejos, it would have cost almost exactly half as much!

Moreover, there is no requirement to actually pay, because no certificate or windscreen sticker is issued. Any rolling debt goes on the car, and is charged to the next owner. It seems a ridiculous system, putting legally due payments on to an almost voluntary system, and that in a country verging on the abyss of bankruptcy.

Sorting out our car insurance was also a bit convoluted. There were the usual big players (Direct Line is known locally over here as Red Telephone, for obvious reasons) and plenty of minor ones too. I believe I am right in saying that about 50% of the islanders do not bother with insurance at all, which can make it all quite interesting in the rush hour, or when it is raining. Insurance rates are expensive in comparison with the UK, although thankfully the insurers did accept our maximum no claim bonus statements from back home, which made it bearable.

Looking back, we did not envisage that we would be needing the car for more than pottering down into the town to the shops or for taking Freddie for different walks up in to the hills, but we have ended up doing more kilometres than you would think possible on an island not much bigger than Rutland.

Now that we had bought our car, we had the option of taking the Spanish driving test to acquire a Spanish licence. It would be a further notch on our belt towards integration. It would probably also help if we were stopped by the police. There seemed to be plenty of them about but because they were all dark and swarthy, wearing the inevitable sunglasses, there could actually be very few of them, swapping roles around on a daily basis.

Some came dressed as *Trafico* police, some as the *Guardia Civil*, other as the *Policia Local*, and yet more as counter this or that squads. All had different livery on themselves and their vehicles, and all with different responsibilities. For example, the *Policia Local* didn't stop you for minor traffic infringements, such as parking on a zebra crossing; that was the job of the *Trafico* police.

Quite often, about once a month, we would come round a corner on a main road, and there would be a road block. A couple of large police vans would be straddling the blacktop, and half a dozen officers, all dressed in formidable black, and even more formidably toting machine guns, would "invite" us to show the contents of our car. Our trick was to fall back into English and then we would just be waved through. Goodness knows who they were looking for, but I would not like to have been one of them when they found them. We would drive off very carefully, one eye on the rear view mirror, and rather dry mouthed.

Each car in Spain carries its own paperwork, and by that I mean literally carries it. By law, you should have the originals of everything in the car at all times. Tax receipts, insurance certificate, accident forms, our Spanish residency forms, our Spanish NIE identity forms, certified copies of passports and much more. This means that if your car was stolen, all your documents went too – barmy! But that is the law, and woe betide a driver without all the paper backup when stopped by the police. It means an instant fine and the probable application of the thumb screws.

The words "Spanish" and "Inquisition" always come to mind.

The Spanish driving test, which is similar to that in the UK with the exception of a more rigorous written examination, appears to be an arduous process. Miguel, a young chap we know, has been at it for over a year now, and has yet to actually step into a motor car. He has failed the written examination FOUR times! Perhaps that is why so many do not actually bother to take it at all.

For people such as ourselves, coming over here to settle and already having a UK driving licence, it is slightly different. My UK licence was unfortunately due to expire the following year, and so I elected to go for the driving test as it would apply to non-Spanish residents. There were a couple of places in our town that offered this service. I went along to one – only to find that it was a medical centre.

"*Buenos dias*. I am told that you offer a service for taking the driving test here?"

Indeed they did, and I had to fill in a long form in duplicate and have a passport photograph taken electronically for inclusion on to the form. They also took my UK passport number and photographed the back page, as well as my NIE Spanish residency document. Oh how the Spanish love their paperwork.

"Come with me now," said the friendly young lady. We went from consulting room to consulting room, each offering a different opportunity to have my eyesight checked on a hugely expensive machine, my blood pressure checked, my general health checked, and then I was inserted into an amazing soundproof booth where my hearing and reactions were recorded to various electronic stimuli.

All the results were recorded on to the form, with comments appended. I could not believe just how healthy they thought I was!

Finally we came to the last and biggest test, one that I had heard about, and I quaked with trepidation.

"Come along, and I will introduce you to the rolling road machine," smiled my tormentor.

In yet another room there was a fearsome electronic beast. I was instructed to sit at the console and grip the two handlebars whilst peering at the screen ahead of me.

"In a moment, when I activate the machine, two rolling roads will appear in front of you on the screen. You have to move the two handlebars to keep the two balls inside the two independently moving rolling roads. Inevitably, you will come off the road, and the machine will measure the speed of your reactions in getting back into place."

"Eh? Is there any chance of a trial run, please?" Have I really understood all that correctly?

"No, sorry!"

And so, with a flick of the switch, we were off. The two rolling roads appeared on the screen, running side by side. Within each road was a ball. My task was to keep the balls within the roads, otherwise a loud alarm would go off. Each road moved independently, sometimes coming nearly together, sometimes drifting apart, and everything in between to make it as difficult and complicated as possible. There were sharp corners and long sweeping ones, sometimes simultaneously, but going in different directions. It was the stuff of nightmares and designed to test co-ordination of reflexes in eyes and hands whilst trying to do different tasks simultaneously.

It seemed to me that the alarm was going off incessantly. I was getting a headache and sweat was dripping from my brow with the concentration.

Eventually it was all over, and I was convinced that I had failed. I slunk back to the front desk where all the data was recoded on a long printout and added to my form.

"Congratulations, you have passed successfully! You did rather well at that last test, actually."

I was not going to argue, so I paid my fee and left as soon as decently possible. All that remained was to take the forms to *Trafico* in Santa Cruz. They would log me into the Spanish system and issue me with a new plastic licence card, after contacting the equivalent authorities back in the UK to see if there were any points against my UK licence that should be recorded here. As there were none, two weeks later I received the phone call from *Trafico* telling me that my licence was ready for collection.

In hindsight, it all seemed fairly straightforward although much more detailed than back in the UK.

7

Home Town

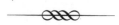

The old town of Puerto de la Cruz has black volcanic sand beaches and a harbour originally built to serve La Orotava, the hillside town some three kilometres inland. There are still the remains of old defensive forts and look-out positions around the beaches. We see it as a town of two halves, the newer, tourist part, and the original Spanish part.

No prizes for guessing which we prefer.

The holiday-makers spill out from their hotels each day onto one of the beaches, or amble along through the side roads, stopping at cafes and browsing in shops selling beachwear and the like. We have often wondered whether many of them ever make it to the far end of town and discover the real Spain on their doorstep, so to speak.

"Our" end of town has narrower, winding streets, and leafy, shady squares. There are three particular squares that we like best.

The first is the main one of the old town, the Plaza del Charco, right in the centre. Large and imposing, with cafés along the sides, it is bounded by large shade trees, with a pond and fountain in its centre, and looks exactly what you might expect on a tourism poster. It could be perfectly cast to appear in a film set. In the evening it really comes alive with twinkling lights wound around the trees, live music being played, and the cooking smells from the various restaurants wafting tantalisingly past one's nose.

The next square that we particularly like lies behind one of the town's many churches. There are formal flower beds there, more shade trees, and locals sitting quietly, watching everyone as they go by, waiting for their friends to arrive and join them for a chat and a cigar or cigarette. At the side of the square lies a smart café where we often take our morning coffee. It is all of 50 metres from one of the main tourist thoroughfares, yet seldom do the tourists explore what lies behind that church.

Although the café has a proper name, Ebano, we always refer to it as "comfy chairs". If we or Peter or other friends are going to be in town, we text a brief message: "Will be at comfy chairs at noon." Freddie is welcome there, and Peter brings Millie and Poppy with him. They create a grand diversion. Babies stare goggle eyed from their prams, children want to come and stroke them, and their parents walk past as far away as possible, a look of horror on their faces. Strange how many Spaniards are still frightened of dogs and try to avoid even small ones.

We all spend an hour or so together, discussing what is happening in the world since we have last seen each other, or to be more exact, probably discussing what the weather is like that morning in Newton Abbot. For a town that we have never visited, we feel that we are on the most intimate of terms with every facet of its history!

The third square that we like is a little out of the way, but very pretty. It has recently undergone a facelift with new palm trees imported from Africa. They have been rooted in but are still bound up at the top so that their fronds do not get caught in the breeze and dislodge the rooting process. At the far end of the square are two restaurants, both with open air seating under large parasols, and seating indoors for cooler winter evenings. One of the restaurants is "smart" and the other "regional", if you get my meaning. The smart one is typically up-market Spanish, but is owned and run by Germans, so it functions perfectly, and the loos are spotless. The regional one is run by a Spanish family and one sometimes wonders how they manage to stay in business at all with that level of competition opposite. But they have been there now for over 40 years, so they must be doing something right!

At our end of town the beach is the Playa Jardin, edged, as the name suggests, by lovely trees and shrubs, like a large flowering garden, all leading down to the beach itself, black volcanic sand, and which has been the subject of much expenditure recently with the receipt of EU money. A preponderance of those on the beach are locals, and it is the beach that they all flock to at fiesta time, and of course at Christmas, when it is the tradition to bathe in the warm Atlantic waters before they all repair home for a day and night long family *fiesta* where they stuff themselves with a gargantuan feast of pork and prawns.

Between the two ends of town lies the huge open-air car park adjoining the town harbour; if you told me it could hold 5,000 cars I would not be surprised. In its midst stands the great lighthouse painted in stripes of red and white, just like an immense example of one of those surgeon-barber's poles of old, when barbers did a spot of minor surgery to augment their income.

In times gone by, large trading boats would dock in the harbour to take on their cargoes of wine and bananas. Now, there are just the town's fishing boats. Only a little remains of the original extensive commercial quays, though we have seen lovely old photographs of them. But so picturesque it all is, with its tiny beach, the old customs house on the quayside, and the jolly, plump lady grilling fresh prawns at her red kiosk, surrounded by red Coca Cola branded chairs and parasols, on the other side of the dock.

Right on the harbour wall is a stall selling fresh fish, and there is also a proper fish shop nearby where the fishermen trade their catch each morning. We are fortunate that there is a daily delivery of sardines, scooped up from the bay beyond the harbour by our local fishermen, together with *boquerones,* (much smaller, a bit like what we call whitebait), and *chicharras,* a little larger than a sardine, and a bit meatier too. All best cooked simply: olive oil, garlic and parsley and a squeeze of lemon. Delicious!

Larger fish are caught further out to sea, and yet others are imported from Africa. So we have a choice of fish of all the colours of the rainbow. Hake is a big favourite and appears on most restaurant menus, done in hundreds of different ways.

There are plenty of mussels to be had, but they come from the Peninsula. Galicia in the north of Spain is a fabulous area for fish, perhaps the best in Europe. Do go there if you can. Their fish is flown down overnight and appears on the counter in our supermarkets the very next day. Fish is taken very seriously here, and so it has to be very fresh.

Our largest supermarket is called Al Campo and is owned by Auchan, the French group. The fish counter is stupendous. There will be a vast array of differing species, big, small, round, flat, as well as live crabs and lobsters, and often winkles, another favourite of mine. Huge prawns are flown in daily from Venezuela or Brazil, and there is octopus and squid in all its many variations.

Further along the promenade is the Lido, the Lago Martianez to give it its proper name, with a number of fresh and sea water pools interlinking around a central island with fountains, all surrounded by a sea of reclining beach loungers. You can spend a full day there for a small charge (reduced even further for the likes of us, Canarian *residentes*), not needing to leave for lunch as there are a number of bars and *cafeterías* within the enclosure. It takes hundreds, possibly a few thousand people before it starts to look overly busy.

Up the hill behind the town lies the old area where the British originally settled. They came and built their homes up there because it was a few degrees cooler than down on the coastline. Here is the English Church, set in Parque Taoro, a most beautiful place, and nearby, the English Library. Within the park is the old Taoro Hotel where Winston Churchill stayed on a visit to Tenerife, as did kings and queens of Spain and other dignitaries. Sadly the hotel is no longer in use, and we are all awaiting the council decision as to whom they might award a 5-star hotel franchise, in order for it to be returned to its former grandeur and pre-eminence in the town.

Whilst we have the little lane behind us for Freddie's daily walks, a couple of times each week we take him down to Parque Taoro. Since it's just round the corner, on cooler days he can walk there, but on hotter ones the pavement might burn his feet and it would be unkind to make him walk. So he enjoys the luxury of going by car.

Down the centre of the park runs a wide straight carriageway, which was originally used for the racing of horses. It is now lit at night by antique type street lamps, and looks delightfully romantic. One part of the park has been set aside for dogs to exercise their owners. Most owners can be let off their leads, and have great fun rushing around chasing each other and their dogs.

There is also a large pond, with a small island of reeds in its middle. The first time, we quite forgot that Freddie had probably never seen a pond before. He just walked in, and his feet were still doing a normal walk as he slowly disappeared below the surface. Fortunately, he had been used to going into the sea back in Lytham, so he did not need his water wings. But he did look very surprised, and has never ventured near that pond again.

Nowadays, whilst our town has spread out to include some of the old suburbs, it still remains a place of grace and beauty, wearing well its patina of age.

While EU money has been helpful in restoring some of the town to its former glory, the Town Hall also came up with its own regeneration plans.

We can always learn from the ideas of others, and here is an idea that met with my approval straight away and I wonder just why it has not been brought into play back in England. The council designated a number of streets in the town that needed re-surfacing or needed the main drain replacing, or both, and threw in the bonus of providing new pavements for everyone as well. They then "invited" those who had been unemployed for a certain length of time, those who had not actively sought out a new job or joined a retraining programme and were receiving monthly state payments, to enter into the new voluntary street repair programme – or they would be cancelling the equivalent of their dole money.

Nearly everyone signed up to it, the streets were repaired at very cheap cost to the town, and the people got paid a proper wage by the Town Hall for doing it. In many cases, they were receiving the advantage of learning a new trade with free on-site training to boot. All of the three main approach roads into the town have been done up like this over the last couple of years, and very smart they are looking too!

To us oldies, the youth of today are an unknown quantity, existing as they do on a different planet or in some parallel universe, and with an almost entirely different language in which they communicate between themselves.

And I hesitate to say it, but sometimes they can be a bit frightening. When we lived in Lytham, a pretty posh sort of coastal town, there would always be groups of youths hanging around on street corners as evening fell, and the evidence of their passage would be there for all to see the next day.

Oh, how different it is here, and how lucky we are to be able to stroll around like everyone else at night time, and in safety. Young people in our home town of Puerto de la Cruz are a completely different species. We might be sitting having a pot of tea, and five or six lads will plonk themselves down quietly at the next table, and order vast ice creams and soft drinks! There will be no loud music machines to disturb the peace. No riotous behaviour to intimidate the elderly populace. No litter will be left behind. Back in the UK, would you find any teenager happy to go out with their parents and sit in a café having an ice cream in the evening, after having paraded around the square? I think not. Total destruction of all their street cred!

How come café society over here is everything that we were told by our political masters that it would be in England, when the alcohol laws were relaxed so unfortunately?

We are seldom out until the early hours nowadays. We are too old for all that now. But we can report that certainly up to midnight, we always feel safe. People will be still sitting in the cafes having a drink, and moving about along the cobbled streets. Never ever have we felt threatened when a group of young people approached. Often they might even wish us good night as they pass, politely acknowledging the older generation.

Family is so important over here, and that sort of respect is widespread, built in from birth. There are very few old folk's homes, or retirement homes, or whatever is the buzz word nowadays. They simply are not generally needed. When family members become too old to continue to care for themselves, they are taken in and looked after. It is just seen as the normal thing to do. So nice and so different from the UK where they seem to treat the old as non-people to be shuffled out of sight and out of our memories.

The culture of the family is just so different, and I have to say that I much prefer it.

Mañana. The word is well known the world over. Literally meaning "tomorrow", it needs no further explanation.

The *mañana* syndrome applies throughout Tenerife in all walks of public life. People are so laid back as to be almost horizontal. In many ways this can be a wonderful state of affairs, and I am beginning to think that a little of it is rubbing off on us.

Your waiter in your chosen bar or *cafetería* might be a perfect example. He will doubtless see you, but not acknowledge you until he is good and ready. He will clear the table next to you, but may continue to ignore you. He might return later and wipe that table, or indeed your own. He may still ignore you. He will serve others who are further up the food chain. Eventually, he might nod as he appears next to your elbow.

The order will then be taken. It will probably be wrong when it comes, because he would not have been concentrating. He would have had his eyes permanently on the *chicas* at the adjacent table, all deeply golden tanned and with endless legs stretching from the briefest of shorts.

When your tea does come, it will invariably be without any milk at all, that which you were so careful to demand as being cold, not hot. Personally, I think it just serves as his opportunity for getting another close up of those *chicas*.

8

Service with a Smile

It may be because we are in a hot country that the dustbins here are emptied so often, but I rather think not. I have been to other hot countries, particularly those along the old Barbary Coast, and the same procedure does not always apply, with fly-blown piles of garbage hanging around for far too long. Here in Tenerife, the litter bins (a bin is a *basura,* which literally means "rubbish") in our town are emptied every single night of the year by 1 a.m. This is helped along by the fact that the smaller bins are swing bins, with a plastic liner in them. The operatives are a joy to watch as they can empty a bin and replace the liner in a matter of seconds. They have it all down to a fine art.

Our own *basuras* are emptied six nights of the week. A big wagon calls round, normally about 10 p.m., lots of yellow lights flashing, with the chaps (and often ladies in the crew as well) hanging off the back as it goes from stop to stop. Back in England, Health and Safety people would be having heart attacks. But here one is expected to act reasonably and be responsible for one's own actions.

The bins are quickly emptied, and then they move off to the next stop. All with a cheery wave if we happen to be passing at the time, which we usually are, as ten o'clock is about the time when we walk down to the *basura* with Freddie and then back up our little lane for his final walk of the day.

Perhaps it is all something to do with the fact that the town contracts out rubbish collection to private enterprise. And do you know what the cost to us is for this exemplary service? Well, it is just 32 euros a year!

It really is "service with a smile".

When we were moving into our new apartment, we had to look for all of our furnishings and furniture, because, of course, our new property came just as an empty space, box fresh from the builder. As is the Spanish way, not even a cooker hob had been included.

We ended up being offered two single beds from the estate of an acquaintance who had died rather suddenly. We then bought a large double bed, with accompanying side tables, a large matching wardrobe, a full length mirror and some bedside lamps, from a big furnishing shop in Icod de los Vinos, about half an hour away along the coast. Icod is famous for its immense dragon tree, reputedly to be well over 1,000 years old, and the town is therefore a "must" on the tourist trail, with parking difficult in high season in its narrow cobbled streets.

We selected everything that we needed on our shopping list, and went over to the desk to place our order.

"We would like to purchase the following items that you have in stock. Please, will you be able to deliver this to us? We live in Puerto de la Cruz."

"Most certainly, *señores*."

"When do you think that might be?" We presumed it would be the following week.

"Would tomorrow morning suit you? We could not be with you in Puerto before 10 a.m., I regret."

"!!!"

It was, after all, about 5 p.m. then.

That level of service is absolutely normal, as we have since found everywhere.

We bought all of our kitchen stuff from Almacenes Siverio in Los Realejos, the next town. People had told us that they gave good service, and then good after-sales service too, should it be needed. We bought our fridge, freezer, washing machine, hob and oven from them.

They too offered to deliver and install everything the very next day. Since then we have bought a dishwasher from the same shop, and that came the next day too, and was installed there and then.

Such a service, whilst entirely normal in Tenerife, is nevertheless still an extremely pleasant surprise.

We had that original washing machine for about six years, and then it died. The springs holding the drum in place had given up the ghost. We ordered a new one, and instead of our old Zanussi, we decided on a Spanish make, Fagor. The new machine was promptly delivered and installed the following afternoon.

After two weeks, it too died, after giving out the noisiest death throes ever. There was obviously something seriously wrong with its innards. Perhaps it had received a knock in transit from the mainland? Who knows? I rang Carlos, the boss of Almacenes Siverio, and a *tecnico* was despatched to us to have a look at it. He declared the machine to be terminally faulty and went back to the shop to report. The very next day we had a phone call not from the shop, but from the Head Office of Fagor, somewhere on the Peninsula.

"We are so sorry that you have experienced this inconvenience. This should not have happened to you. It will take us at least a week to get a new drum and fittings to you in Tenerife, as it will have to come over by boat. Our offer therefore is for you to please accept a brand new replacement machine with our compliments. If this is agreeable to you, the shop will deliver it within twenty four hours."

And indeed it was, and they did, and it was also a more expensive upgraded model at that.

The doctor that I signed up with when I first moved to Lancashire was a nice man, and I am sure also a very good doctor, but he had one crucial failing. It was abundantly clear to me that once you were over the magic age of 60, there was less keenness to bother to repair you.

"Ah, well, at your age, you know…"

"One must make the best of it."

"Well, what do you expect…?"

At that surgery back in England, they were lovely people, but they all seemed just too busy to be bothered with their "customers". An appointment with my doctor was scheduled for a maximum of five minutes unless you booked a double appointment in advance. Getting past the staff on the front desk was a nightmare, and as things were inevitably "modernised" you even had to check yourself in automatically on a horrible new-fangled machine. It made me wonder just what all those receptionists were still needed for.

The worst bit was the fact that, prior to the doors opening at 8.30 a.m., a huge queue would form down the road. Bearing in mind the cold and the rain that was the norm in Lancashire, I reckon that most patients got worse rather sooner than they got better.

I asked the receptionists why they could not open the outer door and allow us to shelter inside in the waiting room area. They looked at me as though I was completely mad, and nothing ever came of it.

Things go rather better on this island.

We were lucky enough to have had private health care schemes when we lived in England. We wanted to transfer them over here and have similar benefits. As you get older, you never know. The international sections of big UK providers, including the one that we were then with, wanted an arm and a leg, so we went to a big Spanish company and signed up with them. They offered good cover for a fair premium. We have not needed to make a claim yet, but we have each needed to see a local private doctor, pending that application to integrate into the Spanish state system. We did the usual thing of asking around and eventually settled on one particular practice in the town.

Our Spanish doctor at the clinic devotes as much time to you as you wish. Nothing is ever rushed; you take as long as you need. You pay your fee at the end of your visit, but should you need a follow up call, there is no extra charge. In his clinic he has three qualified nurses, naturally all multi-lingual. There is also an in-house dentist, physiotherapist, reflexologist and other more intimate services.

Back in England, it was impossible to get to see a specialist consultant without first having been referred to one by your own doctor. I had never understood that arrangement. It was just putting another layer of delay and time/cost into the equation. On Tenerife, if you want to see a specialist, you make an appointment and go and see him or her. It's as easy as that. Speed of service is astounding, but quite normal. One day I made an appointment for an ultrasound check at the suggestion of my doctor.

"Come back in tomorrow, when the radiologist is here, and we will sort it out for you then."

And so, next morning, I presented myself at the front desk.

"Yes, we are expecting you. Just wait a moment, and the radiologist will be with you."

I had hardly sat down before a smart white coated doctor asked me to go through to his room. I was examined very comprehensively whilst lying flat out on one of those uncomfortable beds.

"Any pain here? Or here? Or there? OK, now here comes the messy bit."

And with that he slapped a load of cold gel on my midriff. He scanned about hither and thither, chatting through what he was doing. He did seem to spend a bit of time on one area.

"OK, you can get up now, and please go back and sit in the waiting room."

"Thank you very much."

Only five minutes later I was called back into my own doctor's room. In front of him was a typed report. "Well, there is good news and bad news. The bad news is that you have the start of a kidney stone. The good news is that it is less than five millimetres across."

A kidney stone? Where had that come from?

"Sadly they are not unusual over here due to the high levels of calcium in the tap water. Don't worry, though, just drink a lot of mineral water and it will probably dissolve in due course. Start to buy bottled water that is specifically low in calcium."

And with that, off I went, clutching my report.

From checking in, to my examination, the radiologist writing his report, it being passed back to my own doctor, then it all being explained to me by him, I was back outside in the street in just under an hour, clutching a copy of the report and the photographs of my innards.

The same procedure applied when I later needed an x-ray after a bad fall near to the swimming pool. In and out within the hour, complete with the written report. I could not begin to contemplate the timescale back in England: three months to accomplish all of that? It took me months to get an appointment for a strained back about three years earlier in Lytham – I had no option but to go to a private clinic in the town and I got it all sorted out in a couple of visits; by the time that the NHS appointment came through, months later, I had completely forgotten what it was for.

You can't afford to hang around at my age.

9

Island Vistas

Surrounding our town are banana plantations and old terraces which are being brought back into cultivation. As we travel up the valley, the bananas give way to other crops such as potatoes, spinach, leeks and onions. And, of course, the vineyards. Everywhere, small vineyards. Northern Tenerife is such a beautiful place to live.

The town is situated in the centre of a huge natural valley, the valley of La Orotava, some six miles wide. Everywhere high up in the valley there are those vines, lovely to look at whatever the season, changing colour as the year progresses. The patchwork quilt of cultivation, often still by primitive means because of the steepness of the land, is a never ending joy to the eye.

From the start, we had much pleasure meandering along the twisting lanes, unveiling a new vista back down towards the sea, and finding a small country restaurant where there was little but the dish of the day with bread and olive oil, home cooked by the family, and served by them too. A glass of village wine to wash it all down made for a perfect lazy day out.

On one such outing we ended up in a little coastal fishing village called El Pris. It is not much more than a huddle of houses clustered around a small harbour with a long curving breakwater. You can get there in just over three quarters of an hour, but we prefer life in the slow lane nowadays. The road winds down the high cliffs. We zigzagged back and forth until out we popped onto a tiny quayside and parked the car. A couple of hundred yards away was the unpretentious little village with a couple of (mainly) fish restaurants. It was the sort of place where you eat the catch of the day, whilst sitting under a large beach parasol to protect you from the midday heat.

We asked for the local shrimps, which are known as *camarones*, and were told that we would have to wait a while because the boat was still about 300 yards out to sea. The waiter pointed, and we saw a small open fishing boat, white hulled and with a flash of blue along her sides, slowly chugging her way back into harbour. The skipper was already uncoiling a length of rope ready for welcome hands to catch as he approached the jetty.

It was a nice place to dally anyway, so unspoilt by the 21st century. We enjoyed a plate of *lapas* (limpets), topped with a homemade *salsa*, to pass the time. I do like limpets, but I confess that I am the only one I know who does. Overcook them by a second and they assume the consistency of the rubber on the end of your old school pencil.

Suddenly, Sally pointed towards the beach, mouth agape.

"Just look at that!" she exclaimed. "I just don't believe my eyes!"

I looked too, and nor indeed did I.

A handsome young chap, clad in a black wetsuit and holding a spear gun, was walking out of the sea right in front of us, clutching a large octopus in his other hand. A sheathed knife was strapped to one muscly thigh. It was quite surreal, almost as though we had suddenly been plunged into a James Bond film set and we were extras sitting on the quayside.

"Mmmm. That's a pleasant sight!" grinned my wife.

Well, no thank you, not that octopus. It had to be those shrimps for us, and how good they were, freshly boiled in only a few moments, accompanied by crusty bread and washed down with a glass or two of the cold stuff.

Another time, we went the other way along the coast and came to the small town of Garachico. It is famous because when El Teide last properly erupted, the town was completely swept out to sea, being on one of the main lava routes down from the volcano. It was later rebuilt, and you would hardly know what had happened all those years ago. It is a very pretty place, with shady squares, a couple of small hotels, and a bar or two along the beach lined with rock pools. We sat at one of the bars and ate sardines, freshly caught, and quickly cooked in a pan with some olive oil, a little garlic, chopped parsley and seasoning. A squish of lemon, and what could be better?

We are so lucky in the north to still have so many unspoiled places to go to that have not been overtaken by the tourism industry. I don't think that such can be the case in the south, because of the never ending development that is continually taking place there.

The Anaga mountains are situated right at the northern tip of Tenerife, at the so-called panhandle. It is about 45 minutes by using the motorway, so it is an ideal outing too for Freddie. Despite his lack of a love affair with the motor car and internal combustion engine, he will suffer that excursion along the motorway. On our first day trip there, we found a magic wonderland of old forests cascading down to hidden fishing villages, criss-crossed by mountain trails.

To get there from Puerto, we drove through Tegueste, the centre of market gardening for the north of the island. On the flat plain below the town was a sea of pale green interspersed with rigid lines of purple. When we got closer, we were travelling through hectare upon hectare of lettuces, the darker ones being either Lollo Rosso or Oakleaf. Interspersed with the vast fields of lettuce were fields of other vegetables, leeks, carrots and onions, and, of course, the ever present vineyards.

Leaving that all behind, we started the climb up into the hills. Soon we were surrounded by ancient forest, the road twisting and turning. There was not a lot of traffic, but we did see a trail of cyclists pounding along with calves of iron. We stopped, principally for Freddie, at one of the look-out points and gazed back over a number of valleys and hill villages right to La Laguna de San Cristobal, the old capital of the island. Beyond it, shimmering in the heat haze, we could just see Los Rodeos, with planes reduced to the size of ants, landing and departing.

The little coastal villages are reached by narrow lanes with passing places. It was time for us to make our way down to one of them for lunch. The villages were tiny, with just a few houses, but always there would be at least one place to eat. We pulled up at one that had a tiny shaded terrace, which would be good for all of us, particularly Freddie. On the roadside was a blackboard on which had been chalked the one word *"Viejas"*. Now, I am no fan of the *vieja*. It is a shiny, greenish-grey fish, about 10 to 12 inches long, looking for all the world like an overgrown goldfish or koi carp, and is a denizen of the coastal waters hereabouts. The Canarians love them, but I can give them a miss. And the reason for that is their bones. I love fish generally, and am adept at dealing with their bones, but those in the *vieja* are just so numerous, it is as though the whole fish is bones with just a tiny bit of flesh, rather than the other way around.

We would make the best of it, but there would be none for our canine friend.

Oh dear! When it arrived, the fish had been fried to within an inch of charcoal-flavoured destruction. We pushed it around our plates and concentrated instead on the generous dishes of salad and potatoes that accompanied the serving. Afterwards, we were offered *"flan."* This is the local word for a cross between a *crème caramel* and a *crème brulée*. At its best it is wonderful.

And wonderful it was! Served with pride by the lady that made it, we heaped our bowls and ask for more. She beamed!

Stealthily and most incorrectly, I put down my bowl for Freddie to lick. He had not done well so far with just a potato or two, and the water that the lady brought for him when we arrived. Rather too noisily, he pushed the bowl around the floor.

And then it was time to wend our way back from this little part of Tenerife that time forgot. Up and up we went, hairpin after hairpin, until we reached the ridge where the main road lay. There was a *mirador* here, and Freddie took a breather.

This area is very popular for hiking, and there are a number of trails running along the hilly ridges and across the verdant valleys, often well concealed under a canopy of sun-dappled leaves. Mobile phone signals still tend to be a bit patchy, and not long before our visit a small party of German walkers, out for their "*wanderweg*", had gone missing and the rescue services had to kick in. They were found the next morning, grouped at one of the *miradores* or look-out places, all still hale and hearty despite a night out in the mountains.

We felt have always felt very lucky to see a volcano every day, although I am sure that any feeling would turn to that of abject terror should the slightest puff of smoke ever be seen.

Wherever you are, wherever you look, it dominates everything. It's just… there. You just have to go up there. It draws you to it.

It takes nearly an hour in the car, through all the upward twists and turns, to break through the clouds and to bask in the clear air and sharp sunlight. When you are up there, it is like entering another dimension entirely.

The caldera itself, the outer crater of the original volcano, is miles across from one side to another. Inside that circular rim are lava fields tumbling downwards from the central cone, seemingly frozen in space and time. The rock is surprisingly hard, spiky and jagged, and so heavy. Inner parts of the caldera are taken up by huge pillars of rock, their surroundings having been blasted or eroded away. And around them are flat plains, perfect for the spaghetti western and sci-fi films that have been filmed there.

There is a film being shot up there as I write this and a Mars lunar rover is being tested for NASA. It seems that our island volcano is the best place on Earth to simulate the surface of Mars.

In the middle of all of this is the central upward thrust of the cone of the volcano itself, poking skywards, usually crowned by a corona of snow for part of the year.

Up the side sneaks the cable car. We have always sidestepped all the offers to go up with friends or family. Firstly, it does not quite go right to the top, so what is the point? At my age it would give me a certain heart attack to climb the last few hundred metres in the rarefied air at over 12,000 feet. And with my luck, the old dear would choose just that moment to offer up an earth moving eruption. Secondly, and without wishing to libel anyone, it does look a flimsy contraption; the sort of thing that was originally built and used by the Swiss, but later sold on to the Italians, who sold it off to the Greeks, who had no idea at all that it had to be regularly serviced, and so it finally ended up in Tenerife.

A parador was built up here some years ago. Now, we are big fans of paradors, a really excellent chain of state-run hotels, having stayed in a dozen and visited at least another dozen for a meal or whatever. But I just cannot bring myself to recommend this one, although many stay the night to be up at dawn to see the clearness of the new light, unfettered by smog or industrial haze or the reflective glow from street lighting, the air so pure and clear, so cold and thin first thing in the morning at that height. Outerwear is *de rigeur*. But we live too close by to need to stay there overnight.

But we do want decent refreshment when we have taken friends up there to "ooh" and "aah" at the stunning sight of that volcano. The refreshment offer, alas, is a grotty café, usually filthy, and the loos are the same. Tables are not cleared away after the backpackers have left behind the remains of their breakfasts or lunches and litter is everywhere. It's just all so wrong. So un-parador-ish.

Ah, I hear you asking…But what about those famous *cafeterías* that have been installed into each parador to make them more welcoming and accessible to visitors, offering them comfy surroundings and upmarket service and products for the passing traveller?

Well, every time that I have ventured over the threshold of this particular parador we have been brusquely turned away.

"Hello. Can we have coffee in your *cafetería*, please?"

"Our *cafetería* is closed. You must go to the public café next door." The man behind the reception desk could hardly be bothered to lift his head to address us properly.

"No, no. You misunderstand me. We don't want to go to the one next door; it is not very nice. We have been to paradors before, and like them."

"You still cannot have coffee here."

"Well," I said, brandishing my *Amigos de Paradores* card. "What about this then?"

He just walked away! I instantly started to construct in my mind the stinging email that would go back to the Parador HQ. We took the cup that cheers in a local refreshment house about three kilometres along the road.

But we do have the privilege of being able to see El Teide from our own terrace, and I still look out every day at it and I never cease to marvel.

Once we went up in winter after a fresh fall of snow. Because of its height, El Teide has a capping of snow for a number of months each year, usually shedding the last remains around May. On that occasion, the local TV had reported that there had been severe snow falls not only on our volcano, but on the other islands as well. Cars were sliding all over the place on Gran Canaria, and central mainland Spain had ground to a halt.

The day dawned crisp and clear, and off we set. Unfortunately, so had everyone else.

Everyone on the island must have taken the day off to enjoy this extraordinary sight. Cars had mini snowmen built onto their bonnets, and the drivers were seeing how far they could get back down the hill before they either melted or fell off.

Up in the caldera, fresh snowfields were being explored; with skateboards, old trays and even skis. It was all a fantastic sight, and of course, so unusual for the very young children who had probably never been able to touch and play in real snow before.

Looking out each morning, as we eat our breakfast on our terrace, at the beautiful valley rising above us with its patchwork quilt of vineyards, small farms, banana plantations and white painted houses with shallow terracotta roofs dotted amongst them all, we realise that we truly enjoy a world class view.

Not just up and across our valley, of course, but also out to sea along the northern coastline of the island. It must be serendipity that brought us here, and I sometimes ponder, looking out over the ocean, about those Spanish galleons gliding smoothly across the azure main, their sails flapping idly as they enjoyed their dog days, becalmed for days, even weeks, before the prevailing Westerlies started to blow and brought them safely back home.

It is all so very much a far cry from those rainy days in Lytham where we snatched a hurried meal before doing battle on the M6 down to Manchester.

10

Tea, Tapas & Mushy Peas

One morning after breakfast, having accompanied Freddie on his morning constitutional along our lane, I was idly scanning through the local paper, and an article about the refurbishment and re-opening of the Grand Hotel Mencey caught my eye. The hotel, in the capital, Santa Cruz, was owned by Iberostar, and having been the subject of a multi-million euro restoration, seemed to offer everything that a 5-star hotel should. Being a sucker for proper afternoon tea, I thought that it would be nice to go along with Sally and try the place out. My love of afternoon tea has not faded despite my living in Spain. An hotel that could do a proper afternoon tea back in England was usually one that was generally low in other faults. I emailed the hotel asking about it. After all, the Mencey was now the best hotel in the capital and the Iberostar flagship.

Strangely, I have never received a reply to that email. Still, we decided to go for a day trip to the capital. Although we lived on the other side of the island, we could be parked in Santa Cruz within 45 minutes, thanks to the *autopista* linking the two places, passing the northern airport on the way before descending down to the city on the coast.

Santa Cruz is nowadays best known internationally as a destination on the cruise liner routes to and around the Canaries. I guess that not many days pass when there is not some vast edifice, looking like a block of flats, parked along one of the long quays. Sometimes there are three at the same time. We had friends who came in on the Queen Elizabeth, and they had a really long hike along the quay, past another two huge boats.

A big auditorium has recently been built on the seafront, where international acts can come to delight the locals and those from further afield on the other islands of the archipelago. It has been constructed in the image of the one in Sydney, although slightly smaller, with a vast curving arch over it. I am told that it suffers from leaks.

There is a fantastic, golden sand beach a few kilometres up the road, at Las Teresitas. Millions of tons of Sahara sand were imported on huge barges, a fake lagoon was built out of rocks moved into place there, and with its palm tree fringe, you might well be in the South Seas.

The centre of the city itself is a gracious old place, all elegant avenues and shady church squares, with modern shops and boutiques around each corner. It is a place of yesteryear, which I might call old Spanish colonial, but with some modern trimmings.

And it is bursting with restaurants of all shapes and sizes. Were there enough people there to patronise them all, we asked ourselves? The city fathers publish a *Ruta de Tapas*, where you can go from bar to bar, *restaurante* to *restaurante*, taking a *copita* of sherry or a cold beer, accompanied by a small *tapa* to go with it. Many try to cover all the places listed, but just a few would do for us.

Tapas are small plates of food, and there are thousands of individual interpretations. Each bar on the route will vie with its competitors to produce something new, or of better quality, to encourage people to return. Visitors can mark their card, so to speak, and the winner will receive a much coveted prize. We have the same system in Puerto and one of our favourites, La Clave, was a worthy winner one year. My wife was kissed and my hand was pumped up and down last time we went there, as though we had singlehandedly ensured their victory.

In the old part of Santa Cruz, in the Noria district, we strolled along quaint side streets all with their fair share of bars and restaurants, tables spilling out on to the pavements. By now it was early evening, when people were leaving work (about 7 or 8 p.m. – remember, there is the siesta between 1 and 4 p.m.), so busy business people would drop in for a cold beer or a *copita* of sherry and a *tapa* before scurrying back to the home hearth.

Later on, the scene would change; gentlemen with their ladies dressed in all their finery would saunter from bar to bar, taking a small drink with their chosen *tapas*. In one place the speciality might be squid or olives, in another it might be spicy meatballs, in a third the anchovy will reign; whereas in the next, the humble potato might be elevated to unheard of levels. The Spanish are not a quiet people, so everywhere there would be noise. But all would be good natured, no overt drunkenness to be seen.

Sally gave me a nudge as we strolled past yet another restaurant. "Shall we make an evening of it then?" she enquired.

"Well, Eva did tell us that, if we were going to eat anywhere, it should be around here in the Calle Noria area. But there are so many places to choose from, so let's walk from one end of this street to the other and choose the one that we like the look of best. But only after we've had that *copita!*"

We plonked ourselves down at a little bar that had half a dozen tables outside surrounded by some low bushes planted to offer privacy. We watched everyone strolling by, and watched, too, to see where everyone was headed.

At the end of the street was a smart place called La Buena Vida and its tables were filling rapidly. We got the last table for two outside and enjoyed a meal of lightly dressed avocado and bacon salad followed by a dish of heavenly pig's cheeks for Sally and an equally enticing sea bass with fennel for me. Coffee would help for the journey home, and for a change, Sally drew the short straw.

On the way back, we pondered our day out and decided that the Hotel Mencey would have to bear more in depth investigation on another occasion. Little did I know then that I would, indeed, be staying at that hotel in order to provide a report to the island newspaper.

Another great advantage to living in the unspoilt north is that we have far fewer ex-pats than there are in the south.

As couples, they often sit for ages in complete silence, clearly not enjoying life much at all, slouched down and looking for all the world like a brace of abandoned tailor's dummies plonked down on chairs. When congregating in groups, their demeanour changes and some elderly Britons, and indeed Germans for that matter, most of them with hardly a Spanish word between them, operate on the age old principle of shouting if they cannot make themselves understood. The problem is actually theirs, because not every Spaniard speaks English, or wishes to reveal that they do. After all, we are in their country. Whether it is in a bank or a bar, we have found that it is best to start off in Spanish, even if your vocabulary is limited, because your efforts will be appreciated, and then, with a beam, your Spaniard will switch to almost flawless English and completely flummox you!

But if I had a fiver for each time I have heard the complaint that the locals do not speak enough English…!

We see them, mostly down in the tourist end of town, clustered round bar tables at all hours of the day, empty glasses almost filling the table around which they are sitting. The sun would be well over the yardarm for them by eleven of the clock in the forenoon.

"Hello, old boy! Saw you in the supermarket the other day. Fancy a snifter then? Come and join us and take a pew."

Invariably, I politely make my excuses and pass on by.

Sally and I have always been very happy with Spanish food, its style and the way that it is cooked – and those aromas, so many different ones, so much more sensual than in England! But by way of a change, perhaps twice a year, we go down into town for a meal at The Welcome Café, right in the heart of tourist land, and have their fish, chips and mushy peas. As you may have guessed, the place is owned by an ex-pat Englishman. The cod there is always just perfect; I don't know where he gets it from, but you could not better it, and the batter is always light and crispy, and the chips perfect. And fancy being able to get proper mushy peas in Spain! All in all, a lovely evening out, but so bizarre.

In the town we have also discovered an English bowling society, an English tennis club and an English Rotary club. There is a society that performs English plays and music. They hold lunches where they gossip about all things English, and talk about the "Swallows".

"Swallows" is the term that they use for people who come out to the Canaries to avoid the English winter. Who can blame people for doing that? If they have the money, then why not have the best of both worlds? And they give the lovely volunteer ladies in The English Library much to talk about whilst filling their shifts.

To demonstrate our solidarity, we are members of The English Library. This is housed in a beautiful colonial type of building in the park near to us, and offers one of the largest collections, we have been told, of English books to be found outside the UK.

It costs 30 euros a year to be a member, and we can take out DVDs as well as books. They have a very relaxed view to returns, appearing grateful that we deign to take them back at all. We invariably do, and have also donated many unwanted books to them, startling them even further.

An unknown lady member sells homemade marmalade. She charges 1.40 euros a pot, and operates on an honesty box basis, her pots left on a tray in the library entrance. I hope that she makes a profit. It is very good marmalade, so whoever you are, many thanks.

But the ex-pats will ever be there in full force, talking loudly over the heads of those of us that go there for a bit of peace and quiet, or even, dare one say it, to find a book. The words "silence" and "library" do not go hand in hand in Tenerife at all. I find that intensely irritating.

We walk there with Freddie as it is a stopping off place to the park where he can run around to his heart's content. I tie him to a table leg in the garden of the library, and he howls until someone comes along to talk to him. I am quite sure that he knows full well that I shall only be gone for a few minutes – he just demands some attention. Who can blame him?

A friend had been a library member for a few months and was accosted near to the desk.

"Do I know you?" said this frosty matronly figure, glowering down at him.

"No, I do not think that we have ever met," said our friend.

"Well, what do you do?" she interrogated him.

"Do?" he enquired.

"Yes, what do you actually do?" She was, it seemed, checking on his suitability as a member.

"Well, I am retired now, but I used to own a number of hotels."

"Ah, trade," she said, and marched off.

11

Learning the Lingo

So many people come to live in Spain and never learn the language. I suppose it equally applies in other countries too. We had heard the usual horror stories of couples who have lived in Tenerife for 20 years and not bothered to learn to speak any Spanish at all. When something went wrong, they were snookered. If anything of a complicated or formal nature was required of them, they just could not get their requirements over.

Another acquaintance who had been coming over here on holiday for a similar time, and used to be an apartment owner when he was younger, never got past the "*café con leche*" stage. Nor, incidentally, does he even actually like Spanish food, preferring good old cottage pie. He just used to come for the sun, and put up with the food!

Spanish has now long overtaken English as a world language by the number of people speaking it, and when a guest in this country, it is so rude to expect a Spaniard to talk to you in English. Should you have an accident or need to be hospitalised, then you really do need to be able to communicate properly, efficiently and quickly.

And so, it was time for us to go back to school.

There were a number of language schools in the area, catering for all sorts of nationalities wanting to learn Spanish, and indeed for Spanish people wanting to learn most other languages. Sally was not keen on going back to school. Nor was I, truth be told.

We asked around a bit, and our gardener recommended a local Swedish lady, a *professora de idiomas*. Multi-lingual, she taught

Spanish, German and English and French, and of course Swedish. We really are a multi-cultural island.

Dear Eva was determined to get us up and running. She was happy to come to us, and we started out seeing her five mornings a week. Initially, lessons took place at our dining room table and were centred around text books and computer.

Eva had recently lost her old Boxer, Bobby, and took straight away to Freddie. Freddie, for his part, took greatly to Eva and during our lessons, formed a great attachment to her legs.

As she said to us, "It's a Nivea thing, you know."

After a number of weeks' tuition, we would set off on tours around the area to discuss Spanish life in general, local architecture and the like. We had a fascinating time with her and I hope that she was satisfied with our progress after all her efforts. As a result of her hard work, we are now comfortable in most situations unless they are of a technical nature, when our straightforward lack of a full vocabulary will let us down.

She and her family became good friends, and we have been invited to their house for meals and meet up for coffee regularly. Both of us are pondering how she will take it when the inevitable comes to pass and we press her to take us to the next level.

An alternative to learning the language is the "Canary shrug" which is universally practiced, particularly if you are unsure of something, or do not know what to do, or do not want to become involved. This is the slightly raised shoulders accompanied by bent arms with palms upwards.

If you can master this expression, you can use it in almost any situation, so rendering the Spanish language entirely superfluous. You are instantly fluent in Canarian, and we could have saved a fortune in lessons.

There are a number of variations of Spanish. We have been learning "proper" formal Spanish. Then there's local Canarian Spanish (so difficult), and lastly the old dialect, probably stemming from the Guanches, the original settlers of the islands.

This last is almost completely unintelligible to the likes of us. The dialect uses words and phrases that we cannot get our heads around, and it all tumbles out at the rate of a Kalashnikov on full auto. Pedro, our community gardener, speaks with a local accent, but we have grown used to talking with him, and can work well with our daily exchanges of gossip.

When in doubt, I comfort myself by recalling a conversation that I had with my next door neighbour, a charming (and dog owning) young Spanish man by the name of Adrián. He confessed that when he goes to Santa Ursula, a town only some five kilometres away but further inland, he finds the language there almost unintelligible. So what chance do we have really?

To lisp or not to lisp? That has been a vexing question.

For example, in standard mainland Spanish, *Valencia* is pronounced 'Valenthia'. *Chorizo* is pronounced 'choritho'. And this is indeed the correct and formal way. However, here in the Canaries it is not universally practiced. So we try to drop the lisp to appear more integrated. It is surprisingly difficult not to lisp once you have been indoctrinated.

Spanish is a very lazy language over here. Some words seemed familiar, but we could not quite get them into the right context. This was because the final letter often got dropped from the end of a word. Thus, most words ending in an "s", for example *"entonces"* would come out as *"entonce"*. Really confusingly, "Madrid" comes out as "Madri" with the last "d" being silent. The most obvious one is *"gracias"*, which everyone knows. It comes out as *"gracia"* over here.

We had been told by everyone back on the Peninsula that this was because it was so warm in the Canaries that the locals did not bother to finish their words properly. It could just be true!

Talking of silent, the "h" in the Spanish alphabet is never ever pronounced. That can get really bothering and change your understanding of a sentence completely. So, if it's never ever pronounced…?

One particular day, our Spanish lesson with Eva was to be held out in the open: *en la calle*, in the street, as one might say over here.

Not for the first time, we would be out and about, visiting somewhere else and taking in the sights, learning about our new culture, and all the while, for two hours or more, nary a word of our native tongue would pass our lips until we reached the final coffee stop.

This time, we were going to La Orotava, that lovely old town up in the hills behind Puerto. By then we had learned "La Orotava" could equally be spelt, and pronounced, "La Orotaba", because of the interchangeable nature of "b" and "v". Apart from the architecture of the town, and no doubt to whet our appetite, we had been promised a revelation, which we were already referring to between ourselves as "The Curious Case Of The Revolving Babies".

La Orotava has a most beautiful old town centre, crammed full of gorgeous old houses with typical Canarian wooden balconies, and all reached by a juxtaposition of cobbled streets, too narrow to park in. Further up into the hills by some 500 metres, it is a cooler place to live in summer and where merchants in the 18th century decided that the quality of life would be better than on the coast. Certainly, it remains measurably cooler than Puerto, having an almost English feel to the early mornings and late evenings.

Those grand old traders' mansions look imperiously down towards the coast, perched high on the side of the valley, surrounded by a green sea of banana plantations. The first person to ship bananas back to England was, I am told, a Mr Reid, and he was followed some ten years later by the first large commercial companies, Fyffes, and Elder Dempster. The main banana of choice grown here is the Dwarf Cavendish, sweeter and healthier than those huge tasteless things we see so often in the shops in England.

We had collected Eva, our *professora de idiomas*, from her home, and soon were looking for a parking space in one of the vertiginous streets of the town. The car was eventually crammed in between two others in a very narrow road, and we metaphorically donned our crampons for the ascent into the old town.

The lesson was immediately into full flow.

"Let's stop a minute and look at that row of houses."

Beautiful old mansions with almost palatial facades were being pointed out to us, lying cheek by jowl with older properties which appeared not to be occupied.

"Do you know anyone that lives in any of the big houses?" I asked Eva.

"Yes, I do. That one is owned by my friends Christian and Carolina. They come to our party every Christmas, so you will be meeting them soon. He is a retired architect and now deals in fine art."

"What about those smaller places, that look as though their roofs are about to collapse?"

"Well, that one over there dates, I think, from the 15th century. Nobody knows who the current owners are, so it will just get worse until the government steps in to save it."

"At what stage would the government do that?"

"Well, for the first couple of hundred years, it would have been occupied by one family. After that, ownership would have been split between various parts of the family as sons died and daughters married. Then there would have been an internal family battle to claim sole ownership, with no side having enough money to buy out the other claimants."

"And?" Sally asked.

"Like everywhere else on the island, so many people fled when the famines came, or it became too difficult to earn a living out of the land. Just as in Puerto, warring families could not be traced or found, or could not agree on the split of their inheritance, or indeed had fled to Venezuela and could not be located to learn of their good fortune. Eventually, after all avenues had been explored, in a timeframe spanning generations, the Tenerife *Cabildo* or local government might step in and allow a sale or conversion."

We were engaging in some rather heavy duty Spanish with a lot of new words coming into play. And our calf muscles were killing us.

Most of the streets in the old part of the town were still cobbled, usually one way through for the traffic, and oh so narrow. The town was crammed with cars, because none of these old houses were built with vehicles in mind, and there is no place to excavate for parking spaces due to the steepness of the hillside and the likely lack of any reinforced foundations.

We went next to the Town Hall, which was built in the early 1600s and remained an oasis of calm. Behind it were the Botanical Gardens, and in front was the great square where the sand and flower carpets were laid out each year by the local inhabitants, earning them a place in the Guinness Book of Records. We stood and looked out over the balcony and drank in the view to the valley below, and then further, towards the ocean.

The Town Hall was cool and spacious, full of beautifully carved wood, and the luxurious carpets, which had been specially woven, must have cost the town a fortune.

We stopped next at an hotel, converted from an old mansion, with a lovely interior courtyard. As I'd worked in the hotel industry, neither of us could generally pass one by without some sort of investigation. This one had been remodelled and upgraded, although we felt that some of the reformation would not have been to our choosing. A kind member of staff allowed us to saunter around, looking at all the carved wood on the balustrades and balconies. With all the work that had been done to it, it would surely now have attracted a sale price of at least a couple of million euros. Later, talking with our friend Peter, he told us that it was originally on the market some 17 years ago, and he could have bought it for only 170,000 euros!

Finally, and as promised, we arrived at the Curious Case Of The Revolving Babies, which had been tantalising us all morning.

"What's that all about, then?"

"You will have to wait and see. Be patient."

We rounded a corner, and on the far side of the square we saw an old convent. It stood whitewashed, majestic and silent, the guardian of that old square for a number of centuries past.

Once admitted through the huge, arched portal into an inner court, we peered in delight over the balcony towards the view of the valley below. The day was crystal clear, and the view was superb. Those nuns sure knew where to put down their roots. We could pick out our own home down on the coast, just on the far side of one of the old volcanic blow holes.

"OK. Now you can go and look at the front door. What do you see?"

We turned towards one of the old, original entrance doors. Into the door had been fitted a revolving drum, about the size of an oil drum, exquisitely made out of polished and lacquered wood, which could spin around on its own axis. One side of the drum was smooth, rounded and solid, but when it was spun it would reveal the other side comprising a ledge with a safety up-stand around the edge. A bit like a vertical crib made out of half a barrel. The whole thing was at least a metre tall and almost as wide.

"What on earth was that for?" I exclaimed.

"Babies! It was for putting babies in!"

"No! Are you really telling us that people used to put babies into that contraption? What on earth for?" I asked.

"Well, in years gone by, this being a very Catholic country, an unmarried mother would have been unlikely to have been allowed to keep an unwanted or unexpected baby. Abortion would generally not have been an option for a girl of good family, so here was the answer. In complete privacy, guarded by the huge door and the revolving wooden drum, mother and new-born baby could present themselves at the convent. The baby would be placed on the flat ledge within the drum. A signal would be given, and the nun on the other side would revolve the drum and take the baby."

It was an important procedure enabling a well-to-do family to preserve their good name.

"In this way, privacy would have been maintained, neither the mother nor the nun having been able to see each other, and the passing over of the baby would therefore have been done without the one side knowing anything of the other. The baby would have been assured a decent upbringing. Literally hundreds of them must have passed through that revolving drum over the years gone by."

We all stood there in silence, staring at that drum. Nobody said anything, and I supposed that we all had our own private thoughts on the matter. I pondered whether we should be sad at this mechanism that existed to facilitate the handing over of unwanted babies, or should we be happy that children would be looked after when they were so clearly not going to be accepted within their own family? Just who was at fault there? Was the attitude of the church all those years ago to an unwanted pregnancy outside of marriage the driving force to expel an infant from the bosom of a family? Was the continued "good name" of a family so important as to deny a mother her child, for it to be brought up not knowing whence it came?

How much heartbreak must there have been when the mother saw her child slowly disappear in that drum, revolved by an unseen nun, never to be seen or heard of again?

Eventually, still in silence, my eyes ever so slightly moist, we drifted away and regrouped.

And so, all too soon it was time to end our lesson. We had spent at least a couple of hours walking through the old part of the town. We dropped downhill past yet more fine old houses to a café surrounded by gardens where we took the inevitable shot of coffee (tea for me, please) and relaxed for a few minutes and reviewed our morning, whilst enjoying a perfect clear view of El Teide in the far distance.

It was time to retrace our steps to our car, to drop off Eva at her home and to be reunited with Freddie, who would have dozed away his morning, doubtless dreaming of all those rabbits and squirrels in the woods behind our house at Lytham.

All legs and snout a-twitching in his sleep, we could read him like a book.

12

Keeping Busy

A couple of months or so after we had moved in permanently, I opened up my email account one morning and was surprised to see a message from the editor of the main English language newspaper for the Canary Islands, *Island Connections*, which went very much like this:

"We are wanting to put together reviews of bars and restaurants and the like to give our readers an unbiased opinion of each place, particularly if they are of some sort of special interest and/or out of the way, such that tourists and even residents might not know of. With your experience of the hotel and restaurant industry, I can think of nobody better qualified. Would you be interested?"

I suppose that it was a measure of the effort that we were putting into integration into the local community.

When I had picked myself up from the floor and got over such flummery, I emailed back that I would be interested to meet to discuss it, with one proviso. I would not be interested at all if I was going to be told what to write, and if I did not have full independence as to my reporting. I had seen so many reviews where hotels and restaurants received glowing reviews, usually because they were, in one way or another, paying for them.

The reply came back by return.

"You can write what you wish, about where you wish, as long as it is not libellous!"

My introduction to the readers of *Island Connections* gave a brief précis of my qualifications to be their restaurant reviewer. I had, after all, spent over 35 years in the hotel and restaurant industry, gaining two AA Rosettes for my endeavours, which I had held on to consecutively for a number of years. Because I had also been a director of a European-wide hotel marketing consortium, I had been privileged to stay in some wonderful hotels, and to eat in quite a number of the best restaurants in Europe. I was ready to pick up the quill in my new role as restaurant reviewer (or *critico gastronomico,* as my Spanish business card read, rather fancily).

I fell quite comfortably into the role. I could be impartial, recording the good and the bad of the places that I visited. Restaurants, bars that served food, specialist food shops, local markets, nobody was safe from my probing questioning, my tasting of produce, or the eagle eye of my camera.

I soon decided to include a "Loo Score" for each establishment, working on the basis that most people like to know if the loos are OK or not, because they are usually an integral part of any night out. A lousy loo would put most people off from any return visit. Anyway, doing that made it all a bit different, and I am pleased to say that this idea has since been picked up elsewhere.

I was more than happy to operate truly independently, never normally revealing any connection to the newspaper until I had paid the bill.

Funnily enough, I had received my introduction to the paper's editor initially through Freddie. We came over to Tenerife on the inaugural Jet2.com flight out of Blackpool (big plane, scarily short runway!) and she was on the tarmac doing interviews. I can remember asking her if she would like Freddie to put together an article about living in Lytham with all his friends and how he would like to move to Spain. She thought it could be a bit of fun for the Pets page in the paper. The article was written, it was published, and we took it on from there. It's funny how things can work out in the oddest of ways.

One of my early reviews covered my visit to our regular market, 12 kilometres away down the coast road towards Icod de los Vinos. My wife has never understood my fascination for markets. I suppose that you either like them or loathe them. So, more often than not, I go alone, unless the lure of a *café cortado leche y leche* can tempt her away from the housework.

I love all sorts of markets. When I lived in Paris, I used to go to the flea market at the Porte de Clignancourt on most weekends. I still have some of the tat that I accumulated there.

We are lucky to have two permanent weekend markets within twenty minutes of Puerto de la Cruz, one on each side of the town. They both rejoice in glorious names. The one at La Matanza de Acentejo is called El Mercadillo del Agricultor, El Vino y la Artesania. The one in the other direction, on the road towards Icod de los Vinos, is just as grand, being called El Mercado del Agricultor de La Guancha.

Both markets supply the freshest of vegetables for sale, grown by the stallholders and their families themselves, a far cry from the stuff available from our largest local supermarket. This means that not only is everything exceedingly fresh, but that we eat by the season. As an example, when plums are in season, we eat plums. When they are not, we do not. I find it very pleasant to only eat according to the seasons and not to consume tasteless stuff that has been chilled to make it last. Back in England, some fruits had travelled half way round the world and were about as old. Nine month old apples? No thank you!

Prices at the market are also strictly controlled. At Icod, you see a large electronic display listing all of the greengrocery on sale that day, with a "from" and "to" price range quoted. It keeps the already low prices even lower and sometimes we have to wonder whether a profit is being made at all.

I really enjoyed taking on this new role as a restaurant reviewer. We were getting out more, discovering new places to go to eat in new villages that previously were just names on a map, and the readership seemed to like what I produced. The only downside was my expanding waistline!

Extract from my review of the weekend market near Icod de los Vinos:

"*It's a perfect Canary day, with a light breeze and not a cloud in the sky as we potter along the main road from Puerto de la Cruz in the direction of Icod de los Vinos.*

Shopping bags at the ready, we are on our way to the Mercado del Agricultor, just this side of Icod, at TF5, Km 49, 38440 La Guancha. Stick to the main road, but keep an eye open for the sign, as it comes along quite suddenly.

It is a regular trip for us, because we love the freshness of the produce, the range of items for sale, and last but not least, the prices!

Having said that, we are aware that markets are not everything to everyone, and we have a dear friend that patronises a different market because of the lack of chickens and flat green beans. You can never please everyone.

Nevertheless, everything that we want can be found here. There are stalls for local cheeses (always a selection handy on plates with sticks in for one to taste), a butcher who specialises in pork (surprise, surprise!) in all its guises, a stunning bread counter, really fresh eggs, a wonderful array of freshly cut flowers, a stand selling local honey, an interesting soap stand (boasting various remedial properties for your aches and pains) and many, many others. In between all of this are stand upon stand of the freshest verduras *(vegetables) that you will see anywhere.*

Today we buy cabbage, a type of broccoli that we have not seen before, radishes, tomatoes, lettuce, a bundle of wild rocket (in flower) some freshly dug beetroot, perfect baby spring onions (so unusual round here) and potatoes still with fresh earth on them. Of course, we also patronise the pork man, the bread counter, and pick up some eggs, too. The tally for everything is less than €12.

Afterwards, we take the lift (!) up to the top floor to the in-house café, where for €2.20 we have a cortado leche y leche *and a large bottle of Nestea (nicely served with ice and a slice of orange). If you like orange, then this café will be just perfect for you because the tables, chairs and awnings are all that colour!*

And the smiles are everywhere. People seem to be so happy. It is a family outing for locals, and the stallholders show that they are really pleased to see you and do business. We notice this every time, but cannot believe that group training has been going on. It must be something in the local water.

There is a large tarmac parking area in which we always find a space, and the spaces themselves are of a reasonable size, the whole building having been built fairly recently, and in a very modern style, hence that lift. There is also a small underground car park.

Go along and give it a try. The local people will welcome you with a smile. You will also save a lot of money, and get the best of produce.

See you there next weekend!"

Despite my writings for the newspaper, which had taken up a lot of time quite apart from the necessity to dine in a number of restaurants, some good, some less so, Sally had suddenly come up with the idea that I needed to have another new hobby.

I thought that I already had a hobby, or even two. Since well before coming over here, it had been my declared intention to get our family tree going. Now I had the time to make a start on it and had no excuses to delay it further.

I knew all of my immediate family, because, frankly, there were never that many to know. And all, sadly, were now dead. All the questions that had been in the back of my mind to ask about my history were now consigned to dust, and I would never know. It had never been a source of interest to me whilst I was young, and now I'd left it too late. Why, oh why, did I never ask the questions when I could have? I really hoped that my son Marcus would raise some interest to take it forward, or it might be lost for ever, despite the knowledge that can be gained from the internet nowadays. But the young are always too busy.

Our microclimate here in the north is governed by El Teide, he who dominates our lives in so many ways. Sometimes, the clouds roll down the hills behind us, cutting off all visibility to La Orotava, just above. This grey blanket of cloud is known by the locals as the underbelly of the donkey, the *panza de burro*.

So, one morning when the *panza de burro* was in full swing, I took the bull by the horns (mixing my metaphors) and signed up to one of those heritage/ancestor sites. They make it look so easy, but the reality is that you fumble and fudge for hours before making even the slightest sensible headway. I started putting in all the relatives that I knew of, into the tiny boxes. Later, when I was more used to the dratted system, I found that I could put in notes regarding dates of birth or death, occupation and the like. It was all hard work though.

I contacted some long lost, semi-forgotten distant relatives by email and received some interesting responses. I was further unwittingly helped by receiving, out of the blue, an invitation to the funeral of a very distant relative by marriage, on my late mother's side. Here I met a number of people that I didn't know even existed. They pointed me to others, until I was finally stalled at just over 360 people on my tree. Due to the numbers involved, my original "free" entry on the system had to be upgraded to "premium" at heavy cost and, although there were instructions as to how to print out my family tree, I have never discovered exactly how to print out one that must stretch a couple of metres in both directions. And that was without the inclusion of any of the extra notes. The only plus side was that I had traced my family back in an unbroken chain to the early 1500's.

During all of this I discovered that my ancestors were a Royal Navy captain at the battle of the Nile, a cordwainer, a master plasterer, magistrates (both in England and in New Zealand), a brewery owner (a number of those, mostly in or around Hatfield in Hertfordshire), a county surveyor (one in England, one in Ireland), solicitor (quite a number of those, too) a master builder, a land agent, various army officers and quite a lot of gentlemen farmers... The list went on and on.

Most interesting was the discovery of, and communication with, relatives in New Zealand, all descended from a direct ancestor who went out there in 1842. Although I was temporarily stuck, and laid it aside, it was still an on-going project, and would be for months, if not years. There were still areas that I wanted to research and fill in. It was not something that I could have done had I not been retired from work, and of course, I now had the perfect environment in which to do it.

Anyway, for the life of me I couldn't understand why I needed yet another hobby, because our lives were full of activity, and since we had arrived here in Tenerife there had not been a spare day in which to become bored.

Sally mooted the idea of starting to play golf again. We had both played in the past; indeed, I used to have a handicap in single figures. She pointed out that we were but half an hour away from one of the earliest courses constructed in Europe. How about a game?

The rugged coastal scenery... the views over the mountains... the freshness of the air blown in bright and clear from the Atlantic... She painted a pretty picture.

The lack of golf clubs... the cost of membership... the time and commitment... I responded.

"Let's try again and look for something else," we both agreed. After all, there was no hurry.

And there, again, was the point of being retired in a place like this. Island life here runs at a very definitely slower pace than that which we had suffered back in England. If we didn't do it today, then we could do it tomorrow. If something else crops up tomorrow, then we might leave it till next week. The sun will still be shining. *Mañana!*

But there is one of the three of us living here that has never got the hang of this *"mañana"* attitude. Freddie can only operate on the basis of NOW. When he wants to do something, then there can be no cause, in his eyes, for any delay. He has an inbuilt clock which is accurate to the minute. He knows exactly when his morning constitutional will take place, when he will go out for a brief walk at lunchtime, when his longer late afternoon walk is due (when it is cooler for his paws), and last but not least when it is time for dinner.

When he judges that moment to be, he gets up, walks into the kitchen, and issues forth one bark. His timing is always impeccable, to the minute. Of course, to a dog's owner, that is really nothing exceptional, but it never ceases to amaze us how perfect is his timekeeping.

In between times, he can give the impression of being dead to the world, the deep rumbling of his snores echoing around the lounge or the terrace, depending on where he has settled. But the slightest movement on our part will mean that the snores will stop and an eye will open to see if something is going on. Just how do they do it?

In the meantime, we pondered anew on the hobby issue.

Sally is also a bit of a petrol-head, and knew full well that I shared her enthusiasm. Over the years, we had both owned a few desirable cars. Surely it should be possible to buy something that would give the two of us some pleasure? Perhaps something older, classic, and hopefully a bit sporty?

Because of the climate here and general lack of rain, cars last much longer than back in the UK. It is unusual to see rust buckets, and quite normal to see cars that went out of production 30 or 40 years ago, looking almost like new. No day would be complete without the sighting of the likes of a Singer Gazelle, Hillman Husky, Triumph Herald, Ford Anglia or a range of Mercedes covering every decade from the 40s.

There would be no point in having anything like we'd had before, because once you were away from the main roads, north

Tenerife was quite unsuited to hand-cut Michelins; so the requirement fell into the more "sensible" category. Less power, more comfort in approaching old age. What a depressing mantra.

The island seemed to have an absolute plethora of old cars. We trawled advertisements and visited garages specialising in the type of vehicles that might interest us. Each week we added to our sightings of old classic cars, but nothing took our fancy. Nothing we saw enthused us. How about one of these? Or what about one of those? Even one of those! The list went on. But without exception, everything that we saw that had any sort of sporting pretentions had been hammered and looked tired. Not for me a heavy restoration project in the autumn of my years.

So, what about trying to import something? I bought Spanish and German classic car magazines. I trawled through the pages, and identified lots of cars that would have satisfied my personal criteria, if not necessarily very sensibly.

Then I saw a word that has never failed to stir my imagination… Abarth!

Carlo Abarth founded his factory in 1949 and between then and 1971, when he sold to FIAT (the race division being sold elsewhere), the factory produced some of the most magnificent racing, rally and fast road car machines that the world has known. Even to the present day, Abarth is a major automotive name, particularly so in Italy.

Oh so stupid for one of my advancing years, but if one does not at least try to stay young…

I had long wanted a "proper" Abarth, but they were so expensive nowadays, even bad ones. A good one was for sale in Bergamo in northern Italy. Tony Erker of Superstrada in Switzerland was handling the sale, and the car came, as anything did from Tony, with an impeccable provenance.

It had been immaculately refurbished and repainted, and was in perfect condition. The pictures sent over by Tony did it full justice. It was love at first sight, and all sense and reason went out of the window.

I could have asked myself at this point why I was even considering it, had I had any of my senses left. Sally was quick to point out that there would be no room in it for us and the shopping, let alone Freddie trying to access the rear seats via the roll cage. Our backsides would be scraping the tarmac, but the noise, oh, the noise! Whilst the noise was a plus for me, it was a clear minus point for my significant other. I retaliated with the immense fun factor – and the fact that we already had a SEAT people carrier, so what was the downside of a car with a roll cage?

Apart from the problem of Freddie navigating his way through the roll cage, where would the shopping go? Absolutely and totally impracticable was the majority decision. And yet…

Emails flew back and forth. Questions were asked and properly answered. More pictures were sent. Tony even sent scanned copies of the car's matriculation papers in Italy for the customs engineer to appraise at this end.

I had needed to engage with a specialist import agency and an engineer approved by the Spanish equivalent of HM Customs. One look at a picture of the engine in that Abarth with its beautiful Weber trumpets was enough to give them all a fit of the vapours.

The car was mint, priced accordingly at usual Abarth rates. We established that costs of transportation by RoRo (a roll on/roll off type of vehicle ferry, usually used by car manufacturers to send large numbers of their vehicles to far flung places) ex-Rotterdam would have been another 2,500 euros, and all the technical fees involved would have been another 2,000 euros. Then came the killer punch… import duty would add another 30% on top.

Until then, I had only just prevented myself from jumping on the next plane, but a quiet note of caution crept in and asked the question: this was all getting way over budget, and what were the import rules over here, if they could do you for another 30% on top of the asking price?

The basic rule turned out to be simple. In the same way as new cars are overpriced, the authorities do all in their power to make sure that it is well-nigh impossible to import anything at all, let alone anything interesting. Even importing a classic car from mainland Spain, already correctly matriculated and taxes paid, would attract a swingeing import duty that would put up the cost by that same 30%.

What finally decided the matter was the flat refusal of the Spanish customs engineer to technically approve the car in advance of its arrival on the docks, so it could hypothetically have been refused entry and put on the next boat back out, with me urgently having to look for a buyer whilst it was on the high seas.

My dream of howling round the hills up to El Teide had gone up in smoke.

I had long concluded that I only really enjoyed cars with a slight "edge", but perhaps in retirement, and on roads such as these, it was not to be, and I must perforce lower my expectations, and start to think laterally.

But, rules like that, especially in one's retirement, seemed there to be challenged. Although I failed at the first attempt, I was determined to triumph next time around.

Quite by chance, the very next month, whilst still languishing in the slough of despond, I ventured upon an outfit in Holland selling, amongst other classic cars, Mercedes SLs from the 70s and 80s. The pictures were stunning and the cars obviously well-presented and fettled.

I knew little about those particular models and so I decided to ring them for a general chat, to learn more. And so it all began again…

The SLs that they specialised in were all R107s, that iconic two door convertible of yesteryear, much coveted everywhere. Almost anyone would like to own one, but with my serious head on, what would one be like to live with long term on an island with limited backup if (or rather when) something were to go wrong? Everything that I learned about them pointed out their desirability, image and asset value retention. Nothing was mentioned about any downsides, other than the likelihood of rust.

It's strange how some things click into place. I then happened to notice an advertisement on the internet by a classic car business called The SL Shop, in the Midlands, back in the UK. I rang them up and had a chat with the owner who was candid and helpful. He appeared to love his SLs and had a number in stock.

Crucially, he asked if I was really looking for a classic type of ride, and classic handling to go with it, as well as having that quintessential classic look. This really meant old fashioned, with a bumpy ride and loose steering, and we had a further chat about all that. If that was what I really wanted, then I was going to be spoilt for choice with him.

But if I wanted something a bit more comfortable and reliable, the next generation as it were, then why not consider the newer model, the R129? It looked a bit "new" to me. But I did learn from asking around that it would be a lot better for long term ownership for us in Tenerife than an R107, and I also learned that the R129 was the last of the properly built Mercedes before the bean counters got to work at Mercedes Benz. Later SLs were rated as not a patch for build quality. So it should live me out.

What a surprise! They had one coming into stock, a left hand drive example in bright red, with hard and soft tops, lots of extras, and it had had only two owners, both traceable. I was told that the condition was excellent, that it had been well looked after, and the electric soft top roof was brand new, fitted recently by a UK Mercedes dealer.

We decided to fly over there and to have a look at it. We were made very welcome on our visit, and we liked what we saw, both the car and the people involved. We were invited to take the car off for a drive by ourselves, with the car having had no special preparation at that stage.

"Take it for a long run. Be as long as you wish. Just get to know it."

It was reasonably sporty, yet comfortable and sensible. It was very appropriate for life on the island, and I had seen a few around back here, so I reasoned that spares should be available locally. I haggled and made an offer, which was eventually accepted. Within the offer I included a list of my requirements to further refurbish the car, and it was confirmed that these would be included in the already agreed price.

The wheels were taken off and sent away to be chemically dipped, stripped, and repainted in the correct Mercedes shade of silver. A new set of tyres was ordered. A full service was undertaken with attention to heavy duty greasing of all parts, bearing in mind where it was going to be living. The list went on and on, and it was all attended to with good spirit by The SL Shop.

But it was, after all was said and done, twenty years old and was more than 2,500 driving miles from our new home, with a lot of water in between!

We both felt that this new hobby was going to be something that would engage us both with a shared interest and which would be practical to boot. The car was old enough to be seen as a classic, but young enough and practical enough to serve us for motoring trips in style and comfort.

13

Our First Visitors

Think sunshine, think holiday island… think free holiday. It is a truism that the moment you move abroad, you will be bombarded by friends and relatives (some of whom you hardy know, or have long forgotten) wanting to come and visit. It can raise all sorts of problems, particularly when wanting to let someone down lightly.

But we do have friends that we really do want to come to stay with us. Georg and his wife Eta, hotel owners in Bavaria, will always be more than welcome here. We have known them for years and years, and we were so pleased when they accepted our long standing invitation to come and see us. The quid pro quo was the required return visit, but it is never any hardship to go to Oberammergau.

The day dawned bright as we prepared for their arrival. I had offered to collect them from the airport, but Georg, another confirmed petrol-head, told me that he had already booked a hire car. We arranged to meet in the first layby off the *autopista,* at the Puerto turn.

Although we had done everything that we could think of to make our place just right for them, we were still slightly nervous. How would we all get on living in such close proximity for a week?

The tone was set from the very first moment that they pulled up in the layby. A huge bear hug from Georg, and kisses from his very attractive wife, Eta. And then straight into the café, one of our regular stops, in that same layby. A few ice-cold beers later, and everyone had unwound and we were all at ease. They are one of the nicest couples that we know, and so kind and generous.

We convoyed to the apartment and settled them in. Knowing just how much food the inhabitants of Bavaria can put away, I had prepared a meal which vanished in an inkling. Would that I had made twice as much. Then it was time for *siesta*.

In the evening we dolled ourselves up and descended into the town. They had both been to Tenerife before, when some mutual business had brought a meeting to the island, and we had stayed in Santa Cruz and hired a meeting room at the Wine Museum up the road. I remember it being bitterly cold for that meeting, and the group photograph that I still have from all those years ago showed everyone in overcoats with thick scarves. The meeting room, hundreds of years old, and with a stupendous carved ceiling, had no heating in it. Nobody seemed to know what to do if there was a cold day. Tenerife can catch you out unexpectedly in so many ways.

Our first stop in town was the Plaza del Charco. We wandered around the old square, the evening sunlight shafting down through the trees on to the bars and cafés, whilst Georg and Eta got their bearings, remembering this and that from their last visit. Finally, we all settled on a restaurant whose menu appealed to us and the rest of the evening passed in an amiable blur before the taxi took us back home up the hill to our eyrie in the park.

And so the week flew by. For the most part, the weather was clear and sunny, and during the day Eta made the most of the sunbathing facilities on our terrace.

No visit to Tenerife is complete without a visit to the volcano. Georg being Georg wanted to do the drive, so every hairpin on the way up was taken at maximum attack. I was feeling quite safe, as we had both been competition drivers in earlier years, and I knew that we were in the very competent hands of a professional. Eta was so used to it she did not bat an eyelid. Sally on the other hand was pleased to get to the top for a coffee and a cigarette before her breakfast joined the scenery.

The cable car to the final summit was closed for the day as new parts were awaited to make it serviceable again. I for one was very grateful, and happy to just drink in the scenery around the caldera, which never ceases to amaze me.

Mind you, it never ceases to amaze me either, the fact that we have voluntarily chosen to come to make our home on a small volcanic island, where, if the pundits are to be believed, an eruption of serious proportion is long overdue – by some sixty thousand years. We have often wondered what we would do if El Teide should blow. We have come to the conclusion that we would be gassed, fried or drowned, with no chance of escape. I have become a bit fatalistic about it all. If he blows, he blows, and I will spend my last few minutes with my wife and dog and a serious bottle of claret. Who knows, as in Pompeii of old, I might be found clutching that bottle a thousand years later.

Whilst Georg and Eta were with us, Sally broke the catch on her large leather handbag. Purchased many years ago in a moment of madness in the Cotswolds, the bag had been so hideously expensive that it would have to be sent off to a proper repair shop, probably back to the UK agent of the manufacturer, in order to be brought back into tiptop commission.

And so we would have to go down into the town because she needed an interim replacement. Generally speaking, shoes, handbags, all things made of leather are less expensive in the Canaries, no doubt in part due to the low VAT rate and partly to the fact that one is expected to do a bit of haggling and not pay the tourist rate indicated on the sales ticket. It is helpful to establish that we are proper permanent residents at the outset, so that the seller is under no misapprehension as to our gullibility.

But first, the old bag had to be unloaded.

"What on earth do you carry around with you in that portmanteau of yours? It weighs a ton!"

She started fishing about in it. "Well, you sometimes need a tape measure when we are out. So I always carry one with me."

And so it went on.

"I carry a pack of sweeteners for you."

"I bring along the diary in case we have to make an appointment or if you want to know when we are due somewhere."

"If either of us gets a headache, then I have pills with me. I also have packets of Paracetamol, Gaviscon, Imodium, a small packet of tissues and your funny pills. You never know when something might be needed, do you? What happens if a loo has no paper?"

"If we get separated whilst shopping, I have a spare mobile phone."

"I carry a notepad and pen in case you can't remember something whilst we are out."

"Then there is all of our identification. I have certified colour copies of both of our passports, *Residencias* and *Padrons.*"

"And there is my wallet and cards, in case you have forgotten to bring yours."

"Then there's some personal stuff."

"And last but not least, most importantly, I have my cigarettes, lighter and that tin box that doubles as an ashtray!"

I was glad that she added that last bit. I was beginning to think that it was, as usual, all going to be my fault. Georg and Eta were rocking with laughter.

One day, feeling a bit mischievous, we took our German friends to visit a place that has come to be known locally as Hitler's Bunker.

The name had come about because there had been built, high up on the side of the valley a few years ago, an elongated, grey, pre-stressed concrete structure. From a distance it looked just like one of those concrete abominations that you can still see near to the

Normandy beaches or indeed in the Channel Islands. In the centre of it, you could easily imagine gun emplacements where Big Bertha would have swept a trajectory across the valley to protect it from marauding tourists.

In reality, neither was it anything to do with Herr H, and nor was it actually a bunker.

If one could get one's mind past the WW2 bunker idea, it is actually a very pleasant place to stop for a coffee or a light lunch. We sat under the garish pale green parasols and sank a few beers and then put away a decent meal. We were fortunate in that the day was crystal clear, and our friends could see the amazing view right along the northern coast, and the top of El Teide. It was the same view that had inspired Humboldt, the famous explorer, to pause on his trek up the valley towards the volcano and to state that, in his opinion, here lay the best view in the world.

Months later, I went back to the *Mirador* with Marcus and the family. The charming waitress managed to spill two beers at the same time all over his £900 camera and drenched Tina into the bargain. For some bizarre reason, her official compensation was the offer of a free Beatles T-shirt! It was hardly the moment to complete a review for *Island Connections*, so I had to go back yet again, a couple of months after that.

Extract from my review of the Mirador de Humboldt:

"After a number of false starts to get off the ground, the Mirador de Humboldt, on the road between La Orotava and Santa Ursula, has finally made its mark and become a 'must stop at' destination for the weary tourist, despite the strange shape and love of pre-stressed concrete that has garnered it a more colloquial nomenclature locally.

One can quite see why Mr H, when on his trek up the Orotava valley, paused and declared this spot to have one of the best views in the world, or at least of the world that he had by then seen. The view across the valley, down along the coast, and up to the unimpeded vista of El Teide looking down over everything, is truly world class.

Whilst the food here might not quite be in the same league, you will be sure of friendly service in a clean and smart environment, with your choice of snacks or light meals being more than satisfactory.

We went there for a light lunch and ordered a gloriously and extensively described Hamburguesa de Cochino Canario (lechuga, tomate, cebolla, queso blanco fresco y miel de cumbre) and an Ensalada de Lechugas bio, Jamon y aliño otoñal. The ham salad was exceptionally good (both to look at and to eat) coming complete with nuts, crystalized ginger and other treats as well as with the ham and bio lettuce leaves. After the big verbal build up for the hamburger, it was a disappointment that, for some unknown reason, the base of the bun was burned almost black. The rest of it was good. We ordered a couple of (small) glasses of the white house wine to go with it. I had to ask, and was told that it was Despunte, but it was not as good as the same wine that we had enjoyed so much at El Acueducto in Los Realejos (IC Issue 675). For all of the above we paid the reasonable price of €13.50. It would have been worth that for the view alone.

Other items on the menu that might have attracted our fancy were a range of tapas and bocadillos, all priced between €2 and €8. There were fillings of pork, salad, cheeses, tortilla, mixed sausages, and topping out with a plate of Jamon Iberico de Bellota at €15. Other dishes were available too, together with the usual teas, coffees and infusions. All in all, there was an enviable choice to suit most palates. The clientele seemed to be evenly split between those just dropping in for a coffee, a late breakfast (some nice fixed price choices) or just for a freshly squeezed orange juice, and those arriving for something more substantial. They do a very fancy speciality cappuccino topped with a lot of whipped cream.

The proprietor clearly has a love for the colour green. All of the parasols are a fairly lurid shade of pale green, as are the napkins and the chairs, but once you are seated, you tend not to notice them too much. Mind you, on a clear day I can actually see those parasols from my terrace, at least three

*kilometres away! You should therefore not get lost when seeking the place out
from lower down the valley.*

*But I would suggest that they throw away their menus and invest in some
new ones. I do hate frayed edges and stickiness.*

*Next to the cafetería there is a small shop selling Tenerife knick-knacks
and wines. Bizarrely, it closes at lunchtime, just when most of the prospective
clientele are around."*

Despite being one of the Canary Islands, this is really an island of
parrots, and when we got back home with Georg and Eta, we had
another visitor.

Everywhere you go up here in the north, you are likely to see
parrots. Apart from the wild ones, they are bred in Loro Parque, on
the far side of town, where they are also on display, trained and flying
free, with shows, feeding times and the like. In the streets there are
hawkers with parrots on their shoulders, doing their best to get
tourists to have their pictures taken.

Often as we are sitting on our terrace in the early evening we
will look up to the sound of beating wings, as a flock of wild parrots
swoops past. They are noisy birds, parrots. Chatterboxes, one and
all. Particularly in the evenings, just before they roost. After a
number of years over here, we still find it strange to see wild parrots
on the wing.

But this evening, when we went out onto our smaller terrace
there was a baby parrot, fully fledged, sitting on top of the wall,
peering at us inquisitively. He or she showed no fear, and Sally made
a beeline to go and stroke it on the head, and then to offer a morsel
of bread soaked in milk. This was gobbled up and more was
requested. A small bowlful was provided, and soon emptied.

It allowed me really close to take its picture. We stood there and
admired its plumage, the colours all bright and clear. The little bird

perched happily for an hour or so, and then, when next we looked, it had taken flight, to who knows where.

And all too soon, the time came around to say goodbye to our friends Georg and Eta. Bags packed and hugs and kisses completed, their hire car sped off, bearing them back south to the airport.

Very much later that evening, we got a call from Georg:

"We are just coming up the hill from Oberau into our valley. We have about six kilometres left to go to Oberammergau, and it is snowing! Everywhere is completely white and I am making fresh tracks along the road. Thanks again for everything, love from both of us, and we will see you soon over here."

14

Family Fun

───── ❧ ─────

The time fast approached when my son Marcus, his wife Tina, and their children Josh and Sam, would be coming to stay for a fortnight. I was all of a dither, despite maintaining the firm outer countenance as fathers should. Freddie picked up the vibes and knew that something major was afoot.

You know that aching feeling when you are going to see your son and his family after an absence?

The July school holidays would soon be upon us, and plane tickets had been bought. We were all on a countdown to the big day. Everything must be just so. Our days were full of questions that must be answered:

"How will we fit them all in this time?"

"What will the grandchildren want to do, now that they are a bit older?"

"What shall we feed them on?"

Our lives, therefore, immediately became full of different lists. Lists were pinned up everywhere in our kitchen, as well as the reminder: "Don't forget to put ketchup on the shopping list for Marcus." Hideous stuff!

When we settled down and thought of it properly, how would it work with all of us being that much older? They had been twice before, whilst the kids were smaller, and we had all crammed in together, but that was before we were actually living here full time, and when it was just a holiday home with less of our imported

110

clutter. And we were two summers younger then and the boys were now five and seven.

We decided to surprise them and rent the apartment next door, which was currently empty. It would be wonderful not to be all packed in like sardines. It had been vacant for a few months since Herman the German and his wife had gone back to the Fatherland. They were lovely people, and we would chat over our communal wall as they sat out each afternoon under their sunshade, playing cards or chess.

Despite having to pay out 650 euros to the developer who owned the apartment (for just a fortnight!), it would be so convenient with them being next door. That apartment was smaller than ours but at least it had two bedrooms and a terrace opening out down to the pool. Heaven for the kids, they would be seldom out of it. It also meant that they could come every morning to have breakfast on our terrace, which was super for us.

As usual, they wanted to go to Loro Parque, which also had an immense variety of other birds and mammals. A particular favourite was the whale and dolphin show, where the grandchildren demanded to sit at the front despite knowing full well that it was the water splash area when the whales took off. In vain did their father buy yet more plastic macs; they still got soaked, but is that not all part of the fun when you are five or seven?

Another day we drove along the coast to Bajamar, where we had been told that there were huge sea water bathing pools jutting out into the sea.

A funny place, Bajamar. It was not a town to fall in love with, more a weekend overspill from the capital, Santa Cruz, where you could go to escape from the city. But it was dominated by those huge pools. When we went there, they were chock full of people. There were immense flat concrete areas around them doubling as sun bathing areas. The sun shone, the ice cream café was doing a roaring trade, and it all looked like a perfect throwback to the 1950's. So much so that when I took a photograph of Marcus in one of the pools, he looked so very much like I remembered my father in his younger days. Quite uncanny, and it gave me pause for thought. A shiver went down my spine and it was a very poignant moment.

Sally and I are lucky to have a lot of those special moments when the family come to stay with us during the grandchildren's summer holidays. The fish restaurant at Los Silos is a place that we all go to, with great enjoyment, every time that they are here. Even Sam, the smallest amongst our group, is in seventh heaven at the plates of shellfish that are put before us to be nibbled, picked, cracked or slurped. After the meal is over some hours later, the boys go down onto the foreshore below the restaurant and investigate the rock pools which, if they are lucky, and the tide is right, might contain a baby crab or two. In vain do I tell them to collect some of the salty crust around the edges to use as our own sea salt.

Extract from my review of that superb fish restaurant in Los Silos:

"The family have arrived for a fortnight's holiday, and so we are all going to Los Silos, where there is a fish restaurant that they like so much that it has become a regular rite of passage. Coals are heaped into the boiler room of the old Mercedes, and we all set off. It takes us about 45 minutes to drive there from our home base in Puerto de la Cruz, pootling along whilst admiring the stunning views as we move along this northern coast of Tenerife.

We pass by a number of our regular stops, but this time we have only one particular destination firmly fixed in the Mercedes gun sight atop the front of the long bonnet of the car.

Restaurante El Mundial 82 is actually situated right on the rocky coast by the old village of La Caleta, cheek by jowl with Los Silos. We reach it along a bumpy road, passing by what I am told is an old abandoned sugar factory. A fine mist of sea spray is making the windscreen opaque, testimony to the closeness of the sea.

The restaurant (the clue is in the name!) pays visible homage to the year that Spain hosted the World Cup at football, and every wall is adorned with posters and photographs of teams and players. If, like me, football leaves you just a little cold, then just go there for the best and freshest of fish, all served professionally and with a smile.

It is one of those places that seemed to be a la mode about 50 years ago. Blue and white checks in abundance, plain upright chairs, and panoramic glass windows overlooking the sea. When I was much younger, I used to go to a place very much like it in Wimereux, in northern France, which had at that time, I seem to remember, a Michelin star.

I have pre-booked a table in the window, overlooking the rocky beach and the pounding surf. The tide is on the turn. Piping hot bread and a garlic dip are laid before us whilst we peruse the menu. I sidle up to the kitchen counter where I can see trays of camarones *(tiny red shrimps), sardines, various whole fish (*sama, dorada, lubina *etc.) and I watch a lady mixing a large bowl of octopus with onions and colourful peppers.*

So, our order is placed: a tapa *of those camarones, a* tapa *of the octopus salad, and then main courses of* paella marisco *(for two of us), a plate of mixed grilled fish, an enormous* sama *(for Marcus), a plate of hake and salad, and a bowl of mussels accompanied by a coleslaw type salad with a bowl of bright green tangy coriander sauce. With all of this comes a mound of salted wrinkly Canarian potatoes (*papas arrugadas*), unasked for and therefore hopefully included in the price. With all of that going on, it is pertinent to remind that there are six of us rather than the usual two!*

The menu is extensive, but this place is island-famous for paella, which comes in differing guises according to your tastes. Definitely not the usual tourist offering, which so often gives paella a bad name. Needless to say, there is a delay whilst it is expertly prepared and cooked and the rice soaks up all of the tasty stock.

No matter, the camarones and octopus are devoured, and I am pleased to see that the younger members of the family, Sam and Josh, are prepared to try everything that is put before them. That dip is really good too.

We have ordered a bottle of dry white Viñatigo, from just along the coast, and a 1.5 litre bottle of still water. I have drawn the short straw and so I am perforce abstemious, needing to pilot my trusty old steed back home afterwards.

Now it is time for the main course and the waiters engage in a spot of theatre for our benefit. Plates, piled high with fresh fish, are transported above their shoulders to the table and laid before us with a flourish. The two boys gasp with pleasure at the cornucopia of seafood covering the table, and, with a united front, we fall upon it.

What seems quite a long time later, there is virtually nothing left on any plate other than bones and cracked shells. All remains of the bread have long since disappeared, used to mop up fishy juices. The pile of detritus pays testament to the succulence of our meals.

It is time to call for our bill, and to stagger outside into the heat, so that the boys can research the contents of the rock pools on the shore below, before they are covered by the incoming tide.

Our bill is a mighty 91 euros including IGIC, but it is cautionary to remember that this is for two courses for 6 persons, the two boys feasting like trenchermen of old. That is about 15 euros a head, and stunning value for what we had. We could have chosen cheaper, but no matter. For example, the plate of camarones came in at 5 euros, the octopus salad at 5.90 euros. Both were sufficient as starter portions for the 6 of us to nibble at. The paella for two was a grand total of 14.95 euros, which is frankly cheap for what we received. The hake was 6.50 euros, the mixed seafood platter was 10.60 euros. Only the whole sama *burst the bank by coming in at 16 euros, but there was probably over a kilo of it. Those potatoes did actually make it on to the bill, but enough for the 6 of us came to only 2.50 euros.*

We had arrived early at 1 p.m. for the sake of the children. By the time that we left, there was hardly a table remaining free.

All in all, a truly memorable and splendiferous couple of hours at the table.

El Mundial 82 is not the easiest of restaurants to find, but if you aim for Los Silos, then onward to La Caleta (well signed) you only have to get to the little road along the beach and you cannot fail to find it. Not much comes closer without actually being in the water! If you fancy an expedition followed by a superb fish meal, then this is surely the place for you."

I may be a sentimental old fool, but going to places like this, with my family all around me, creates memories for me to treasure and it gives me great pleasure to think about them as we sit at home on a winter evening.

This time round, Sally and I cried off the visit to El Teide, wanting to give the others some time on their own. On the way back, they came round the long way, because Sam, the youngest, wanted to collect some of the huge mountain fir cones that he had collected on his last visit when he was only three. How on earth do children of that age remember such things? I have a problem nowadays with remembering what I did last week.

Marcus likes barbeques. Indeed, as far as I am concerned, he is the barbeque king. Whenever he has offered us a barbeque at his home back in the UK, he has effortlessly, it appeared, produced mountains of perfectly cooked foods of differing types. Grilled perfectly, charred perfectly, and just cooked through so as to retain some moistness, he turns out tasty food time after time. Even fish, for heaven's sake!

Why can't I do that?

We love barbeques, but despite all of our efforts, we have managed to acquire absolutely zero skills in that department. As regularly as clockwork, burnt offerings skitter off the grill and, as like as not, are hidden behind various plants to be discovered by the cleaner who probably thinks that we are into some sort of weird fetishism.

On a previous visit to the island Marcus had bought us a large barbeque, which, after his departure, we carefully cleaned and packed away. It did not see the light of day again until he came back. I hope that he never finds out.

A couple of evenings, therefore, were taken up by the barbeque and chef Marcus. Scrumptious food, and the evenings slowly drifted along. Freddie thought that he had gone to heaven, what with all those delicious meaty smells, and, of course, the little treats of sausage or the like dropped by various persons who shall remain unnamed, just when they thought my eye was elsewhere! The grandchildren stayed up late, but eventually caved in, and then we opened yet another bottle, chatting away as the sky got inkier and the stars got brighter. It was all a very, very, special time for me.

As we all know, the Spanish eat very late in the evening, often not before 10 or 10.30 p.m. Quite how their stomachs then allow them to sleep and be wide awake and at work at 8 a.m. the next morning, I have never understood. My grandchildren learned that this was a bargaining tool to avoid being sent to bed at anything like a reasonable time.

"Can we go down into the town now for a yoghurt ice cream please, Grandpa?!"

Or alternatively, "Well, all of the Spanish children will be playing down in the square at this time. It's not fair!"

And finally, "But we don't have to go to school tomorrow anyway!"

The inevitable result was that we often wandered down to the main square after dinner, strolled around people-watching, and the children played with instant friends that they seemed to be able to make. We watched fondly as we sat at a café, coffee, beer or yoghurt ice cream to hand. Eventually we crawled off back home to bed, to be awoken at almost first light next morning by the grandchildren, all ready to rock and roll yet again.

After a leisurely breakfast on our terrace followed by a swim in the pool for the boys, we would usually pack things up and set off to explore somewhere new on the island.

Tenerife is a duty free island, or duty free zone, depending on whose bit of literature you happen to be reading. Certainly, customs in the UK have decreed that it is not part of Spain, and therefore not part of the EU for duty-free purposes, which leads to the most ridiculous anomalies. Sally was once stopped at Gatwick for having a few too many cigarettes and I thought that I would be locked up when I invited the mean looking officer to tell the King of Spain that Tenerife was no longer part of his dominions. He just happened to be on holiday at that particular time at his usual penthouse apartment in Puerto de la Cruz.

But because prices can be so much lower, we spent time with the family trawling along through various shops, picking up bargains from shoes, belts, electrical goods and perfumes.

A spot of pavement pounding would be followed by lunch. Fortunately, the grandchildren were brought up from a very early age to accompany adults to restaurants, so, for the most part, they did the right thing until boredom set in. Josh would eat almost at the speed of light, something that he has picked up from his father. Sam was the complete opposite and, whilst his plate would be cleared, it was sometimes painfully slow.

"Sam! Why are we STILL sitting here? Everyone else finished long ago!" This from Tina.

Sam smiled back beatifically. He long ago learned that parental admonishments whilst on holiday would hold no threat for him.

Long lazy days all gave me wonderful opportunities to stock up on my memory bank of all that my family means to me. As I grow older, I realise that my memories are something to be cherished, stored away and to be retrievable for when the time comes that I am less flexible in that department of my brain. I want to keep my thoughts of what we all did together on any one particular day alongside others which can be simple things like a particular bird song that affected me, or the smell of newly cut grass, or even the whoosh of air made by the owl that whizzes across our terrace most nights, just a very few feet away from me. My memories are the stuff of keeping me sane as my faculties will wane in later age.

Time flies by when you are having fun, as the saying goes. For me it was particularly awful as the dreaded day of their departure drew ever closer. We had got so much closer to their lives during those last two weeks, and enjoyed so much together. But it had to be, and they had to go. I took them to the airport and, as I waved them goodbye, I had to look away. I hope that they never saw the tears in my eyes.

15

Marathon

By now we had been in Tenerife, as formal residents, for about a year, and we both thought that it was time for a bit of a holiday; indeed, part of our original plan had been to maximise the opportunities for travel in our retirement, despite the fact that we would be living on a small island. What better opportunity, I reasoned, than to drive our new acquisition, the Mercedes, over on an extended tour down through France and Spain, rather than just having it shipped over.

"It will be the trip of a lifetime, seeing all those sights and visiting all the places that we have read about. Much more fun than shipping it over in a container," I enthused to Sally.

"Yes, I suppose that it would," she retorted, "but are you forgetting that I've been seasick on a rowing boat on the Serpentine?"

"Oh, come on. You know that ferries nowadays are like ocean liners, they are so big."

There was little that I could say that would convince her, until I threatened to do the whole journey by myself. Her face dropped, and I could see that a bit of compromise was needed. Plan B had to be put into operation. But what was plan B to be?

"I know, I'll fetch it down from the Midlands, and meet up with you in northern Spain. We can then drive down through Spain together, and you can fly back from Seville whilst I come the long way back on the ferry. That way you avoid the two ferry crossings. How about that, then?"

"Mmmm." She was not totally convinced. I could see that half of her liked the idea of missing out on the sea crossings, but the other half didn't want to abandon me, or miss out on what could be the trip of a lifetime.

We finally decided that we would fly to Birmingham, stay somewhere overnight, pay for and collect the car, drive it down to Brighton, well, Hove actually, and stay overnight with the family. The following day we could go on to Portsmouth, put it on the big Brittany Ferries boat to Santander in northern Spain, drive across Spain and embark at Cadiz on the rust bucket back to the islands. Unfortunately that meant missing out on France completely. Still, Brittany Ferries have big ships and should not rock about at all with stabilisers out and so the compromise was reached, agreeable to both sides. Sorted!

Part of the pleasure of future ownership of the car came from working out the itinerary, which I steadfastly continued to refer to as a "holiday". Planning was undertaken like a military operation. Nothing could be left to chance, because once committed (should I have been, I asked myself?) there could be no going back. By then, we would have paid out a lot of money on flights and ferry tickets, as well as insurance and other things, to say nothing of the actual cost of the car. We had to get everything right to bring it back here to our home.

The die was cast. Freddie went on holiday to stay with his friends the poodles, and we left the balmy sub-tropical temperature of Tenerife to arrive at Birmingham, which was freezing cold in late October. Our taxi driver, who turned out to be a part-time employee of The SL Shop, was on time and the pub he took us to was excellent. Called The Boot Inn at Flyford Flavell, we had found it on the internet, and picked it partly because it had been Worcestershire Pub of the year in 2009/10. Our hosts were welcoming and our bedroom spotless and we had a pleasant dinner and an even better breakfast the next morning.

And so, bright and early to The SL Shop, where we were treated to the drama of a formal unveiling of the finished product. The fancy embroidered dust cover was removed with a flourish to reveal the old girl in all her newly fettled splendour. She shone in the overhead lighting, and to all intents and purposes, looked just as she had when she left the factory 20 years ago, although we were paying only about a sixth of her original price. Refurbishment work was inspected, paperwork was completed, money was paid over, a short test drive was undertaken, and hands were shaken. It was time to go.

But before we finally aimed her south, an unforeseen diversion was in store.

In order to be properly street legal, we had previously arranged for six months' road fund licence, although we would only be in the UK for less than 24 hours, so hoped to be able to apply for a five month refund in due course by sending the unused portion of the tax disc back from Tenerife. The car was still on UK plates, and the diversion was to be to the local DVLA centre on the outskirts of Worcester to receive the changeover of ownership papers (the V5) so that we were fully legal should we be stopped en route. We had rung DVLA in Swansea before leaving Tenerife to ensure that the local office could, and would, issue the paperwork whilst we waited.

They had assured us that all would be OK as it was a simple and regularly made request. DVLA Worcester issued us the required V5 but were adamant that they could not issue the taxation documents because we (only) had European insurance cover issued by an international insurer. We had specifically checked this with DVLA Swansea in advance, and they had given us the go-ahead. Also, the insurer had confirmed in writing to us that they would cover us (including vehicle recovery) from the point of collection in the UK right back to Tenerife, should it be needed.

"What is the root of the problem, please?" I was at my most polite.

"You have insurance cover – which does look to be in order – but it is not issued here in the UK." The clerk shuffled through the paperwork, head down, avoiding all eye contact.

"OK. But the insurer is a world-wide name with offices in most EU countries, including the UK! What does it matter where the paperwork originates from, provided that it is within the EU and is correct and valid?" I was doing my best to keep calm.

"It has to be issued by a UK insurer." There were more downcast eyes and shuffling of paperwork.

"But this is a UK insurer. It just happens that the paperwork was issued by their office in Spain." I cried.

"That is not the same thing. We cannot deal with it here. Swansea should not have told you that." This last with a sour face.

"Yes," I said, "but they did. That is why I bought the insurance cover."

Of course, there was to be no swaying the jobsworth who was sticking to her guns. Eye contact continued to be avoided, and the papers were pushed, yet again, back in my direction. Nothing that we could say would make them change their minds, and it was just one of those occasions when one cannot afford to press the matter too strongly, as we feared not being able to sort things out in time to catch our ferry. Time really was of the essence.

A call to The SL Shop resulted in quick reactions and a rendezvous at a very small local village post office where insurance papers were presented and a tax disc obtained. We grabbed the disc and fled the county as fast as the car could carry us.

We pushed on down to Hove to stay overnight with Marcus and the family. The rain poured down on us all the way, but the old girl did not miss a beat. The grandchildren came outside to admire the car, despite it being filthy as a result of 200 miles in monsoon weather.

The next morning we were up bright and early. We stirred the car into life and sashayed on towards Portsmouth. Coming into the town, I saw a sign for a car wash.

"I'm going to pull in over there." I said to Sally, pointing out the car wash.

"What on earth for? We have hundreds of miles to go and it will still probably be raining like this when we get to Spain anyway." Sally clearly thought that I was bonkers.

"Yes, but it will be nice to drive off the boat in Spain with a sparkling clean car, won't it?"

The car was restored to gleaming sparkling cleanliness and as a result was much admired in the queue lining up to get on to the boat. I was happy too, particularly so because I had persuaded Brittany Ferries that we should be offered a classic car discount from our fares.

We drove on and parked down in the bowels of the ship, and got our pass to our allocated stateroom (aka poky cabin). It was to be a twenty-four hour crossing, so much of our stuff had to be lugged from the car to the cabin. First port of call was the posh restaurant to book a table for dinner that evening.

That done, it was time to go out on deck and to wave goodbye to Albion as we progressed slowly into the murky Solent. All around us were the sad remnants of our Royal Navy, reminding us that we used to be a great sea power. Over there was an aircraft carrier, looking as though it was being stripped bare before going to the knacker's yard. Yonder also was a line of boats, perhaps destroyers or frigates, all looking so sad and probably destined for the same fate. Then, saddest of all, was a warship being hauled along by a couple of tugs, seemingly unable to reach her final berth under her own steam.

We turned away, wondering what had become of our once proud country, and pondering anew the reasons for leaving it all behind.

But we had covered a lot of ground in these last forty-eight hours and we cheered ourselves up by realising that we were on our way at last, ready to enjoy our great adventure.

Well before dinner time, Sally had turned a whiter shade of pale. "You know what I'm going to say, don't you?" she moaned.

"No. What?" Was I really that unobservant? It seemed that I was.

"I told you that I would never get to that restaurant this evening. Why don't you ever listen!"

And so I was sent back to the restaurant to cancel our table. Yours truly later dined in the cabin on a bottle of claret, a plastic sandwich and a packet of crisps. Sally lay on her bunk bed and dined on fresh air, glaring across at me from her prone position as she saw me tucking in.

Dawn broke on another day.

"The damned boat must have broken its stabilisers, or the captain just forgot to deploy them. It rolled about all night." said Sally, determined to wake me.

I had missed it all, sleeping the sleep of the just, possibly aided marginally by the claret.

The Bay of Biscay looked just as it usually did, faintly aggressive and grey hued. Murky clouds, the colour of unpolished pewter, scudded from one horizon to another. Rain was on the wind, but we stayed on deck to catch the first glimpse of Spain, the city of Santander, a welcome sight at lunchtime.

The boat berthed right in what seemed to be the centre of town, and getting off was quick and easy. This was the first time that we had driven our left hand drive car on the right hand side of the road, and, although we were used to driving in Tenerife, it did feel strange for the first few kilometres.

We had pre-booked to stay at the parador in Santillana del Mar for that night. Leaving Santander behind in the drizzle, we came almost immediately onto the coastal *autopista*. Before we knew it, we were approaching our turn off, so we drove straight towards the hotel in the centre of the pedestrian-only village. Inevitably, we were flagged down by the *Policia* but, waving our parador reservations in front of them, were smilingly waved on. It was still raining. Why had it followed us all the way from Birmingham?

Parador hotels, all state owned, are sited mostly in lovely areas and generally housed in stately home type properties, sympathetically converted. We had booked to stay at a number of them on this journey. My only gripe with the parador system is that they invariably charge too much for dinner, and so must lose a fortune from the tourist sector for that odd corporate decision.

The parador in Santillana del Mar (which oddly is not by the seaside, though it may well have been in days of yore) was called San Blas, and we found it to be excellent in all respects. We were graciously shown to a lovely large room looking out over low rolling hills and an orchard below our room, and with a large and well equipped bathroom. A decent sized bathroom after a day on the road is always appreciated.

After the restorative glass of wine in the hotel bar, we wandered out into the main square to explore. Here we found a most attractive looking restaurant, quickly filling up with locals. It looked regional rather than tourist, with a well-constructed menu, and was but a stone's throw away from the hotel. We enjoyed it so much that, if we could find nowhere else better for the second night in Santillana, we resolved to go back there for a return match on the morrow.

Santillana, being a car-free medieval village, has for the most part remained unspoiled, and we enjoyed our two nights there exploring all the side streets and shops, as well as motoring out to discover the countryside. Nearby were the famous Picos de Europa, a heritage area of picturesque mountains with jagged peaks and verdant valleys. Unfortunately, as we cruised along, we could see neither the tops of the mountains nor the bottoms of the valleys, as all continued to be shrouded in mist and rain. We changed our plans, fetching up at Cangas de Onis where an old monastery just outside of the town had been converted into a parador. Sprinting from the car to the front door (yes, it was still raining), we opted for lunch in their *cafetería*, which was excellent and decent value, although we were the only customers.

As we set off the next morning, it was only threatening rain, but by the time we by-passed Bilbao, the heavens had well and truly opened yet again. The hardtop was doing sterling service without a leak showing anywhere. As we turned inland, however, the rain faded away and we came into one of Spain's most famous wine regions, La Rioja.

We were booked to stay in Laguardia, right at the heart of the area known as Rioja Alavesa, in the province of Alava. Rioja Alavesa lies between the Cantabria and Toloño mountain ranges and is bounded by the River Ebro, which further along its course becomes one of the mightiest of all Spain. Laguardia was founded in the 10th century as a fortified stronghold under the control of the Kingdom of Navarre. You can still see the defensive churches at either end of the walled town and the medieval street system has been almost perfectly preserved.

This region of Alavesa has over 13,000 hectares of vineyards, and some 400 wineries delivering 100 million bottles of wine each year within the Rioja *Denominación de Origen* (DO). Many of the wineries are now state of the art operations with each one seemingly trying their best to outdo their competitors in terms of size, futuristic new buildings and number of immense stainless steel tanks. In the smaller rural villages, though, you can still visit places where everything goes on in cool cellars deep down underground, as it has done since Roman times.

We stopped for a light picnic lunch (parked on the edge of a vineyard, the vines all russet coloured now) before arriving at the hotel. We were booked for two nights into the hotel owned by, and immediately adjacent to, Bodegas Cosme Palacio, just outside the town walls. Although our reservation had been made on the internet at a discounted rate, we were welcomed like royalty and shown to the best room in the house, overlooking the vineyards to the hills in the far distance. We were quick to note that "our" bedroom appeared on all their publicity material.

After unpacking, we aimed for the town in the late afternoon but were quickly beaten back by the incessant rain. Laguardia being a fortified town on a hill, the water ran down the roads in torrents towards the outer walls. To our surprise, the hotel restaurant was closed that evening, so we were forced out to find somewhere to eat. Our shoes were soaked through yet again as we braved the torrents cascading along the cobbled streets in order to find a regional type of *restaurante* or *tasca*. I suppose it was inevitable that for once we drew a bit of a blank, ending up snacking in a bar and drinking a bottle of the local brew. Hey ho.

Next morning, the day dawned bitterly cold, with a covering of snow over the mountains in the distance. But at least it was dry, so we decided to tour around some of the famous wine villages during the morning. At lunchtime we found ourselves parking near a little bar in Elciego, the town most famous for the vineyards of Marques de Riscal. There are a number of other *bodegas*, but Marques de Riscal is the main one, and it is internationally renowned. The *bodega* has a piece of architecture by a famous architect, which you can see from miles around. It looks as though some giant has dumped a load of multi coloured sheets of bent aluminium on top of a lovely old building. To my mind it's quite revolting – I think that it ruins the place – but I am clearly a philistine.

Anyway, lunch was to be mainly a liquid one, but not as you may think. We had parked in the village and I had bought a postcard of Elciego in the snow, most appropriately, because it was cold enough for more snow that day. Into this little local bar we retreated (anywhere would have done to escape that bitter cold), looking around to see what was what, and I noticed a large thermos flask on the bar, with cups in a pile around it. Next to it was a large sign saying "*Caldo*".

Now, we knew from our time in Tenerife that the word *caldo* is a generic one for a type of stock, either meat, fish or vegetable that you add to your stews, sauces or the like, if you happen to be too lazy to make your own.

"Good afternoon. What does *caldo* mean, exactly, on that sign please?"

"It is a piping hot broth, made every day by my mother, and everyone round here drinks it at lunchtime. It is the speciality of this house. It will keep out the cold for you!"

Well, if it was good enough for the locals, it was good enough for me. Some of the said locals were looking across to us and smiling a welcome.

I ordered a cup of the steaming brew to try it. It was superb and I am sure that it was properly homemade. Sally tried a sip of mine, and that made it two cups, please. It was jolly hot, but equally, it was a very cold day, so we stayed there for another cup each with a chunk of oddly shaped homemade seedy bread. As we were in La Rioja, a bottle of white wine was brought over, and we were told to put a little into each of our cups, at no extra cost.

Cheap as chips, as the saying goes, but a memorable meal for all that. I can dine out on the story of that *caldo*.

In the afternoon we had already been invited, as hotel guests, to enjoy a free tour of the Bodegas Cosme Palacio winery, followed by a tasting session.

We were in their tasting room with a Belgian couple, to master the art of swishing the different wines round in our mouths before spitting them out into the Victorian china bowls provided. When she thought that nobody was looking, I caught Sally downing the stuff instead of spitting it out.

"Hey! I saw you swilling it down. Why aren't you spitting?"

"It's too damned cold out there, and in here as well. I need it for the warmth!"

Afterwards, our guide finished the tour by taking us to the shop where we were invited to purchase some of their wines. I was much taken by their Glorioso, although it happened to be one of their less expensive wines. Their best red, Cosme Palacio, I had already seen in the speciality area of my local Tesco back in England. We bought three bottles, one of Glorioso and two of Cosme Palacio, explaining that we were driving down to Tenerife, and space was therefore at a premium. Not for the first time did we receive stares of incredulity.

"You are really driving all the way from England to Tenerife?" chorused the Belgians and our guide in unison.

"Yes, indeed we are."

"But in that sports car with only two seats? How will you manage it?"

I was not yet sure that we actually had the answer.

Dinner that night was to be in the hotel. We still had not got used to the Spanish way of waiting until nearly 10 p.m. before feeding. We turned up and the room was freezing, and the sole staff member obviously startled to see us as early as 9 p.m. But a blower heater was quickly found. It was a huge commercial affair like they have in a factory, and sounded like a jet engine being fired up. But it did heat that room quickly. We took our meal in solitary splendour, washing it down with one of the finest of the Cosme Palacio wines, though needing ear muffs to blot out the noise.

Up in the north, and particularly in La Rioja, wine is also a natural accompaniment to breakfast. As well as the usual croissants and preserves the next morning, there was a hot offering of bacon, chorizo sausage and eggs nestling in large chafing dishes, together with a help-yourself option of red or white wine.

As everyone else seemed to be at it, who were we to refuse?

It gives you a pleasant glow as you fire up the motor on a cold morning, and so for the first time ever, we came to drink wine at all three meals of the day.

We began to push a bit further towards the south that day, down towards the next famous wine region, the Ribera del Duero, named after the river Duero, which eventually crosses the border into Portugal – that absentee from all Spanish maps – and transmogrifies itself into the Douro of port wine fame.

La Rioja, with all its constituent parts, is the largest single wine growing region of Spain. It is so much larger than you would believe unless you had driven through it. The Ribera del Duero is smaller, though in the opinion of many Spaniards, it is the producer of better wine. Something along the lines of quality versus quantity, we have heard a number of people say, but never by anyone from La Rioja!

On the way, we stopped for morning coffee at the huge parador at Lerma, which had to be seen to be believed. You could see it from many kilometres away, perched on the top of the hill in the centre of the town. It turned out to be market day, and we could find no parking space anywhere near the parador. We had fought our way through the market traffic to the top of the hill, only to find the huge main square entirely full of tented stalls, and so had to turn round to park in the next parish.

A brisk stroll brought us back to the parador. A vast 17th century ducal palace, it was latterly owned by the dukes of Lerma, who used it for retreats and for visits and festivities by King Felipe III of Spain. A huge central covered atrium was surrounded by soaring arched cloisters, and we sat in the comfiest of armchairs. The courtyard was so large, and each table had a small circular electrical contraption on it.

"What on earth is that thing that you are fiddling with?" I enquired.

"Dunno. No idea. You have a look."

I picked it up and turned it round. It looked a bit like an old fashioned bell push that had been reincarnated into the 21st century. Should I push the button? Yes!

A few seconds later an apparition shimmied into view and

stopped at our table. The waitress was the spitting image of Emma Thompson, the actress, all in fancy dress, sorry, medieval local costume. I blinked and stuttered.

After we had given our modest order, I realised that the contraption was the latest craze for calling a member of staff when sitting in such a big courtyard. Zany, but it worked very well.

I wonder if it was really Emma, and if she was moonlighting?

Afterwards, pushing out through the old doors to join reality once again, we mooched round the market stalls and bought some pasties in the square. They looked a bit like Cornish pasties, but they had much more exotic and spicy flavours bursting out from them. We sat in the car in a quiet side street overlooking the lower part of town. Whilst munching our food, we saw our first stork's nest, for which Lerma is famous, just like a mini thatched roof perched on a chimney opposite to us. Unfortunately, the nest was vacant. The birds had already flown south, just as we were doing.

Leaving Lerma behind, we had booked to stay that night in a converted nunnery, the Hotel Convento Las Claras. A magnificent job had been done of the conversion, turning it all into a tip top hotel with spa facilities, right on the banks of the river flowing through the very nice little town of Peñafiel, and providing us, from our room, with a direct view to the floodlit fairy-tale castle atop the hill opposite and dominating everything below. We were now slap bang in the Ribera del Duero.

It had become very cold by late afternoon as we walked around the town. We needed something piping hot.

"Look," I said. "What's that place over there?"

"No idea. It's got an ice cream sign outside it."

"Let's cross over the road and have a look. If it sells ice cream, it might do hot drinks as well."

It was called the *Centro Social El Mirador*. And therein lay the clue. We stood outside, peering in through windows that were steamed up from the inner warmth. From the doorway we could see the place was busy with people having drinks, coffee, what have you.

An elderly gentleman paused at the entrance and shuffled up to us. "Can I help you?"

"Is this place a café? We are not quite sure. We are looking for a place to get a hot drink."

"Of course they serve hot drinks, coffee too. Come inside with me."

And so in we went, and all conversation came to an immediate stop. Everyone stared at us. I don't think that there was anyone under 80 in the place, and they were all men. We stuck out like sore thumbs.

Our new friend introduced us around, and coffee was produced for Sally, and tea for me. There was no charge.

"Do tell us, what is this place, then?"

"It is the town's senior citizens club, and I have just made you honorary members for the day!"

Handshakes all round, a number of toothless grins, and we were welcomed into membership.

We bought some drinks for our new friends, and were still sitting there at a large communal table swapping stories about our travels and the local area when some of the wives turned up for the evening cards session with their men. A number of black looks were cast our way, so we judged it to be the right moment to beat a tactical retreat.

It had been a couple of hours to savour, and not just for the coffee.

Next day, as we moved on, the autumnal weather was starting to loosen its grip. The rain had faded away, and fewer layers of clothing were needed, at any rate during the day.

Still in the Ribera, we motored past a small sign at the side of the road which announced on it the hallowed words "VEGA SICILIA." I slammed on the brakes and pulled over to the side of the road. We fetched up outside the heavily barred gates to an imposing mansion.

"You know where this is, don't you?" I said.

Sally, who always looks everywhere except where she should, had missed the sign, as usual, so I explained.

"Vega Sicilia is one of the most famous wines of Spain, perhaps of the world."

Small production of the highest quality ensured sky high prices. Two hundred euros a bottle would not be unreasonable just for one of their second wines.

"Let's see if we can get in."

The car was filthy, and we were in comfy travelling clothes, nothing smart. I walked to the gate. There was a barrier manned by a stern looking employee.

"Good day to you. Is it possible to visit? I realise that we have no appointment."

"I am sorry. No."

It seemed to be the moment to go into grovel mode. In vain I pointed out that we were English travellers driving through Spain; that we were ex-hoteliers and that the name of Vega Sicilia was music to our ears; that we promised to purchase a little wine, even at their stratospheric prices. Even that we thought that he was a very nice man.

"No."

No, there was to be no admittance. No, not without a prior appointment, and these were rarely granted, unless your name happened to be Robert Parker, the world famous wine guru.

And so we drove slowly away. Butting up to the verges of the road we could see the vines of Vega Sicilia, and in November they did not make a pretty sight. They looked nothing special at all, but deep down I knew that they were, and I was sore dispirited.

Turning almost due south now, pointing the long bonnet along the empty roads, our minds turned to the coming evening. Our stop tonight was scheduled to be in a hospital; well, an old converted hospital, to be absolutely correct.

But would we even get there?

A few hours and various speed cameras later, we suddenly became aware of a dearth of petrol stations as we cruised along on the *autopista* and the orange warning light on the petrol tank gauge was lit steadily now. A certain amount of nervousness was setting in. If things had been left to Sally, we would have filled up on a much more regular basis, as she was keen to point out to me for the umpteenth time.

"You really should have filled up at that last petrol station. Why do you always have to cut things so fine?" she grumbled.

"We have seen plenty of petrol stations along the way so far, so stop worrying."

"Maybe, but what happens if the gauge is wrong?"

"Why should it be? It's been OK so far."

"It's twenty years old."

There was not much of an answer to that.

Then a sign appeared at the roadside, indicating a fuel station a couple of kilometres off the *autopista*. We dived off, heaving a collective sigh of relief.

Yes, and there it was. But... but... it was closed.

It was totally deserted at five o'clock except for a single phlegmatic lorry driver chewing the cud after his siesta. His elderly wheezing lorry was parked right across the access ramp, belching noxious fumes as he coaxed it back to life.

So, off we went again, with 20 or so kilometres to go to our destination, and nothing more marked on our map, nor shown on the satnav. We must have been running on fumes by the time that we turned off into town and saw a sign for a Shell station. Oh, the sighs of relief.

The converted hospital was a member of a small privately owned group in Extremadura (for that is the area in which we now were) specialising in the conversion of lovely old historic buildings. It was called the Hospederia de Ambroz.

The Hospederia was sited in what used to be the Jewish quarter of the old town. We looked at the menu in the hotel, but yet again it was ridiculously expensive, so we settled for a drink in the bar instead, wondering what to do next. We set off to explore the immediate vicinity and dined later in a tiny bar, enjoying, on the recommendation of the proprietor, such dishes as marinated strips of pork (Jewish quarter rules seemingly did not apply!) and jumbo prawns in garlic with sea salt and olive oil, very homemade bread judging by its shape, and all washed down with some local red wine.

The picture hanging over our huge double bed was a bit strange, even for an old hospital: a line drawing of doctors in olden times, showing them in far too much detail dealing with a corpse. Not for the faint hearted but, I suppose, totally in keeping.

On the morrow we woke to bright sunshine, a cloudless sky, and snow on the hilltops on the other side of the valley. Strangely, Mr Garmin, who had failed dismally to find the hotel in the first place, took us out of town and back to the *autopista* perfectly. It was the only time that he had let us down. It had been a good move on our part to purchase a European coverage Garmin; the machine was equipped to alert us to all the hidden "safety" cameras along the *autopistas*. For £100, I reckon we got our money back at least tenfold.

On and on we pushed, further south, well past the level of Madrid, to the old Roman town of Merida, high on Sally's wish list of places to visit on this journey. There was an enormous Roman arch surviving in the middle of town, and a whole area complete with an amphitheatre and other buildings. The town was founded at the time of Caesar Augustus and sits on the banks of the River Guardiana.

Pulling up at the parador in Merida for a coffee stop, all of a lather because of the confusing directional signs, we were met by a very smart uniformed sentry in a hut at the entrance to the hotel car park.

Entry was denied!

We stood, or rather sat, our ground until eventually the barrier was raised, on the basis of a small white lie that we were going to be eating there in the restaurant, which in fact we were not until we found out inside just how delightful it all was, with a lovely shaded courtyard, and an appealing ancient wood panelled *cafetería*. We did the decent thing and had some food and, after a walk around the hotel, we were soon outside again in blistering sunshine (how it was hotting up now) to explore those Roman remains. Sally was quite captivated by it all and put it down as a place to revisit on our next Peninsula excursion.

And then ever onwards once again, pushing ever further south. Spain is just so BIG!

Our overnight stop was to be, for a change, in a *balneario*, a three-star hotel converted from an old bath or spa resort, called the Hotel Balneario El Raposo. We had booked it over the internet as it looked interesting, and it was near Zafra, a historic town with a parador, which we thought could bear a bit of exploration.

We crammed the Mercedes into the only space remaining in the leafy square just below the parador and walked in through the towering wooden front doors, just like those of a castle, which indeed it had been. Effusively greeted, we were passed along a rank of welcoming officialdom, and handed a large "goodie bag" each. With us were about another 100 people jostling to check in…We had arrived right at the start of a medical convention!

A minute later, we were back in the square, admiring the old fortress from the shade of a nearby café, and still clutching the goodie bags. However, little did we envisage the even stranger goings on that we were about to encounter back at the *balneario*.

We arrived at this huge yet attractive old building, way out in the countryside, and try as we might, we couldn't find a space amongst the sea of cars in the large car park. A number of cars had full covers over them, with a layer of dust and fallen leaves, which we thought a bit odd. Eventually we found an overflow parking area on the other side of the lane. We finally got to the front entrance and trundled our bags into the foyer, and so arrived at the reception desk. We were politely checked in and handed a map, carefully highlighted in green, to find our room. The map was two sided, one for the ground floor, and one for the first floor on which our room was to be found.

"Are we really going to need a map to find our bedroom?" asked Sally.

"Do you have a better idea? This place seems huge!"

"Who are all these people shuffling about in long terry-cloth white dressing gowns? I'm getting a funny feeling about this place…"

In truth, so was I. I had had the funny feeling ever since I first saw all of those sheeted up cars in the car park.

"I think that they are here for some sort of treatments, aren't they? It looks a bit like a spa of some sort," I whispered back to her as we walked down yet another long corridor. We followed the highlighted route on our map, and passed by a fully staffed medical centre, then a pool complex where people were doing synchronised exercises in the water, then went through a lounge area, the contents of which Oxfam might have rejected many years ago.

"What on earth goes on here?"

"It looks just like some old folk's home from the 1940s." Everything looked so dated, although it was in good order and spotlessly clean.

Down yet another corridor was a spa area, offering all sorts of massages and all the other treatments that I supposed may be found in such a place. All were busy with very elderly people, uniformly clad in white dressing gowns. Just what was going on? Had we undertaken a seismic shift into some parallel universe? The internet booking site had made no mention of all this stuff.

We found our huge bedroom, which incidentally was very nice, though rather austere. There was a vast bathroom en suite and the heating was full on. We gasped for breath and flung the windows open wide. After unpacking, we returned, again needing the use of the map, to the main reception area. We were told that this was a health retreat which had originally been set up at the turn of the last century to provide treatment facilities "for those of a lower social order".

I promise you, their words, not mine!

And it was all still functioning and going strong. The place was packed.

We could but enter into the spirit of it all, and had a memorable time. Dinner was to be served at a really early hour, and the dining room appeared to have no spare tables, so we opted to eat later in the bar, ordering a bottle of wine, much to the amusement of the other "guests". The bottle of wine met with frowns from the serving staff, who I believed were more used to handing out a small glass each to their more deserving patients.

After a slightly uncomfortable night on a very hard mattress, we got up the next morning and Sally opened the door to our room to find a surprise. She hurriedly closed the door again.

"John, come here," she hissed.

"Eh? Whatever for?"

"Just come here. NOW!"

She cranked open the door again, and there they were: two very elderly white be-gowned people sitting in silence on two chairs right outside. It made us jump. We could not imagine why they had chosen that spot. Perhaps they were just having a rest? We smiled nervously and hurried down to breakfast. When we came back, they had disappeared, and so had their chairs, and we never found out what they were doing there.

Peering out of our bedroom window we could see a very strange low building, which had intrigued us on our arrival. Shafts of sunlight played through the branches of the overhanging trees onto what looked like a line of 30 or so sentry boxes or cubicles, without roofs or doors, built all together in a long terrace. There were no fronts to each cubicle, and the backs were only half built up. We had seen odd buildings like these on our travels before, but this time I just had to ask what it was all about.

"Ah!" said Matron, when I button-holed her. "It's for the healing with the mud. It is a specialist treatment. We have been doing this for the last hundred years."

"Excuse me?"

"Well, we put the patients that want this cure into a long line, one in each cubicle. They must be naked. We put the men and the women all together in one long line. Then we cover them from neck to toe in the healing mud. Then we leave them for two or three hours to dry in the warmth of the sun. When the mud starts to crack, the nurse comes along with a hosepipe, and washes them all down, one by one, along the line. And so they are cleansed of their impurities. It is very popular with our clients!"

All this was said, straight faced, and without a trace of humour.

"And you still do this, do you?" I ask, eyeing the nurse and the hosepipe , which looked more like an old water cannon to me.

"Yes! Do you have time to try it out? We may be able to find you a couple of spare spaces in the line-up. It's normally part of our package deal, but as you are staying here, I will be happy to make you a special price."

We fled.

Our final target on the long road home was Jerez de la Frontera, the home of sherry.

Although Seville is a "must" for any visitor to the Peninsula, we had previously agreed that we would by-pass it on this trip, since we could get cheap air fares from Tenerife using our *Residencia* discounts. If there was to be a highlight to our trip, then we expected that three nights in Jerez might be it. We had pre-booked into the only modern hotel of the whole journey, the five-star Grand Hotel Prestige Plaza Jerez. What a mouthful of a name, but would it live up to it?

The hotel was set in its own large gardens, and we enjoyed being shown to a beautiful large bedroom with a stunning bathroom and separate vast marble wet room. Sally wanted to take it home with her. Our room looked out over the central garden area towards a beautiful old converted *bodega*.

Parking was at premium in the small courtyard, but we had been found a space under one of the arches when the staff noticed our car. The space was smilingly vacated by one of the receptionists, and we wondered just how often that would have happened back in the UK.

Much later, after we had relaxed and then put that wet room to the test, a ten-minute stroll brought us right into the centre of town. There were some very fine restaurants there, tucked away down side streets. We started off with a *copita* of that internationally famous sherry, La Ina, whilst sitting outside a wine bar. Well, when in Rome, as it were...

Later, we ate in a smoky *restaurante*, with all the diners talking at the top of their voices to each other. At one end was an open plan kitchen, and all the way down the side of the place was a great long bar, where customers were packed two or three deep enjoying their evening *tapas* with a glass of sherry or a cold beer. Many spilled out to the pavement tables, and the little paper napkins supplied with each *tapa* were spread around like confetti on the floor of the bar area. By the time we left, we had contributed quite a few bits of paper to the growing piles.

No trip to Jerez would be complete without a visit to one of the internationally renowned sherry *bodegas*, and to the Royal Equestrian School.

A number of famous *bodega* houses offer tours, and we chose to visit that of Gonzalez Byass, the home of Tio Pepe. Mr Byass was an Englishman from London who bought into the business when sherry first started to become popular. He must have made a fortune out of it. The *bodega* was almost in the centre of town, yet the site itself was huge, and a miniature train was used to transport us from one area to another. We were shown buildings housing vast quantities of sherry in various stages of production, given an insight into their production methods, and even ferried around a vineyard within the walls. It was a fascinating couple of hours and at the end of it all, we were treated to a sampling of the various sherries the company produced, and naturally were offered the opportunity of buying some.

Jerez is one of the famed winter homes of the stork. Those empty nests that we had seen in Lerma were empty because their occupants were now perched on the roof of the *bodega* opposite our bedroom. Neither of us had seen a real live stork before, and so we were surprised that they were smaller than we had assumed. I could not even begin to guess how they were supposed to be able to transport a fully grown baby in their beaks! I snapped away, taking pictures of storks walking on the roof, perching quietly, and doing all the things that busy storks did. Their nests were vast things spreading out much wider than the chimneys upon which they had been built. Not even a high wind would dislodge them. I suppose that they have had enough centuries of practice, their storky skills passed down from generation to generation.

Bright and early the next day, we walked to the world famous Royal Equestrian School, less than a kilometre away. We found that it was a training day there, rather than an exhibition day. For Sally, a keen ex-horsewoman, that was just perfect. We sat in the main arena and watched amazing horses going through their paces with practised ease, guided by equally skilled riders. She was able to point out to me the finer points of dressage. The training course for the riders was, if I remember correctly, four years long. Each year some 200 expert riders applied to join, and only four were accepted. They received no pay, and if they could not stay the pace, or please their instructors sufficiently, they were sent packing back home. Trainees came from all over the world.

Then, on we went to the carriage driving area where we saw people learning the skills of carriage driving. What is it about tall, dark, handsome men in jodhpurs cracking whips, I mused? Sally swooned again. Afterwards, she mentioned a couple of times in passing that she really liked Jerez and would like to visit that horsey place again.

I wasn't fooled for one moment.

The next day I headed the car out of town on the last lap towards Cadiz and the ferry back to our archipelago. It was already hot as we set off, and it reminded me that for the last few days we had been looking for shade instead of sun, just as we normally did back at home in Tenerife, where only tourists walked down the sunny side of the street.

Before we reached the old town of Cadiz we needed to negotiate our way through seemingly endless road works and diversions before at long last we burst out from dreary suburbia and into the old port area. We were much too early, but it left us time for a nice light lunch accompanied by Sally grumbling about the Acciona ferry, the regional transporter of cars, lorries, passengers and freight to Tenerife and the other six islands.

There was a *restaurante* at the terminal, virtually empty despite the queue of cars and lorries in the parking area. One lowering glance, shot from between bushy eyebrows that met in the middle, from the surly waitress ensured that her day would not be further disturbed by our custom.

So the satnav, in pedestrian mode for once, showed us the way into the old town, and after strolling about admiring some lovely architecture, we end up in a spotless modern wine bar which served us artistically presented plates of food and glasses of quality wine, all for a reasonable price.

Ambling contentedly back to the car park we found that it was well past the time to move on. Most cars had already pulled out. We joined the end of the snake of vehicles – strange to see local Tenerife number plates again – moving towards the ferry.

The closer we got to the ferry, the more Sally talked of seasickness.

How do you get seasickness by just looking at a boat whilst you are still on terra firma?

We were all parked in a line on the quayside, awaiting our turn. By chance, we were level with the front of the ferry, and casually looked up to see its name, *Albayzin,* proudly painted in large blue letters for all to see.

But what was this? Just below the nameplate, there was another name in raised lettering, *Maria Grazia On.* Although it had been painted out, the raised outline of the words remained. It was the perfect excuse for Sally to assess the fact that we would be travelling for nearly three days on a second hand boat that had previously been in the ownership of Italians, sailing, as we soon found, through the Mediterranean for so many years before coming into new ownership. Her confidence about boat travel, already low, expired with a long drawn out shudder.

"Do we really have to go on it?"

"Yes!"

How else do you answer such a question when there is patently no other option?

The queue of lorries all took precedence and were loaded first, trundling down into the bowels of the boat, parking on what might be called the lower ground floor. Lots and lots of lorries there were, carrying everything that could be needed for the islands that could not be produced or manufactured in situ. How could this boat take on board so many of them without sinking?

Patiently, we bided our time, then were called forward, and directed to mount a very steep ramp to the open top deck. The brand new VW Golf in front of us failed dismally at its first attempt on the ramp. There were clouds of tyre smoke coming from its spinning front wheels, and a general slipping and sliding slowly downwards, back in our direction, to much guffawing and merriment from the crew and onlookers. Tension set in and we held hands and prayed, for it was our turn next.

The Golf revved up again and took as long a run at it as was possible and just crested the brow at the top, aided by a friendly shove from the chaps strategically sited, I guessed, to assist daft foreigners.

My thoughts were centred round the fact that we were seriously overloaded now with everything that we had accumulated over the last three weeks or so, and we were depending on a 20 year old engine, regardless of it displacing three litres.

With fingers crossed, I fired her up, engaged low gear, piled on the revs, released the brake, and cruised gracefully up to the top, to the massed cheers of myself and Sally. We were directed where to park on the open deck at the rear. The car next to us had an enormous rabbit in a cage on the back seat. Many people were already busy applying waterproof car covers, and we began to wonder at the expected height of the waves to come.

Walking away from the cars, we saw that the passenger seat of one of them was still occupied. It was nothing to do with us, so on our way we went. Much later, having a look at our car to see that it had not shifted from the pounding of the non-existent mountainous waves, we saw that the passenger was still sitting there. Strange, because we had seen the driver alight and walk away quite a while ago. We had to be nosy. What we found in the passenger seat was a full size bronze statue of a naked woman, draped strategically in a flowing bronze robe!

This was a two night, three day, voyage because of the stop-offs at the intervening islands on the way, so once again the cases had to be hauled out of the car. By now, we could win awards for packing and stowage in small inconveniently positioned spaces.

"Tiny little tub." muttered Sally.

"No, dearest one, it is over 20,000 tons, so not that much smaller than the Brittany Ferries boat that you enjoyed so much."

Still grumbling, I steered her to our cabin which once again demonstrated that our luck was holding. It was larger than we had dared to expect, and was sited exactly in the middle, facing forward, and just below the bridge. We seemed to have been allocated the best one on the boat.

"Is this glass thick enough to keep out the waves when they break over the front?" grumbled Sally.

Did she really think that they had to replace all the window glass on each trip?

Our unpacking was interrupted by a loud banging on our door. Whilst on the car deck previously, we had encountered a very vociferous disabled lady, clad in multi-coloured leggings, spinning around in a wheelchair, complaining to one of the crew about something or other. Tied to the wheelchair was a small apology for a dog, endlessly tripping itself up as the wheelchair rotated. Nothing seemed to be satisfying her, and she and the couple with her were grumbling and making themselves unpopular, as only Germans can sometimes do, such as when they are trying to pinch our sunbeds.

It was indeed she at our door.

"I have come to see your cabin!"

"Er, OK. How do you do?" We were stumped for words.

145

"My cabin is unsuitable. Yours may be better for me."

"Er?" again. This was verging on the surreal.

She wheeled herself forward and crashed against the sides of the beds. She became stuck. We had to push and pull to ease her backwards. Still attached to the wheelchair by a lead was the small yapping dog. The lead became further entangled as she tried to navigate herself backwards, and everything ground to a halt. The dog panted.

"You shall come now to my cabin. It may be better for you."

We interpreted this to mean that our cabin might be better for her.

Despite the fact that the intruder could see that we were almost unpacked, Sally went along to see her cabin. It was right on the front corner of the boat, about three doors away. It was a very nice cabin, a bit wider than ours, because of that corner site. Sally said that she could of course have ours, but whilst she could turn her chair and her dog in her own, she would not be able to do so in ours, as she had already demonstrated by the dents to our woodwork. Disgruntled and still grumbling, the woman took herself off, with not one word of thanks for our time or our offer. Later that evening, we saw her again in the restaurant, and she was still complaining about something or other.

Dinner was by courtesy of the inclusive meal voucher included with our tickets and was of a buffet nature. Smiling staff heaped our plates with the advertised hot dishes that were in fact almost cold on delivery, let alone when we had got them back to our table. Chaps wearing chef hats proudly looked on and changed dishes and trays as they became emptied. It was painfully obvious that most of the food had been prepared well in advance and not properly reheated before being brought to the chafing dishes. It was all pure idleness on the part of those chefs.

The mountainous waves never materialised at all, and I for one slept well on my surprisingly comfortable bed. Not so my significant other who grumbled as usual; but I heeded her not, also as usual.

During the next morning, we passed a happy couple of hours or so watching dog owners being exercised by their dogs. We moved towards them and we passed some time in gentle petting and conversation.

In the evening, and to celebrate the continuing calm seas, we booked a table in the a la carte restaurant, hoping for better fodder by paying the required extra. When I say a la carte restaurant, that is a euphemism for a small separate roped off area with the bonus of a tablecloth to the tables. The food turned out to identical, and worse, still at the same temperature. At least here we could send it back! And so we did.

During the night the boat docked in Lanzarote to offload cars and passengers, and no doubt to take on new faces for the onward journey. In the morning, taking a stroll to check that nobody had offloaded our Mercedes, we saw our car park neighbour busily attending to the needs of his giant rabbit, which was hopping around on the deck, whilst all the travelling dogs were howling to join in a rabbit hunt. There was much amusement all round. The bronze lady still sat in her seat, inscrutable as ever.

In the late morning we pulled into Gran Canaria and were met by a colourful procession of new Nissan Jukes coming aboard. We had never seen one before, so idled some time away on inspection. They looked really rather funky in their different hues. Much later we learned that Jeremy Clarkson had given the Juke the thumbs down, so we may safely assume that it is really quite a good car for ordinary people in the real world. Certainly, they have now appeared in significant numbers on our Tenerife roads.

The boat was due to stay in port for a few hours, so we disembarked, clutching our town map, and walked what seemed like miles to get to nowhere particularly pleasant, though we found a huge beach, all lovely yellow sand.

Then it was time to set off again. The excitement was building as this would be the very last leg of our journey before coming home. Soon, Tenerife hove into sight round the northern headland of Gran Canaria. It seemed so near, though it took us another couple of hours to get there. We chugged along – I really enjoyed my trip on that ferry – and we were swiftly overtaken by the inter-island Fred Olsen wave-piercing passenger catamaran that does the trip in half the time between the two islands. Next time….

Sally was so pleased when we pulled into port in Santa Cruz, where we were overshadowed by two vast cruise ships tied up opposite our berth.

"How about going on a cruise next year?" quoth I.

I interpreted the piercing glare as a "no".

Now the big test was to begin. Would we get the car through customs?

We were on UK plates, but we were also left hand drive. Would some eagle eyed customs officer stop us to ask too pertinent a query? But it was now getting quite dark, and this might not be noticed. We had valid insurance covering us for holidays in Europe and a new UK MOT. All was technically in order other than actually having the required vehicle entry inspection certificate in our hands. The conundrum was that we could not have got it because the car was only just arriving here and it could not be issued before the inspection in Tenerife, our final destination. We had been told beforehand by our tame engineer that the car could be impounded until the documentation had been issued. We could shortly be finding ourselves at the centre of a Spanish puzzle of epic proportions.

We had rehearsed our message that we were just tourists visiting the island for a holiday.

Oh, yes? With a car full of everything bar the proverbial kitchen sink?

Thank heavens for the all-concealing darkness. We crawled along in the line of vehicles, trying to look as inconspicuous as one can in a bright red Mercedes sports car. Not an easy trick to pull off, but, oh, the sighs of relief when we were just waved through, the customs officers having descended en masse to pounce on the motorcycle immediately in front of us. We did not have to show even one scrap of paper. It was, in a way, a huge anti-climax.

The sport button on the gearbox was swiftly engaged and we sprinted (relatively speaking, you may understand) for safety in the anonymous dark streets of Santa Cruz.

And so, just over half an hour later, we came home. We parked the car in its new home down in the underground garage and left it ticking away nicely as it cooled down from its epic adventure. It had seen us safely through 2,445 kilometres with no dramas, no accidents, no breakdowns, and we had enjoyed a trip that we both agreed was replete with a lifetime of wonderful memories.

We could not have asked for more.

16

Traffic Idiosyncrasies

We had to apply for Spanish number plates for the Mercedes. But you cannot apply for them until your car has passed the Spanish MOT, known over here as the ITV (*Inspecciòn Tècnica de Vehiculos*). We therefore had to undergo the rigours of the Spanish system to obtain the certificate, despite still having over 11 months MOT from the UK. Although Tenerife law allowed up to six months for a car imported by a foreigner to be matriculated onto Spanish plates, with all the appropriate paperwork completed, it made sense to us to apply for it right away.

In the UK you just go to an MOT approved garage, pay your fee, and trundle out half an hour later with a certificate (should you have passed), and that's that for another year. You then pop down to Halfords and they make up the plates.

The Spanish system is so different, we were to learn.

In Tenerife, ITV stations are entirely independent of garages. There are only four on the island, serving nearly a million cars. Huge places, with three aisles for cars and vans and one for lorries, like a continuous conveyor belt, but one which moves slower than a snail.

The test itself was to prove significantly more rigorous than that in the UK. That is probably why 50% of cars don't bother and are only caught out when stopped by the police, which is a regular occurrence.

You cannot just turn up. Booking in advance is via the internet (unless you want to spend half a day listening to an unanswered telephone ringing) where you reserve your slot, usually for some two weeks in advance. The internet booking system was quite handy, but fell down on one crucial point. The Tenerife system was developed around the original ITV station in Santa Cruz which was a lot bigger than our local one. It therefore accepted as many bookings as it would have coped with at Santa Cruz, with the inevitable result that there was always a severe backlog at our local one, with cars jammed everywhere. It was therefore quite normal to spend half a day up at the ITV station, fairly bursting with pent up frustration as one manically suffered the cut and thrust firstly of the check-in process and then the dodgem-like activity of trying to join a queue where 50 others were trying to do the same and were not prepared to give an inch or indeed a front bumper!

On our first visit, despite having taken advice, a vital piece of paper was missing (an import document issued by Madrid in respect of cars brought into Tenerife on foreign plates). It seemed that it was a new requirement, only brought in a month ago, but they were already only too aware of it. Off we went, not quite slinking away, because it was rather tricky to excavate our car from the growing pile of those behind.

We re-booked for a fortnight later. Still no certificate had been delivered to us, so we cancelled and took up yet another booking a fortnight after that. The certificate then arrived but it was a completely pointless bit of paper issued by some jobsworth in an office in Madrid about a vehicle that he had never seen and which could have been to a completely different specification.

But the man at the MOT station nodded approvingly and allowed us to join the lengthy queue of cars. Queue 1 for us, and we took it to be a good omen. An hour later, and it was finally our turn at the front. Pull this, push that, twiddle everything that was twiddlable and lo and behold... we failed.

Failed!! How come? This car had had so much advance preparation in the UK, it was in tip top condition; everything worked, and it had a brand new UK MOT.

"So what's the problem, then?" I enquired.

"Aha, *señor*, alas it is your headlights. They are no good. They dip the wrong way. They do not comply with our regulations. You must change them for Spanish headlight units. I cannot pass your car. *Hasta luego!*"

And that was that.

We went home and tried to unravel the problem. The first owner of the car had been an officer in the British Army stationed in Germany, and he had purchased the car new from a Mercedes dealer in Dusseldorf. Without doubt the car had the correct dipping lights at that time. When we first saw it, there was a box in the boot clearly marked "left hand lights" so we and The SL Shop both reasonably assumed that the car now had had an exchange of headlights for its life in the UK. They had agreed to swap the lights back over as part of the preparation of the car, and confirmed that they had done so on my check list that they handed back to us. Clearly, they had not done so, as they later acknowledged. We were left with the wrong set on the car.

So I changed the headlight units over and made a new appointment. Another fortnight passed. We turned up and were nodded through into the queue. We went through the full test all over again, and... failed again!

"What is it this time?"

"*Señor*, your lights dip in the wrong direction."

"No, no, that is not possible, I have changed them over."

I opened the boot and extracted the other set of lights. "See, here are the old lights, in the boot."

"I cannot help that. You have still failed. Here, you can look on my machine; see, they dip incorrectly."

"Bloody hell!" So they did. It just could not be possible!

A specialist mechanic was drafted in to check both sets of lights. He confirmed that both were wrong. At this point, words almost failed us. What to do next?

In the end, to break the impasse, I ordered two complete headlight units direct from Mercedes in Germany, based on their original specification on the car's build card held by them. They had a pair of light units in stock, and they went from the Mercedes factory to the Mercedes main UK depot in Milton Keynes, from there to Mercedes Worcester, then to The SL Shop, who posted them out to Tenerife. And, no, before you ask, they could not be shipped direct to us.

Yet another appointment was made and along we went. This time, no queue, no waiting; the head chap there looked at the car, gave it the nod, and we got our stamped ITV with the certificate to follow in the usual way. We shall never know, but was it because we had taken Freddie along with us that time, and he had fixed him with his beady stare?

Now we could apply for our Spanish plates, and these were made up and fitted within the week. We had wanted an old registration to suit the year of original manufacture, but instead were awarded brand new numbers and letters, as for a new car. Hey ho.

Oddly, looking back on that episode, we realised that we had never driven the car at night. On its first day in our ownership we arrived in Hove just before nightfall. For the journey south through Spain, we had always arrived at our chosen hotel before dark set in. It was just one of those things.

Does anyone want two spare sets of UK headlights for a R129?

Driving, traffic, the rule of the road; almost everything is different in Tenerife to what we had been used to in England. The most obvious difference is driving on the other side: the nuances of road

153

behaviour need to be learned all over again when piloting down the right hand side of the carriageway.

There is now a rash of roundabouts developing in Tenerife. They proliferate everywhere, even where they are not really needed. No new road, or the resurfacing of an existing one, will be complete without the construction of a new roundabout. It has only been in recent years that these strange road works have been introduced to the native population and there is a particular drawback; that is, that nobody has bothered to tell the population how to use them.

Nobody, but nobody, uses the inner circle of the two lanes round a roundabout. Whichever exit you want to use, everyone goes round using the outside lane. As you approach the roundabout where there are two lanes, everyone pulls over to the right and squashes into the outer circle. There will even be a filter sign on the tarmac on the right hand side. So, why did they bother to tarmac the inner circle at all? Thus there are always longer tailbacks at roundabouts. Should you have the temerity to actually go into that inner lane, then nobody will let you back out, and you might well be consigned to everlasting circulation.

Of course, the building of a new roundabout is another excuse for building something next to it, adding value, you might say, to its very existence. A brand new petrol station (for a major international petroleum company) has been built hard by a local roundabout, complete with pumps, car washes, lavatories and a shop, all with an extensive parking area. It is massive and impressive. But, there is a big problem. It was completed and opened before full planning permission had been granted. Someone jumped the gun! And so, there it is, with no permissible entrance from the roundabout, and therefore a singular lack of customers. Only in Spain…!

Zebra crossings are another nightmare area for the unwary.

A pedestrian in Tenerife has the absolute right to cross on a crossing. He or she takes precedence over the car. Most pedestrians have taken this to an insane extreme. They literally do not even bother to look in the direction of the traffic. They just step off the kerb and go. Those of a really venturesome nature appear to deliberately look away as they are doing so, like children playing a game of chicken. A few really brave, or stupid, ones actually start the crossing process well before arriving at the zebra, striding along and never faltering. You, as the driver, just know that they will not stop or look, and you learn a sixth sense to slam on the anchors.

That, it seems, is why a lot of cars in Tenerife sport bashed in rear ends! I was determined to ensure that this fate was not going to befall either of our two cars, and immediately adopted the Spanish signal for slowing down prior to stopping at a junction or crossing, by giving three winks on my offside indicator. It works a treat.

And a zebra crossing, to a Canarian, is merely an untaken parking space that will enable him to park nearer to his destination than otherwise he would have been able. If two Canarians can, between them, manage to block it entirely, so rendering it completely useless on both sides, then so much the better. And nobody complains! Pedestrians just walk round the blockage, never giving a second glance, and the police just drive on by.

Conversely, something that the Canarian driver is good at, is letting you in at a junction. We had been to Guernsey, and seen that the formal rule of the road there was to let alternate cars in, so there was no build-up of traffic queues. I don't know whether that is actually a rule of law here, but it is invariably applied, and very nice it is to be able to pop out into the main road without grumpy BMW drivers blocking your way.

We have no traffic wardens up here in the north that I have ever seen. There is no need for them. The traffic, and it can be heavy in town, keeps on rolling along, everyone double parks, and the world goes on turning.

But there is therefore an unofficial system for double parking, which we have learned. You pull up where you want to shop, or stop for whatever reason. If there is no space left, you simply double park and block the properly parked car beside you. You understand that you must not go far, and if you hear a couple of urgent toots, you must go back and let him out. When you have let him out, you can take over his space, and then you can go off for your extended lunch or whatever.

I like to imagine the glee on the faces of UK traffic wardens. faced with all that.

17

Exploits with Pedro

Each year the community of owners of our building hold an annual general meeting, where the accounts are presented, and income for the coming year is aligned with expenses. Individual petitions can be put forward, and those owners that are in arrears are named and shamed, and excluded from any voting process. The meetings are almost interminable, a complete shambles, and are frankly best avoided unless there is something of import to you personally. Admittance on the door is strictly controlled, and sadly that's all that is strictly controlled.

The last meeting included the curious case of Pedro, our gardener.

Pedro, who is Canarian, is the gardener retained to maintain our community complex of lawns, flower beds, shrubs, trees and other flora. He is well trained, friendly and very competent.

In my humble opinion, no other person could have wrought the magic that he continues to do on the large tract of his responsibility. In addition to these duties, he has been trained in the black art of swimming pool management, so not only can he feed the beast with the right amount of chemicals, sufficient not to give any of us a chemical peel, but can also repair any dislodged tesserae that might from time to time come loose. He is also a general handyman and tasked with keeping a watching brief over all the garage spaces as well.

Sally and I are both Pedro fans. We have always got on. We have learned quite a lot of Spanish from him, because despite his local accent he will talk slowly when required, and he has clearly been well brought up and educated.

In previous years, he also monitored the visitors at the swimming pool at weekends, because really good pools can be magnets for young people who climb over security railings, almost impaling themselves as they do so. But his own children, two lovely daughters, are growing, and he does not want to continue to spend his summer weekends away from them, whilst pursuing those of others. Not even for some modest extra remuneration.

So our community has engaged an outside security company to offer a patrol service during the summer months. And very posh we are, with notices all around telling the world that we have a security service in operation. The employees of the company are dressed in smart navy blue uniforms with peaked hats and badges. They look the part, and it is strange how it gives a feeling of comfort to have them about, although there is absolutely no reason for it.

One afternoon, the vigilante on duty, Sergio, had most of his time taken up by trying to get rid of a herd of goats that had somehow managed to breach the outer defences. Such excitement there was, everyone running around laughing and crying, children racing hither and thither making it all worse, and Freddie barking away as though it was all a personal affront to his space to have the goats at such close quarters.

But I digress from the matter in hand…

In some way, I know not how exactly, Pedro had fallen foul of one of the Spanish apartment owners. Allegedly, he was caught napping. Just once, you understand, and in his defence, the temperature can often rise to over 30 degrees at midday. Whether it was true or not, I do not know. Nor do I consider it to be of much import. If a Canarian cannot take a snooze, then the world will cease to turn on its axis.

That particular owner is what is known as a *macho Iberico,* a huge hunk with bulging muscles. You would not want to pick a fight with him, although I must say that he has always been very kind to us.

Unusually, Pedro was in attendance at the meeting. It opened with our neighbourly *macho Iberico* having a go at Pedro and calling for his immediate dismissal. He also accused him of cutting the shrubs leading up to our main entrance, which strictly speaking are not owned by the community, but by the *Ayuntamiento*. Pedro responded that whilst this was true, he had a few minutes free one day, and so he tidied up the area, as it would be nicer for the rest of us owners. As for the falling asleep on the job, Pedro denied it completely.

The denunciation dragged on and on. What a meal was made of a snooze and a few shrubs. A couple of stooges waded in but they looked all too obvious to us, right out of an old Laurel and Hardy film. And after an hour we still had not got to item one on the agenda.

But Pedro was well off the hook by then. Too many people stood up and said what a good chap he was, and if he went, we would surely need two persons as his replacement. Also, he had been responsible for helping a lot of people, ourselves included, when there were minor repairs needed, or addresses to be found or suchlike, and we all said how helpful he had been over the last year. He might be a bit of a gossip, but he is much liked and admired both for his expertise and friendliness.

At last the meeting came to some semblance of order and the agenda proper could be started.

I had little interest in most of it but kept a weather eye open for anything of personal interest. One such was that there were some broken lights within the gardens. Instead of the community board doing the obvious thing and just sorting out replacements, there had to be a lengthy debate about it.

Someone opened the batting. "What about the broken poolside lights, then?"

"Yes, they are a disgrace," grumbled another.

"How much shall we have to spend on repairs?" said a third.

"Who broke them?" said a fourth.

"It must have been somebody's children, clearly."

"Are you accusing my children of vandalism?" A middle aged lady stood up, waving her arms, steam coming out of her hairy ears and nostrils.

"No, I'm not," said the other woman. "But it must have been somebody's children, and you do have two."

The lady sat down again, only slightly mollified. The slur had been cast, and was not to be so easily deflected.

Nobody knew who was at fault, or certainly nobody was saying.

"What sort of replacements should we have?" Here we go again.

"Well, the same, why not?"

"No, something more robust, perhaps? And less of an invitation for children to swing on?"

"Well, what are the costs of these replacement lights?"

Nobody knew that either.

There was a lot of shrugging, Canary style.

And so it went on. There was no order or control. People talked over others. Some people went outside for a smoke, and yelled back through the doorway across everyone else. After three hours, we sidled out to go for dinner somewhere close by, and left them to it. They finished about 11.30 p.m.

Pedro was nowhere to be seen on Monday morning. He had wisely gone to Lanzarote for a week's holiday while it all calmed down. On his return, all would no doubt be as before, the furore long forgotten.

Extract from my review of a restaurant on the outskirts of Puerto de la Cruz:

"It is Canary Day. Almost all of the shops and businesses are shut, and,

with the lovely weather, everyone will be going to the beach. A mass migration will take place.

Not so your scribe, who languishes in some pain with an ingrowing toenail. Little did I realise that this was going to lead me towards an excellent dinner, albeit by a somewhat convoluted route.

I had emailed my podologo (podologist) the day before and she emailed straight back reminding me that every business, including hers, would be closed. But since I was in pain, then she would open up at 6.30 p.m. on Canary Day just for me, as I was departing for England on the morrow.

On the dot, as I am pushing the bell to the surgery door, her car screeches to a stop, double parks, hazard lights flashing, and she opens up the surgery. Ten minutes later, with me breathing a sigh of relief, we are all back on the pavement. Money is firmly offered, and just as firmly refused. She zooms off, back no doubt to her family fiesta.

Once again I am stunned at the generosity and service of local businesses here in Tenerife.

After all that, a quick drink in the Plaza del Charco is definitely needed and we decide that Tito's Bodeguita sounds just the place for a relaxing meal. A little out of town, this is a lovely old restored Canary building on a sharp corner just off the TF5 autopista at Junction 35.

Lined up outside are taxis galore, disgorging a hungry populace, and it looks as though the place is going to be packed. There are two terraces and a large indoor room with bar. All the tables on the terraces are already taken and, not wanting to eat indoors on such a lovely evening, we are resigned to being turned away.

But just then a table is vacated, and we swoop. We are two, the table is for four, but no matter, the staff smile accommodatingly and menus are brought. There is a nice level of choices here, not so many that you are convinced that a lot is going to have to be taken from the freezer.

Our waitress bustles about, all jeans and a ponytail, but smiling the while, and very professional.

Bread and a dip (almogrote) is brought. The bread is outstanding. The dip is made up of smoked red pepper, cheese, olive oil and a touch of garlic. It is altogether excellent.

We decide on the octopus as our starter. This is really a dish large enough for two, and the octopus is meltingly tender, served as a tian *topped with an orange jelly and fresh ginger. If that sounds a bit different, then indeed it is, but I cannot wait to go back to sample it again. It is accompanied by an excellent salad of endive and lamb's lettuce with cherry tomatoes, perfectly dressed and seasoned. We demolish the lot.*

For the main course my wife opts for fish. She goes for the cherne, *lightly cooked. It is accompanied by a ratatouille, albeit rather heavy on the peppers for her. But then, we are in Spain…*

Miss Ponytail is keen for me to have the rabbit, which she says is a house speciality. I succumb to her blandishments, and a plate heaped with conejo en salmorejo *is put before me, surrounded by* papas arrugadas. *The rabbit just melts in the mouth, no knife needed, and it's a portion larger than I can manage.*

And it is very, very, good.

The while, live music is being played behind us at the back of the terrace. I cannot remember what it was, but for me that is the plus point, nice music without being overly intrusive.

There's a party of local people nearby, and between them (including their well-behaved children) they seem to be going through the card. Plates of pimientos de padron, Iberico *ham, mixed cheeses and so on are being distributed as their starters, and everyone we see is clearly enjoying themselves.*

At a secluded table for two, an elderly couple, romantically entwined, are working their way through – yes, the same octopus starter – followed by a steak of serious proportion, and a plate of calamares a la romana, *served with a mountain of chips. I take my hat off to them.*

We have no room for postres, *and call for our bill. It comes to €44.21 including IGIC and covers two main courses, that large (main course sized) starter for two, a bottle of water, half a litre of red house wine and bread with that excellent dip.*

My brief when writing this column is to include the good, the bad and the ugly. But, in truth, I have nothing but praise for this establishment. The food is good, the service is good, the setting and ambiance is good, and the price is reasonable. I cannot wait to go there again."

In my review above, I omitted to say that during the meal a crown had fallen out of my mouth. It was just one of those things, and certainly nothing to do with the quality of the rabbit that I had been eating. It was by then well past 9 p.m. and I sent a text to our Danish dentist, Cristina.

"Any chance of getting to see you early tomorrow morning?" and I explained the problem.

"Be here at 8.45 a.m.," came the swift response.

You can't say fairer than that!

A month or so later, it's Monday, just before lunchtime, and the sun is beating down out of a cloudless sky.

The garden gate rattles, and there stands Pedro, hopping from one foot to the other, clearly in some discomfort. I go to meet him with his usual tumbler of cold water, because he eschews our coffee, deeming it to be inferior to anything that a self-respecting Spaniard would ever allow to pass his lips.

"*Qué pasa,* Pedro?" I said, pointing to his twitching legs.

"Oh, it's my legs and backside. I was up in the mountains yesterday with my father and the horses. We went riding all along the top ridge, and it took us six hours. Fantastic, but crippling!"

Pedro's father, as we had learned many months previously, owns a *finca* up near La Florida, a hill village about half way up the mountains towards El Teide. We had seen his horses when we went to the village *fiesta* last year. I remembered that he had won one of the show classes.

"You went right along the top?"

"Yes," he said. "We often go out riding the horses at the weekend to give them a thorough exercise. The trip that we do is right along the top of the ridge that you can see from your terrace. Look… over there!"

All a-shimmer through the heat haze, we could see right along the ridge. We have never been up there, although we have been told that there is a track that runs right around the top of the valley. It's still on our "to do" list.

Pedro knew from previous chats over our garden gate that Sally used to be a keen horsewoman in her younger days. I guess that most young girls are, but Sally continued to ride until more mature years overtook her. But we were a bit stunned when he came out with an invitation.

"Why don't you come up to my fathers' *finca* one evening and have a look around. You can have a ride if you want to, as well. Oh, and could I have a refill of that water, please?"

Sally declined the ride, but we did fix with Pedro to meet him after he finished work on Friday, and to travel in convoy with him up to the *finca*.

When that day dawned, I went to find Pedro, in case he had forgotten, or the date had become inconvenient.

"No, all is OK. Meet me on the corner at five p.m."

So we travelled up into the hills, the temperature dropping a degree every 500 feet or so as we climbed ever upwards. Leaving the village of La Florida behind us, we pulled up outside a pair of large wrought iron gates. The Canarians love wrought iron gates, and often build a couple of gigantic stone or brick piers each side of their driveway, just to hang these wrought iron monstrosities on. You see them everywhere, often where there really is no visible need for them to be at all. Weirdly, there is usually no wall either side of the gates, so anyone can just walk around them.

Pedro opened the gates, and we all motored through, bumping over potholes, rough stones clattering around in the wheel arches. An unmade winding track led us to a long single storey house, attached to which were a series of barns forming an L shape with an open courtyard. We pulled up and had hardly got out of the car when three large dogs of indeterminate pedigree bounded towards us baring enormous fangs, but with what we hoped were friendly grins.

Pedro, like many Spaniards, had never made much of a fuss of Freddie, so we were surprised when he greeted them so warmly and made such a fuss of them. He explained that they were outdoor dogs, used for working and guarding the *finca*. Having taken one look at them, I certainly would not have put the place on my list of premises to burgle.

Inside the house, all was cool and cluttered, the shutters closed against the warmth of the sun. Nothing seemed to have been thrown away that might conceivably be of use within the next couple of decades. Nevertheless, there were big squishy armchairs grouped around a huge stone fireplace, which was obviously in regular use. We moved through to the kitchen, and we saw clearly that this was where the family spent most of their time. A huge refectory table could seat about a dozen people and the antique range-type cooker could probably manage a feast for a hundred, it was so large. Pans hung over it in random fashion, hooked to the large beam with old S-shaped butcher's hooks.

"Come and meet the family," said Pedro. "They will still be out in the fields."

We went out onto the terrace, and Pedro let fly a piercing whistle. Not only did it bring the dogs back to us, hurtling round the corner of the house, but heads popped up over the top of a nearby wall, and waved in greeting. Pedro's father was lean and weather-beaten, and like all working people in their working clothes, with a ready smile and warm handshake. He had been hard at work trimming back the largest and lowest-growing vine leaves from the rootstock in order to give the budding grapes a chance to catch the most sunshine. The pruned twigs, once stripped of their leaves, would have a further use. Nothing here would go to waste.

He had not a single word of English, and spoke with a very local dialect. He obviously knew that we were coming, and was very welcoming, but Pedro had to act as an interpreter despite my asking him to slow down a bit as he spoke.

We all walked downhill past their small vineyard, a larger banana plantation, and so came to some pasture, where half a dozen horses were taking advantage of the shade under a lean-to, swishing their tails to ward off the flies. Four of them were work horses, but the other two were clearly something special. Seeing Pedro and his father, they all ambled over, and the two special ones whickered a greeting whilst Pedro scratched their necks.

"Surely you would like to ride one, Sally?' he asked. "They are big, but they are also gentle."

"Er, no thanks, Pedro. I'll pass this time round. Old age has overtaken any skills that I might have had."

When we got back to the house after a lengthy tour to meet not only the horses but some Canarian black pigs, the scruffiest chickens that you have ever seen, and last but not least a family of goats, it was time for something to eat.

We had not realised that food was going to be on the agenda, but working families up in the hills still eat early on workdays. I suppose it is a relic of going to bed when it gets dark and getting up as soon as it is light, before the advent of electricity, which would not have been so long ago up in those hills.

With his father, Pedro, Sally and myself, another couple sat down at the long table. We never really found out who they were, but we smiled at them and they smiled at us, and we passed some desultory conversation between us. Like Pedro, they spoke well. The meal was a simple affair, a vast iron tureen of goat stew with onions, black olives and bacon lardons, wafting tantalising garlic infused scents from the cooking range, and accompanied by crusty bread, washed down with their own wine from last year's harvest.

I didn't like to ask if the contents of the stew had been part of the family grazing outside, but I had to assume the worst.

Pedro told his father how I too cooked goat stew, and there was a lot of mirth at the fact that an Englishman had learned to cook a Canarian signature dish. But Pedro stood up for me and said that he had tasted it and that it was very good. I hope they believed him, but I expected not.

All too soon we thought that the time had come to leave them to it, to enjoy their Friday evening all together, and so we thanked them most effusively and they all came out to wave us off.

"Have a good weekend, John and Sally, and I will see you as usual on Monday morning. Do you remember the way back?" called Pedro.

"Yes, no problem!" We waved back, and as we motored off down the driveway, the guard dogs stood and stared after us carefully until we were out of sight.

18

Storms and Tempests

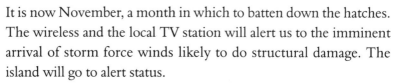

It is now November, a month in which to batten down the hatches. The wireless and the local TV station will alert us to the imminent arrival of storm force winds likely to do structural damage. The island will go to alert status.

I am in no way exaggerating when I say that the first storms we encountered were really frightening. Both of them destroyed roads, uprooted trees, created mudslides, washed away houses and cars and created absolute mayhem. Electricity went on the blink in some places, and the phone lines collapsed in others. The damage to the banana plantations we love so much ran into millions of euros as whole swathes of trees were decimated.

For once, the Fortunate Islands were not living up to their name.

The storms were so bad and the damage so severe in the archipelago that the Spanish governmental central rescue scheme kicked in and repairs were paid for centrally from Madrid, rather than through individual insurers. The airports were closed on all of the islands, and we were glued to the local Spanish news for days following the storms. The pictures were awful and other places on the archipelago seemed to have taken the brunt of it equally with ourselves.

Most lost the food in their fridges and freezers, unless they possessed their own back-up generators. Family and friends back in the UK rang to ask how we were. We hadn't suffered damage ourselves, although the roof of our building did suffer over 4,000 euros worth of displaced tiles. A couple of weeks later, Sally's hairdresser told her that she had lost the entire roof from her house. Not just the tiles, but the entire roof! It was picked up and scattered further along the road. Water came in through the ceiling of her hairdressing salon from the apartment of the landlord above her, and he refused to sanction any repairs, although he did take her out for dinner!

A storm is never a good time for a dog, or, I suppose, any animal, although Freddie used to love the high winds back in Lytham, and would almost fly along the seafront, his ears stretched out like mini wings, wearing what I swear was a huge grin.

Over here, all is very different. I think that perhaps it is the noise. Firstly there is a gentle soughing on the wind, a rustle from the palm trees in the garden to announce its imminent arrival. And then it comes. Not only does it come with the force of the hand of The Almighty, it makes a thunder like that of a runaway express train. At its peak, it would be madness to go out, and Freddie has learned this fact for himself. He retires to one end of the settee, does his best to cover his ears, and stares and stares at us. In the end, we are all on the same settee, trying to give each other comfort until the worst is over.

What Fortunate Islands?

Some hours later, the noise will drop away as quickly as it started. Freddie will be the first to know, exercising some sixth sense, and move himself from the little burrow that he has made for himself, towards the front door.

"Time to risk going out, then?" I enquire, knowing the answer already.

"You bet! I really can't wait any longer!" And he is gone, disappeared into the garden, to return all smiles a few minutes later with an empty bladder, as though nothing at all has happened for the last few hours.

A friend who lived in the next town called me in some panic.

"Did the storm hit you?" he enquired.

"Yes, some of our hibiscus bushes have literally been stripped back to bare twigs. I suppose that the wind caught us because we are on a corner. And I can see tiles on the ground all over the place. It was really frightening. Otherwise, we are OK. But how about you? All OK with you?"

Apparently he'd been up on to his flat roof that morning, only to find that the large, heavy plastic sun loungers which he kept up there for his visiting friends had completely disappeared.

"Apart from my sun loungers and other bits and pieces which have gone, my car has been damaged. When you have a moment, could you pop round and have a look at it for me, and tell me what's to be done? The kettle will be on!"

It was two days before we could get our car out to the main road because the lane was blocked by fallen trees. We urgently needed some shopping, and then we went straight to look at his car. I stood in the road and stared at it. All down one side, and over the roof and boot areas, the paintwork had either been stripped or heavily scratched.

"What on earth have you done with it?" I said to him.

"It wasn't me… Just look at that palm tree down there." he said, pointing down the road. "It came flying past and thrashed itself against the side of the car. What am I going to do?" A fully grown palm tree had become uprooted in the storm, taken flight down the hill, and attacked his car before coming wedged to a standstill, conveniently next to the *basura*.

I went off to visit an automobile paint and repair shop that I had heard of.

Going back through our town, we pulled up in amazement when we saw about 30 cars and vans all piled in a great heap at the lower end of one of the *barrancos*, the steeply carved ravines where from prehistoric times water had run down during storms from the mountains and escaped to the open ocean, eroding the land a little bit more each time. Two great *barrancos* run down through our town.

On the flatter part of one, the 30 or so cars that had been left parked overnight were found the next day about 200 yards away lower down the slope, actually piled up nearly at the edge of the sea in a jumbled tangle of scrap metal, such was the force of the water in the flash flooding. We counted ourselves very lucky to have escaped all that catastrophe.

The man from the paint and repair shop eventually came along and quoted 1,000 euros to re-spray every panel of our friend's car, and two weeks later, all was as new again. He never did get his sun loungers back, although a few days later he saw a big bit of plastic in the high street about half a kilometre away, and it looked suspiciously like a part of his paraphernalia. He quickly walked on by, pretending not to have noticed anything.

Good wet weather driving has never been a skill easily learned. We all know the principle of driving a bit slower in the rain, and, of course, leaving more space between us and the car in front. It is drummed into us, starting with the Highway Code, through years of experience, possibly augmented by taking advanced courses. When I was much younger, I was lucky enough to drive a variety of high power machinery in various competitions that taught me a lot of respect for the damage that a badly driven ton of metal can do to myself or others around me.

When it rains here in Tenerife, there are always, but always, pile-ups on the *autopista* and elsewhere. After a prolonged period of dry weather, the roads have become coated with rubber deposited from the passing of thousands of tyres. The moment that it rains, the road surface turns into a skating rink as the surface downgrades to little or no grip.

Is this something for the average inhabitant of the island to take into account? No!

The usual plan is for Canarians to keep on driving at the same rate in a downpour, preferably at the maximum speed for the particular bit of road, but to put on hazard lights whilst remaining as close to the rear bumper of the car in front as is humanly possible. If one has a mobile phone, then that will usually remain clamped to one ear and hands will be used for gesticulating.

Why slow down, or leave more space between vehicles? No, not a thought that appears to cross the mind of the average Canarian when on the *autopista*. He will be far too busy trying to see out of the steamed up windows!

On such days, when we must be out, we have learned that it is much safer to grind along in the slow lane, taking our time. The only problem with that is that we live in terror of being written off from the rear by a car whose windows are fogged up and who cannot see us at the suicidal closing speed deemed the norm.

I look across at Sally. She glances back at me…

"!!!"

"!!!"

No words pass between us, but we both know that the maniacs hurtling past us have virtually ceded any control over their vehicles, and may well involve us in mayhem and destruction if the next corner does not catch them first.

Days such as those create happy hunting grounds for the *gruas*. They are the large breakdown trucks with cranes that seem to nest in groups near motorway junctions and other likely spots. The *grua* will be driven by an immense woolly mammoth of a man with arms like tree trunks. Instead of an assistant, he may have an equally large and shaggy dog sitting in the front passenger seat. I sometimes wonder if the two are completely interchangeable, and I have had dreams of being winched up on to a low loader by an Alsatian.

Fortunately, however, rain is the exception to our daily lives here. We are able to sit out on our terrace most evenings and marvel at the clouds, like giant puffballs, slowly drifting across our sightline.

They pop up over the crest of the hills at the top of the valley and almost immediately vaporize to nothing as the pressure changes. A gentle breeze, just sufficient to cause a ripple on the front edges of our sun blinds, will herald a perfect view of the sun setting further down along the coast as its fiery orb dips into the red molten sea on the far horizon.

And the air here is said to be some of the purest in the world. After all, what is there between us and the Americas? Only 3,000 miles of nothing at all other than the Atlantic Ocean. No wonder that all of our friends who have been to stay sleep like logs and have difficulty in getting up in the morning.

19

The Importance of Goats

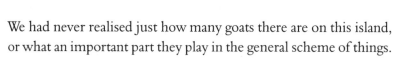

We had never realised just how many goats there are on this island, or what an important part they play in the general scheme of things. Living in England, one was not accustomed to a couple of hundred goats descending on your garden, or clogging up the road as you hurtle round a hairpin bend up in the hills.

In Tenerife, it seems, the goat is king, and now that we are playing our part in island life, we are coming to terms with their immense importance.

There are goat festivals, where people come to celebrate all things goaty. There are other festivals where entire herds, each some 100 or so strong, are invited to participate with their smelly brethren. Just like extras in a film, a herd will suddenly appear over the nearest hill and before you know it, they have taken over.

Goats' milk is on sale everywhere. So is goat cheese, in all sorts of flavours. Goat cheese back in England was usually to be found for sale in a roll, with a uniformly strong flavour whether it came from Harrods or Tesco. Not so here on the island. There is a whole range of flavours from the mildest to the strongest, some mixed with herbs or nuts, some smoked and some not. I defy anyone not to find one to their taste.

And, should the wind be blowing unfavourably, we are sometimes assailed by the odour of goat, something all of its own. One particular herd passes along our lane every Sunday afternoon, mustered along by a couple of dogs that do not seem to receive any commands at all, presumably on their way to seek pastures new, or at least a scrap of anything remotely edible. I have even seen them eating plastic.

The goats also appear to enjoy a special goat law. A herd can go anywhere that is unfenced on the island, with no fear of reprisal. You may return home to find your garden absolutely flattened, since those goats will eat anything at all. The phlegmatic goatherd will just stand by, leaning on his long crook, and give his version of the Canary shrug if you dare to remonstrate. His couple of dogs don't even bother to flick their tails in the heat.

Once, a friend lost an entire hedge of mature hibiscus in that way. It had been his pride and joy, that hedge, and just the stumps were left after those trenchermen had moved on.

Goats can, and will, evacuate their bowels anywhere without penalty. You see huge trails of droppings on country roads. If I do not pick up after my dog, I can be fined, but how do you pick up after 100 goats have passed by? Think of the number of poo bags to be carried around!

Once a year, all the thousands of goats are driven down from the valleys behind us to be immersed in the waters of the harbour, and blessed by the clergy to ensure their on-going fertility. The goats travel to town in their own individual herds, moved along by their herdsman accompanied by their mangy looking dogs. By the time that they have all arrived at the harbour, there may well be 20 herds, some with up to 100 goats in each herd.

Tourists are bussed in from miles around to watch the spectacle, and they cram into the small space between the beach and the square, wondering what on earth they are there to witness. The harbour is decked out with bunting for the occasion, and locals are keen to do business, elbowing their way through the throng, hawking cold beer or soft drinks.

Can you imagine the pandemonium?

Suddenly the crowd parts and a herd of goats approaches the

harbour side. The older ones (assuming that goats really do have memories) start to look a little hesitant and nervous. As they get closer to the water's edge, a dozen strapping lads clad only in swimming trunks and, bizarrely, wellington boots, rush forward, each grabbing the horns of a senior goat, and either ride it or drag it into the water. Legs flail and the poor animals momentarily go under. It's just enough to satisfy the feudal requirements, and they are released from their purgatory and allowed to run back up the beach, where they stand placidly and watch the torment of their brethren. This is repeated until every goat in the herd has been immersed.

The dogs, the real goat minders, keep perfect law and order whilst this is all going on. When the dowsing of the herd is completed, the entire herd, with a dog fore and aft, melts back through the tourists and vanishes.

One minute the town is full of goats, the next there is just that lingering goat odour wafting on the breeze, and all the tourists are wondering if it has all been a mirage.

And all of this comes to pass because one year, back in the mists of time, the patron saint of goats decreed that they would be more fertile if they had an annual dip.

But, there is a bonus for us, with the animals becoming so fecund from their immersion in the water of the harbour. We very early on discovered that goat tastes wonderful! If you have never eaten goat in any of its variations, you really should.

On the menu up in the hills in the autumn and winter, goat stew is served, rich with wine and herbs, spreading its aroma round and about. So enticing when flavoured with a hint of chilli in that rich dark sauce. Crusty bread to mop it up, and all for a fiver a head in old money. Absolute heaven!

We were determined to seek out somewhere where we could obtain goat meat, because it is never on sale in any supermarket. The hunt was on, and we tracked down young goat meat for sale in a small village butcher further along the coast. A bit like the tale of London buses all coming along at the same time, we have now found a number of outlets and been offered a number of new recipes.

One day when our gardener, Pedro, walked past our terrace, he paused in mid stride, his nose all aquiver, and called out to me.

"*Hola, señor* John! What are you cooking? It smells very good." He knew that I did a lot of cooking.

"*Hola* Pedro! Come into the kitchen and try some of this." I called back out through the window.

In he came, and was surprised when I offered him a spoon and lifted the lid from a large cooking pot. "What is it *señor* John? It smells like *cabra*!"

"Yes, it is goat, Pedro."

"But you, you are English, and you are cooking *cabra*?" I could see this going on for ever.

"Dip in and try it." I was very confident.

"Mmmm. This is wonderful. Where have you got it from? You must have bought it!

"No, Pedro, it is all my own work!"

"But it is better than you can get in a restaurant!"

"I know!" I preened myself.

Goats, I can forgive them all their misdemeanours.

Pedro the gardener came a-knocking on our door again one morning. He had been sweeping up the leaves in our *calle*.

"What are you doing this Saturday?" he asked.

"Nothing special, as far as I know. Why?"

"Are you going to La Florida?"

It seemed that twice a year there was a *fiesta* or *romaria* in La Florida, a small village some kilometres uphill from La Orotava. As at most village fairs, the goats play a significant part, either being on the market for purchase or actually on the spit for lunch. But here there would be a show area for local cattle, horses and those scrawny mountain sheep as well. It was not an event known to the tourist sector – and long may that continue, please.

Pedro would go there because not only did he have family up that way, but his father would be entering some horses for the show.

"So come along. I will see you there. We can have some village wine together."

It sounded good to me. We made it a date.

We found the village by the simple expedient of following the local people making the pilgrimage there. When we arrived there was no parking to be had anywhere nearby, and we had to turn around (not easy when the crowds were so dense) and park in what seemed to be the adjoining parish. By the time we had walked back, things were well underway and the temporary bars and roadside stalls were doing a roaring trade. We stopped for a cold Coca Cola – just one between us as we did not know where there might be somewhere to "go" later on.

Walking up the main street in front of us were four Red Cross workers in their bright red uniforms. Was this a good or a bad sign? Was it an omen of things to come?

The crowds were getting thicker. There was nobody that looked remotely like a tourist. At the side of the street the stalls were selling beer and soft drinks, others selling local straw hats, and one or two firing up their burners to provide hamburgers and the like.

Riders on horseback clattered past us. A man stood on the pavement with a fully grown iguana on his shoulder. It flicked its tongue at us as we walked by.

Herds of goats were parked on every available empty space,

closely penned in by their doggy custodians. Were they really going to be part of the show? How would so many herds be moved around by their owners without trampling the rest of us underfoot?

At the top of the street, the central part of the village widened out to become a square. On one side there was an area where cows and bulls were going to be on show. Under some shade trees, beautifully groomed horses were tethered whilst their owners, clad in their best riding gear, discussed this and that. Tight jodhpurs and cigars were the order of the day. We looked out for Pedro, but he was not to be seen anywhere. Perhaps we were too early, or perhaps too late?

Soon it was time for judging to start on the cattle section, and stern faces passed from one animal to another, inspecting and commenting. Rosettes were awarded, and the crowd cheered each time.

We decided to visit one of the village bars whilst that was all going on, before they got too busy. It was a press to get in at all, people were taking up every space available, and everyone shouted at each other to make themselves heard, which meant that the noise was deafening.

Miraculously, a couple vacated two seats as we went in. We beat some other people to it, and nothing would budge us. Also miraculously, within a few seconds, two cold beers were set before us. We looked up in astonishment, and there was Pedro, all wreathed in smiles.

"I just knew you would come into this bar!"

"Thanks, Pedro, we have been looking everywhere for you. But how did you know?"

"It's the only one in the square with decent loos! And I have been looking after my father's horses in the show ring. Did you not see me?"

"No. We looked everywhere."

"Just look for the best horses! I'll be seeing you at the village feast afterwards?"

"Perhaps, but probably not. But we have had a super time; thanks for letting us know about it."

We had our beers together, and then he was off, back to the horses. We did not think that we could wait another two or three hours there before the feast was ready. We had seen the preparations on the way into the village, and sauntered back to have another look.

On a large bit of waste ground, some fifty or so cooking pots had been placed over a line of open fires. Each pot was nearly two feet across. They would provide a special festive stew for the whole village, and a number of men wearing aprons were going to each pot and tasting the contents. A touch more of one spice here, a touch more of another one there. A quick nod and the advice was taken up.

On a big table, sides of pork were being butchered. There was also some suspiciously fresh goat meat in evidence. A line of women formed up, took buckets full of the cut pieces away, and handed them to the people in charge of the pots. In it all went, and there was later yet another repeat of the stirring and tasting.

The process was repeated for the addition of chopped vegetables, and everything was left to simmer and reduce. The fires were stoked, and continually fed from a huge pile of wood that had been collected by the villagers. There was going to be pork stew and goat stew in industrial quantity. The whole process looked positively medieval, and indeed, it probably was.

We left them to it. The pungent aromas were wafting up to us as we peered down at the bubbling cauldrons, making our tummies rumble, but it would be a long while yet before the dishes would be served.

We left, but were pleased to hear that Pedro's father later won a first place rosette with his best horse, as Pedro proudly told us on the following Monday morning.

20

La Gomera:
The Island that Time Forgot

La Gomera is the next nearest island to Tenerife. We had heard and read so much about it and had always wanted to visit. We thought that it was now the right time to go, but decided that the trip was not one that we could take Freddie on, as it would involve a sea crossing, much travelling round hairpin roads, and a posh hotel to boot. The poodles kindly extended an invitation to him for a couple of nights, and we knew for sure that he would prefer to be there with them rather than suffering the indignities to his person by accompanying us.

La Gomera has a tiny boutique type of airport; but going by boat is a lot cheaper, even when you include taking your car. The departure port for the ferry is Los Cristianos in the south of the island.

The weather forecast was good for the coming week, and the best hotel on La Gomera had a special offer in the local paper. We decided that the time had come for the Mercedes to have a good outing, and we would be able to tootle about in the sunshine with the hood down.

We knew people who had been to La Gomera, and they had all said, without exception, that it was a wonderful experience. So we decided on a couple of nights away. In hindsight we really should have booked for three, or even more.

As usual, the car was packed to overflowing with unnecessary paraphernalia. The weather was bright and sunny as we pulled out of Puerto, up the long hill towards Santa Cruz, on our way around the island to fetch up in Los Cristianos and the ferry port.

On our right as we drove along, was the great majestic curve of our valley. Above the terraces of small farms or vineyards was the forest leading up to the caldera of El Teide. We drove past the small town of La Victoria where, as the name implied, the Guanche forces had repelled the advance of the Spanish invaders, and then on to La Matanza de Acentejo, *matanza* meaning slaughter, where the situation had been finally and irretrievably reversed.

Everywhere we looked as we drove, there was that patchwork of green hills covered either with vines, or higher up, forestation. Some of the forested land must be primeval, but quite a lot has now been planted with differing types of conifers. The forested areas are strictly controlled, as you might imagine in such a hot and dry climate. Forest fires inevitably spread fast, not least because it is so difficult to get water to the places where it is needed. We have often seen huge containers of water being dumped from helicopters to try to bring fires back under of control. All the forested areas have wide firebreaks, and rangers regularly patrol on the lookout for any hazardous activity. Everywhere there are signs asking you to stub out your cigarette responsibly.

Further up in the hills are large areas cleared for barbeques. Part of family life in Tenerife is the group barbeque, and the island government has provided a series of quite upmarket public barbeque areas, complete with cooking areas and benches, all in well cleared and protected forest glades near to the road network. There is one quite close to us, and on some weekends there will be over a hundred people there, all around their individual barbeques and with their tables and chairs decorated with balloons if the day includes a birthday. It is a lovely family sight, popular because the further up into the hills you go, the cooler it becomes. You have to take your own wood with you, and bags of this are sold at most petrol stations; you aren't allowed to take any from the forest without permission. I seem to remember in my younger days back in England, one would haul any fallen dead wood found in a public forest, back home for the family fire. Not so over here. To be found doing so will result in a large fine for the unlucky perpetrator.

As we motored further along, higher up on the valley side we could see the mouths of caves where the Guanches once lived. Some of those caves were inhabited until less than a hundred years ago.

Driving further along the *autopista* from Puerto, everywhere was the usual riot of colour with flowering oleanders and huge wild poinsettias, some of them up to nine feet tall, lining the roadside. And the temperature was climbing. But as we turned inland at the top of the hill, towards Los Rodeos, the northern airport, the colours started to fall away and the beginning of the urbanisation of Santa Cruz took over. Everything quickly changed to an urban sprawl with long rows of apartment blocks, offices and commercial buildings lining the edge of the *autopista*. Everywhere there were banners and hoardings advertising shopping malls, petrol stations, stores and the latest offers from IKEA and El Corte Inglès.

Leaving the capital behind us, we suddenly seemed to be in a different world again. The road now hugged the coast and we passed turn-offs towards small industrial towns with their apartment blocks tumbling seawards down the cliff side. Nothing much was growing. The odd dusty palm tree tried to make the most of it, but nearly everywhere was barren. It was a relief to arrive in Los Cristianos on the southern coast, from where the inter-island ferry would leave. The town is a holidaymaker's paradise – if you like too much sunshine and too many English bars.

The Fred Olsen ferry is a huge beast of a thing, seemingly immense overkill to get to such a small island. Its name emblazoned on the bow read *Benchijigua Express* which is as difficult to spell as it is to pronounce. We found out later that it is named after a small village on La Gomera, but why, I have yet to discover. Known officially as a Fast Ferry, it is a wave piercing catamaran; it travels at over 40 knots, and can carry 1,200 passengers and over 300 cars and lorries. It looked longer than a football pitch – but there might have been all of 200 souls on board for our trip.

Gliding along, it took just 35 minutes or so of ultra-smoothness from setting off from Los Cristianos to docking in San Sebastian, the capital of La Gomera. Nervous sailor Sally felt nary a tremble all the way.

We were disembarked within a couple of minutes. Off we went, the satnav steering us out of town and onto the road leading to Playa de Santiago, the village where our hotel was situated. It was half an hour away, and the journey certainly packed in the maximum quota of corners along the way. But the sun was shining, the views were stupendous, and the brakes worked just fine as we zigzagged down the steep road to the hotel.

When I had telephoned the Hotel Jardin Tecina, I had cheekily asked the reservations department for a room upgrade, trading on my old life as a hotel owner, and my wish had been graciously granted without question. Pulling up at the main entrance, we were greeted by smartly uniformed flunkies, and the baggage was whisked away to our room.

Sally cannot travel light, so the Mercedes was not the best for even a couple of days away. Packing had to become seriously inventive. But perhaps that's part of the fun? How on earth had we managed for more than three weeks when we drove down through Spain?

We were shown to a front-line room facing directly out over the ocean, complete with a large terrace with a table and comfortable chairs. We decided to unwind and go with the flow, helped by perfect weather and the stupendous cliff top position. In front of our terrace was nothing but blue sea, stretching as far as the eye could see. Beyond that, the next stop would have been South

America. Matching the sea was a big, big sky, its lighter blue blurring with the ocean on the horizon. We sat together on our terrace with a cold glass of wine and marvelled at it all.

After about an hour, with the wine finished, I wanted to have a look round and get my bearings.

"Come on, let's go and explore the place."

"Do we have to?"

"No. You can stay here and just look at the view and the ocean."

"OK. I'll come along."

Just then, idly gazing down to the sea, I saw a pod of dolphins break the surface and dance through the swell. We watched them for about ten minutes before, just as quickly, they dived back out of sight.

"Come on, then, time to go."

We looked around the gardens, the bars, the pool and the different restaurants. We chose the outside one to dine in and asked if we could make a reservation. That done, we went back to shower and change, as it seemed to be a smart sort of place.

Later, sitting out in the moonlight over our *digestif*, we both agreed that we could not have chosen a better hotel, nor a better location. There was just one fly in our particular ointment, and that was that our canine friend was not part of it with us. We looked at each other and I tossed a coin to see which of us would telephone back to poodle-land to check how he was. The call went straight to message, so we guessed that he and the poodles would be out on their last walk of the evening. Enjoy your holiday, Freddie!

The next day dawned with a clear blue sky, so after an excellent breakfast taken al fresco, we set off to explore. The electric roof purred down in the hotel car park, and other guests getting into their hire cars looked on with envy. On went our sunglasses and off we drove.

The island still exists in some sort of time warp, a place that the rest of the world has forgotten. We saw abandoned terracing and entire abandoned villages. The views were just stunning, but the corners, oh, those corners. Never have so many corners been crammed into such a small space.

We stopped for coffee in a tiny village that had but the one café, and watched the world go by – or more truthfully, we watched a completely empty road. Our table was out on the pavement, shaded by a red Coca Cola parasol, and in the half an hour or so that we rested there, nothing at all passed us by.

I worried about those abandoned terraces. There were still a lot of them back home in Tenerife, but we had been encouraged to see many of them being re-cultivated by the planting of bananas. It seemed that European money was flowing in the right direction once again. But over here, in La Gomera, these terraces had almost reverted completely back to the wild. It must have taken whole generations to build some of them, and it was so sad to see them so.

Those lost villages were even worse. Where had all the people gone, when, and why? It seemed that many of them had emigrated to Venezuela to seek their fortune because there was no future for them on La Gomera. Whole families or villages had emigrated, leaving behind groups of houses to rot and decay. They looked like left-overs from an old film set.

We were so sad that its young had deserted La Gomera in droves and gone to find work on Tenerife, or the mainland, or in South America. The population of the island was now less than half than it had been only fifty years ago, hence all those deserted villages and overgrown terraces with their crumbling walls. But who nowadays would want to grow up to be a shepherd or goatherd in that harsh and forbidding environment, seeing paltry financial reward at the end of the day to provide for a growing family?

And so we continued to climb ever higher, the car twisting upwards round a hundred hairpin bends towards the centre of the island, which was renowned as having a prehistoric laurel forest encrusted with lichens.

What on earth would we find when we got there?

Suddenly, we were motoring through a light mist. The sun had gone in an instant.

"It's beginning to rain!" cried Sally.

The climate was undergoing a total change as we entered the enchanted forest up in the volcanic corona of the island.

The hood on the car was electrically powered and could be put up at low speed whilst still on the move. We had never tried it, but clearly now was the moment to do so. That tour bus that came round the corner just then must have been so startled to see our ghostly apparition looming out of the mist, hood half erected, on that narrow road.

It was wipers on all the time now. We had passed from clear blue skies to wet mist and now thick cloud in almost the blink of an eye. Those laurel trees had the strangest of shapes, all twisted and gnarled, and the silver grey lichen coating their boles was all a bit odd too.

By the sides of the road, aided by all that moisture, grew dandelions, but not as we knew them. They were at least four feet high! We passed plants and flowers that we had never seen before at every turn. Sally commented that, should a dinosaur have suddenly appeared around the next corner, she would not have been in the least surprised. It was just that sort of place.

And just as quickly we broke back out of it all on the other side of the mountain, back into glorious sunshine and, it seemed, yet another world.

We motored downwards along the Valle Gran Rey, twisting and turning round those hairpin bends, criss-crossing huge, deeply scarred *barrancos,* much deeper and broader than the ones in Tenerife. We could quite understand how it would have taken a shepherd over a day's march to get from one side to the other, and thus we came to learn the meaning of *Silbo*, the whistling language of La Gomera, still practised to this day by those shepherds who remain and need to communicate with their brethren on the other side of those enormous *barrancos*. The different whistling intonations have developed over thousands of years into a complete communication system, still taught to this day. A shepherd's whistle, bouncing and echoing around those great canyons, can be heard literally for kilometres.

Down and down we motored, and so we came at last to the sea on another side of the island. We parked and went for a stroll through the village before settling down at a table at a beachside cafe for our lunch. It was basic and home-made, the fish as fresh as could be, the potatoes as wrinkly as they should be.

The village of Gran Rey had a large and impersonal hotel of eponymous name, but otherwise seemed to be a haven for backpackers and surfboarders, and we were glad to leave it behind and wend our way to somewhere quieter. But not before we popped into the local shop and bought two jars of sticky Gomeran honey, which we had been told was excellent. The stuff we got was thick and dark, badged as being gathered from bees that had feasted up among those prehistoric laurels.

I had some for breakfast this morning, prior to taking up my quill, and it was very good, but it sure did pack a punch.

To get back home to our hotel, we had to go back through the enchanted forest and the accompanying rain, before the sunshine met us again on the winding road back downwards. We spent an hour or two in the evening sunshine, sitting on our terrace looking out over the ocean clutching glasses of cold local wine, setting the scene for a memorable dinner on the restaurant terrace.

We should have stayed on for at least another day. All too soon it was time for the elderly gentleman driving his electric buggy cart to call in to collect our cases and deliver them back up to our car. A nice service, that.

In our two days, we had only managed to cover a small part of the island. There was so much more to see, and we must go back to see it.

Back in San Sebastian, the capital town, there was a parador so, as is our habit, we wound our way back there in good time to have a coffee before the ferry embarkation process got under way. Reaching the town, we looked at our little map, and lo, the parador was clearly marked. A simple matter, therefore, for us to find it?

At the end of the street there was a right turn only, when we needed to turn left. So, let's go right, right again and try all over again. After a couple of failed attempts, we clicked on the trusty satnav to sort it out. It was no better. These pesky Gomerans must have altered the traffic system since our software was issued. Paradors throughout Spain all have excellent local signage, using the international brown tourist signs to point the way to their door. The moment that you enter a city, you will see the first sign, even if there are still a few kilometres still to go. Here on La Gomera, we were on the island that time forgot, and so, it would appear, had *Señor* Parador.

If in doubt in Spain, we would generally stop at the local *farmacia* (chemist) and ask for directions. There is no shortage of *farmacias* in Spain; they breed on every street. Unfortunately, the chemist that we chose was in the same one-way road (they all seemed to be one-way in San Sebastian) so although we could actually see from her directions where we needed to go, we could not quite get to the correct turning. Tantalizingly, the parador, whilst visible at the top of the hill, remained out of reach.

Stuff like this always brings out the locals. Soon there was a gathering of wizened old men (the ladies stay indoors and cook or are sent to the river bank with the washing), all smoking like chimneys, pointing this way and that, all gesticulating to us with unintelligible dialect words of encouragement. Some of them reached out to caress the curvaceous flanks of our car, admiring the bright red colour, not yet faded by the southern sun.

To get back to the crucial junction, we actually had to go all round the outskirts of town and re-approach it from the northern end. On the final crossroads, there was the gathering of the old folk, still excitedly waving at us and pointing. Up the hill we eventually wound, until, on the plateau we found ourselves at the portals of the elusive parador.

But what a disappointment it was. The door to the lovely old building was wide open, as though to welcome us, but nobody seemed to be at home. We wandered about where we would, past the reception desk, into the gloomy *cafetería*, past the restaurant, and even visited the loos. We saw nobody at all. It was like the Marie Celeste. We popped out the far side of the building into the gardens and eventually peered out over the end of the terrace to the port far below. Nobody came to see us; the place was clearly open, but all of the staff must have gone into hiding. On the way back to the car we discovered a somnolent gardener preparing to shin up a palm tree to prune it, but not a solitary soul other than him. So we retraced our steps down the hill to the port and were the first in a very small queue for the boat.

21

San Marcos

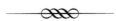

Our idea was to go on a day trip to San Marcos, a fishing village away down the coast with lovely swimming.

We had been there a few times before, but this would be the first time in the Mercedes, and therefore a first also for Freddie, who just loves the space behind the seats where he can be hooked up to a special doggie harness and stick his nose out, catching cool air, and probably a few flies as well.

The day dawned without a cloud in the sky; a perfect Canary day. Everything was so clear that one could see for miles along the coast. On such a day one should make the most of it, so the roof would be down as we trundled along the coast road, at peace with the world.

But first, our usual breakfast was taken on the terrace at the back of the apartment. Although the sun had yet to gain much strength, we sat under the shade of the big striped awning and ate our fruit and cereals, followed by toast and local honey from bees that had feasted on the shrubs clinging to the slopes of the mountain behind us. Sally drank her black coffee and I gulped down a couple of mugs of tea.

Then it was time to take Freddie up the lane for his morning constitutional. As it was warming up nicely, the lizards would be out already, basking in the sun, their long tongues flicking in and out as they sought to catch an unwary passing insect. Freddie enjoyed spending some time on his lizard hunt. We, as well as the lizards, always hoped that he would be unsuccessful in his quest, because the smell that comes out from his rear end after a tasty lizard snack is too terrible to contemplate. We move in unison further upwind.

There was not much that we needed to pack, other than our swimming things and towels and a couple of hats. Freddie would have his own towel and a bowl for his water.

San Marcos is a little cove with a small village and fishing harbour, the front of which is mostly composed of beach cafes and restaurants. We knew a number of them of old. The drive would be spent in wondering which one we should patronise today.

Out of our apartment we went, and into the lift down to the garage. The car was only washed yesterday, so it sat there gleaming, ready for the off. We packed in our bits and pieces, and were ready.

I turned the key. Nothing happened. Silence.

No growl of the engine purring into life, no purr of the electric hood as it slid down neatly into its concealed housing. I tried the key again. There was not even the faintest of electrical activity going on under that bonnet. I played with the fuses, but everything seemed to be in order. Nothing had blown as far as I could see. There was nothing more that I could do. We could not even alarm the car as we left it behind and came back upstairs.

Freddie looked up at me, more than confused. "What on earth is all that about, then? You put me in the car and then you take me out again! But we haven't been anywhere!"

It was taxing me, let alone my poor foundling. It was time to call in the experts.

A local mechanic was telephoned and arrived later in the morning. It was yet another testament to the excellent level of service that is the island norm.

He commenced by jump starting the car so that we had some action and he could apply his electronic diagnostic apparatus to the different areas that might be causing the problem. Yes, he confirmed, all the fuses were fit and well. The battery was as flat as a pancake, but we could have told him that. The engine continued to turn over, hopefully charging some life back into the battery. The alternator was tested, and that appeared to be converting the current properly, so I was told to take it for a drive and see if it would restart again once I had come back here to base.

Off I drove, taking the motorway up towards the town of Tacaronte, some twenty minutes away. There I turned round and came back. In the garage, I switched off, and then started her up again. All was well.

Next morning, I was faced with the identical problem. The battery was flat once again. Back came the mechanic and removed the battery. It would have to go away to have a full 24 hour charge, and he would bring it back the next day. When he returned, he said that he had been checking on the Mercedes website help desk overnight, and was now concentrating his thoughts on the regulator.

After some testing, which went right over our heads, he announced: "You have a lazy regulator."

· "I know what a regulator does, but how can it be lazy? Surely it either works or it doesn't?"

"See, it is not doing its job properly." He was demonstrating on some infernally complicated machine which he announced had cost him 1,600 euros. Graphs with wiggly lines were displayed on the small screen.

"Fine", I asked. "But can you fix it?"

"Let's get it off and have a look."

Fortunately, the regulator was bolted on to the outside of the alternator, so it was only a ten minute job to dismantle it. The inside was worn down, as I could see, and I was told that I needed a new one.

"Do they sell them on the island? After all, the car is nearly twenty-two years old!"

"No problem – if I order one now, Bosch will have one to me tomorrow. I'll call you when I have it and come and fit it for you."

True to his word, that is exactly what he did. There was no further trouble.

But our visit to San Marcos was to be a non-event that week.

It was another perfect Canary day, ideal for San Marcos.

Since the last aborted escapade, it had been a couple of weeks, and the car had never missed a beat since, so we were confident that it was an isolated incident, put down to that lazy regulator, and was all best forgotten. Any car nearly 22 years old, even if in perfect condition, is entitled to the odd tantrum.

We packed the car with our swimming things, hats and a water bottle and bowl, and emerged out of the gloom of the garage into the blindingly bright sunlight. The electric hood purred down, we donned our sunglasses, and Freddie blinked at the glare of the sun. We were off.

It was about a forty minute run along the coast road, the twisting ribbon of tarmac hugging the edges of the cliffs, swooping down to cross the *barrancos,* and twisting and turning over the many terraced hillsides in between. We marvelled at the broadness of the cerulean sky that stretched from one horizon to the other, and realised that our island was just a tiny speck of green land in an otherwise vast ocean of blue.

On the way along the coast lay our favourite Texaco petrol station.

Most petrol stations over here have a café attached to them. Back in England, you might well seek to avoid such cafés. Not so over here. They are deservedly famed, and people go out of their way to stop for a coffee and a cake. The added advantage of this Texaco station is that the café is also a *mirador*, which means that it is in a lookout position with a better than average scenic view.

It's not often that one would admit to going out of one's way to have lunch at a petrol station, but we have been there many times. I am particularly partial to their octopus which they serve with peppers and onions. They have a big range of *tapas* on the bar, and also an even bigger selection of cakes to satisfy the Spanish sweet tooth. Their coconut cake is to die for... But I digress too easily.

On this occasion, we could not stop there since Freddie was with us, and so we drew to a halt a little further along the road at a *cafetería* with a terrace. A Danish pastry was shared between us. A biscuit miraculously appeared from my pocket for Freddie. We humans were not to spoil the lunch that would be in store for us at San Marcos.

Back outside into the sunshine, we saw that a small group of young locals had gathered around the car, much as usual. I could only assume it was because it was bright red and with perfect coachwork that they found it so interesting. Cars, cakes and football are three of the main four Spanish male preoccupations. Spanish boys never laid any sticky fingers on the car. Some flattering comments were received and gratitude was exchanged, and off we went again.

It was only another twenty-minute journey further along the coast, passing through banana plantations lining the sides of the road, interspersed with terraces of lemon and orange trees, and we soon spotted the sign pointing off the main road. The village of San Marcos was down a winding lane and set on a black sand beach, a perfect crescent. In summer you could hardly find a space to put your towel down, it would be so busy. So we mostly avoided it until the summer rush had subsided.

The car was safely parked, Freddie liberally watered a kerbside oleander, and we made our way along the little parade of fish restaurants, looking to see which one would take our fancy that day. The alternative was to go to the restaurant run by an Italian family, which lay at the other side of the beach. Last time we went there was with Marcus and the family, and I remembered Marcus ordering a *sama*, a big chubby fish that fills a large plate all by itself. It usually comes on the bone and is enough for two people. Marcus could demolish one in the blink of an eye.

At the end of the parade, the grandfather of the family had taken the best seat on the terrace of the little restaurant, and was watching us approach. He called out to welcome us, although I am sure that he had no idea who we were. I think it was a trick to encourage his prospective customers to feel welcome. As usual, he achieved his aim, and, instead of going back to one of the other places, we piled in. And how nice it was that Freddie received a grin and a pat, swiftly followed by a tin bowl of water, without anyone having to ask.

Bread was laid before us almost before we had got comfortable in our seats. Did we need to see a menu, or would he do the usual trick of bringing a platter of the catch of the day to us, and telling us to point to what we would like?

No, today it seemed that it was either sardines or sardines, unless we would like a meat alternative. The catch of sardines had just been unloaded from his own boat, so could not be fresher. We had not come all this way to eat the ubiquitous pork chop, so sardines were ordered. Would we like them whole or filleted, grilled or pan fried, accompanied by a *salsa* of the house, or just wedges of lemon? And, to cap it all, could we decide on the salad or the Canary potatoes, cooked in their skins in sea water and heavy with their salty residue, perfect Canarian *papas arrugadas*?

We chose to start with a mixed salad to share, a bottle of water and a small jug of house wine. When these had been brought, we ordered the sardines, whole and pan fried, just with lemon and parsley. Sally opted for the wrinkly potatoes and, since I never had chips at home, I went the tourist route and ordered them. Their wrinkly potatoes were the Canary speciality, like small new potatoes, but with very dark brown skins. Here they would have been cooked in seawater taken from the bay directly behind us. When almost cooked, the water would be drained away and they'd be left to steam in the pan with the lid off. This gave them the faintly wrinkly texture on the outside, and left them with a slightly salty crust. Scrumptious!

Freddie is very good at eating out. After the first couple of goes, he learned naturally that he had to find a place in the shade and suffer in silence until a morsel was surreptitiously passed down to him. The aroma of those sardines was more than he could bear, though, and half way through the meal he was on his hind legs, one front paw raised in silent query for a sample. He got one, and it barely touched the sides.

It is a plain meal at this place, and not a lot of money eventually changed hands in return for the sampling of its simple delights, and the pleasure of whiling away an hour or two on their terrace. We are people watchers, and spend a lot of time either in amiable conversation or pointing out to each other the strange or the odd that may be passing our way. We are by now so attuned to each other after all these years that we often don't need to describe our feelings at that moment. A nod or smile is quite sufficient to do the trick.

We had to take a swim before we went back. Not that we felt much like it now, after a lovely lunch. But we must take the exercise, it is part of the ritual, so we waded out into the bay and launched ourselves into the deeper water. Freddie mucked around near the water's edge and preferred to play with a couple of local Spanish children, until all three of them plunged into the water, paddling about, grinning hugely. New friends!

We emerged brighter and hopefully a little fitter, but with a very wet dog.

Back in the car, we all sat on our towels for the drive home. The Mercedes welcomed us with a perfect start on the button, and off we went. The evening sun was on our backs. Freddie would have much to tell his poodle friends about his canine exploits of the day. And so, we all came home, happily tired from our day out.

We knew that Freddie would later snore the night away, and probably, so would we. San Marcos had seen us right yet again.

Extract from my review of another beach restaurant in San Marcos:

"Today my wife has chosen the venue. We will be lunching in San Marcos, at a restaurant that had received the dubious privilege of our patronage a year ago.

My toe (see a previous issue) whilst firmly on the mend, still precludes me from driving, and so I am chauffeured by my wife along the TF5 from Puerto de la Cruz until it peters out and becomes the main northern coastal road. We are heading west, and soon come to Icod de los Vinos, where we take the bypass instead of heading into town. The sign for San Marcos is soon upon us, and we swing down the twisting road that leads us to the village. On the way, we pause, looking to the left, to see stunning volcanic rock formations where the strata have been bent into scarcely believable shapes.

The village is built around an almost horseshoe shaped bay. Not a match for Lulworth Cove, by a long shot, but you may get the idea. At the far end of the strand is a small commercial harbour, and leading down to it is a string of bars and restaurants. All is overlooked by some unprepossessing high rise blocks, the planners of which should be subjected, in my humble opinion, to the thumbscrews.

No matter. As a whole, the place is pleasing. The black sand beach is thronged with sunbathers, and a goodly number are bobbing about in the water.

Looking directly out over this beach is our chosen destination. We are aiming for La Cocina di Dona Rosa, a restaurant specialising in regional Italian cuisine, fresh fish, pizzas, and some international and Canarian dishes. It is a cheerful, unpretentious place, with good attentive service, and food better than your expectation might allow.

We are greeted by the owner who, although he probably does not remember us, nevertheless welcomes us as though he does. He stares brazenly at my polo shirt, which bears the logo of the German motor sport club of which I am a member. He quizzes me, and we quickly establish that we both spend quite a lot of time passing through Munich airport, he to his family home in the Tirol and we heading to Bavaria for said motor sport reasons. Next time, I tell him, we will come in my old classic car.

The menu, in a range of languages (one of them looked all Greek to me, and probably was) is presented. We have drawn a nice table, being a bit early (well, spot on 1 p.m.), right on the edge of the terrace, overlooking the sea. The sun is shining, and we are looking forward to our meal. We are asked about bread and wine, and choose a half litre of white house wine at 5 euros. It comes from Bodegas Insulares, and is excellent. No need at all to spend a jot or tittle more.

There are a number of blackboard offerings scattered around the place, indicating specials or dishes of the day. Not a small menu, but the kitchen, all stainless steel, looks adequate to cope.

The owner is at pains to tell us that everything that they sell is fresh and/or homemade. I see that there is an offering of lapas *(limpets), which I do like when not overcooked to rubber, but my wife is less keen. We settle for a joint dish of* camarones, *those little red shrimps that are such a delicacy along this northern coast. Here they come with wedges of lemon and a dusting of rock salt. Nothing more is needed. Heads off, and eat all the rest, even though they are in berry. I have seen them at 29 euros a kilo in Al Campo, but here a decent starter portion for two comes to 6.50 euros. Salted Italian bread sticks and lemon finger wipe sachets come as standard.*

The main course for my wife is a large plate of tuna salad, minus the peppers. I hit the jackpot with a veal fillet steak topped with a sauce that includes a selection of wild looking mushrooms. The steak is oh so tender and the sauce, zinging of mushroom, a perfect accompaniment. A large bowl of very hot french fries, already lightly salted, is put down between us.

A group of young Spanish boys, aged between 10 and 13, I guess, arrive straight off the beach, all wet and sandy; they park themselves nearby after having carefully lifted the padded cushions from their seats, and devour enormous pizzas with bottles of water. Their behaviour is impeccable.

A Spanish family is here on a fishing expedition, their table laden with

199

fried calamares *and a heaped platter of mixed grilled fish. It all looks mouth-watering.*

With no room left for any dessert, the afternoon is so pleasant that we decide to tarry awhile over a shared extra glass of wine. And so eventually the bill must be called for. It comes to 40.53 euros including tax for everything mentioned above and also a large bottle of water and two portions of bread.

With it come two tasty little fig and pastry slices, made on the premises, as a sort of amuse bouche in reverse. Then the waitress comes back and, lo and behold, two lemon sorbets as palate cleansers appear as if by magic.

Having paid, I then decide to do what I have never done before, and that is to announce my association with Island Connections. *It results in the waitress being instructed to bring over two small chilled shot glasses of homemade limoncello. And so a delicious end to a perfect afternoon."*

22

Food & Wines

Local people are always encouraged to get involved in the grape harvest as a semi-free work force. Tractors and trailers are laid on to get people out to the vineyards, and the day commences with a vast communal breakfast at about 7 a.m., before the sun gets too strong. After a morning of often backbreaking work, a lunch is offered to us toilers by way of recompense. Back at the *bodega*, long trestle tables will have been laid out under a veranda of vine leaves to keep away the direct sunlight, and out will come bowls of olives, local flat breads, pates, perhaps a rabbit stew, cheeses and so much more. Needless to say, there is always an immodest sampling of the local wine, which will ease the passing of the afternoon labour.

So much of the harvesting is still perforce done manually, because of the steepness of the terrain and the narrowness of the terracing. We can walk where tractors fear to tread.

The free straw hat to take away with you, the food and the camaraderie make for a memorable outing. And, of course, in the coming months, we are able to drink the wines made from grapes that we helped to pick.

So a resounding "Cheers!" to the wines of Tenerife.

We live in one of the five specific regions of the island where there is strict control over production of wine. In the south there are Abona and Valle de Guimar. In the north we have Valle de La Orotava, Tacoronte Acentejo, and Ycoden Daute Isora. Naturally, the ones in the north have borne the brunt of our interest.

We had accumulated a certain level of knowledge of wine generally over the years, but not a lot about Tenerife wines until we came to live here. If I was to remember my schooldays correctly, one W. Shakespeare, Esquire, referred more than once in his plays to the availability and quality of Canary wines. It would seem that wines from Tenerife, and probably from the other islands too, had long been imported into Europe, and particularly to the UK. Importation ceased a hundred or so years ago as quality and quantity fell off for various reasons.

Nowadays, quality and production levels have increased dramatically again. Tenerife wines regularly win gold and silver medals at world wine trade fairs. We have enjoyed first class quality, and very keen prices especially when compared to wine prices back in the UK. It is unusual for us to need to pay more than a couple of euros for a bottle of decent everyday drinking wine.

The nearest wine area to us is La Orotava. This is the oldest vine growing area in Tenerife, with the first vines having been planted here after the Spanish conquest at the end of the 15th century. There are just over 1,000 hectares of vines under cultivation, shared among about fifty *bodegas*. Vines are grown on *cordones*, where each growing vine plant is propped up on stakes and at a height of a couple of feet or so the shoots are then trained to run horizontally along the *cordones,* a system of wires or strings. The famous Canarian Malmsey wine was first produced in this area.

The other area that we know quite well is Tacaronte Acentejo, only a little further away, where there are about 2,500 hectares under cultivation, making it the largest DO (*Denominación de Origen*) area in Tenerife. Mostly reds are produced here, strong and powerful.

Further away down the coast is the area of Ycoden Daute Isora which was in fact a combination of three smaller areas. Because of the prevalence of the Trade Winds, the harvest here often starts early, sometimes as early as June. The wines are mostly young and white.

Last year, a photographer friend on a local newspaper invited us to a food and wine event in a little town down the coast. Sally was not well that day so opted out. So there was Peter of poodles fame, another Peter who lived in the centre of town, and myself. I drew the short straw and was therefore to drive.

It was a lovely day, and down the coast we trundled to the small town of Los Silos, where there is that superb fish restaurant run by a football-mad family. Nearby, on the rocky foreshore of La Caleta, is an area which is known for superb sea salt. The small natural basins in the rocky outcrops above the high water mark produce a fine sea salt which is then further refined locally. These basins, although on the foreshore, have been jealously guarded and handed down within the same families for generations. The local tourist office at Los Silos can arrange guided walks and visits to the salt "refinery" for those expressing an interest in what may be the oldest semi-commercial operation still on the island.

It turned out that the wine tasting was to be held in the Town Hall, facing across the little main square. This was a lovely old building, with a huge central courtyard surrounded by balconies. Inside we met our photographer friend, who introduced us to all the dignitaries present, as well as to some of the suppliers. It turned out that the event was a wholesale purchasing opportunity for hoteliers and restaurateurs!

We chatted to people and were plied with all sorts of pates and cured meats, washed down with much wine. Before too long, we were all well and truly pickled, had all forked out for some cases of expensive wine imported from the Peninsula, enough to need to have had it delivered the following week, and had to retire to the café in the square for the restorative and sobering round of coffees and tea, before the run home.

I drove back extremely carefully.

One day, we were going out for three or four hours to try out a new restaurant that we had been told was worthy of a visit, and decided to drop Freddie off to play with his friends, the big black poodles. We arrived at Peter's front gate, and there they were, alerted to our imminent arrival by the bark of greeting from Freddie. Standing behind them was another big black poodle, almost identical.

Had we drank too much last night?

No. Her name was Dina, and she was one of the daughters of Millie, the elder of Peter's two poodles. A lovely dog, long and slinky, and moving so gracefully, and also with the kindest of natures. We all fell for her immediately, and that included Freddie. He and Dina quickly became great friends, and whenever they see each other nowadays there is much barking, leaping about and general nuzzling between them. It's a sight to behold.

Dina was being dropped off by her owner, who has a large vineyard up here in the north. Each day he and Dina would walk miles together through his vineyards, checking on this and that, whatever one does if one is the owner of a vineyard. He was not too proud to go down on his knees to cuddle his dog as he said goodbye to her. They clearly adored each other.

And so, leaving Freddie with friends old and new, we continued to the restaurant that we were going to try out. Would it be worthy of a good review, or would I have to kiss yet more frogs before finding a princess?

About half an hour from where we lived, higher up in the hills, was the small village of Pinolere: for the most part, unremarkable, with little to differentiate it from many other hill villages. It had the usual winding main street, a tumble of houses, mostly with flat roofs, not for sunbathing but for the drying and airing of the washing. Some of the houses were painted in rather garish colours, as though their owners had bought a cheap job lot of bright blue or mauve paint. There were two or three shops. As we passed along the village street, a bevy of elderly ladies, clad all in black, were standing in the shade chatting to each other. A group of their menfolk were sitting outside a café, playing cards and drinking rough red wine. Through the open car windows we sniffed, and the rich aroma of cigar smoke tickled our nostrils.

Strange, is it not, this segregation? All the men at one bar, all the ladies elsewhere.

But what made this village different was its restaurants. As we approached the centre, we saw the sign for a French restaurant, the name of which is El Refugio de Maria. A strange name for a French restaurant, but very French it is. The proprietor is French, the setting could have been in Normandy, and the white wine that we drank with our scallops came from the vineyard of his brother in Provence.

We were not heading there this time, nor to another smart *restaurante* nearby, and so passed by, reaching the other end of the village where there was a more regional *bodega* with a dining terrace. We sat under a shade tree and enjoyed a marvellous time whilst looking out over their vineyard and down the valley back towards the sea. Behind us was a line of large new stainless steel tanks for their harvest. We had a simple meal of suckling pig, potatoes and salad, all washed down with their own red wine, and were charged a fraction of what we would have had to pay back down in town.

Finding your way round the hinterland of this island surely does pay handsome dividends.

When we got back to collect Freddie, he told us how he had entertained his harem of poodles with tales of derring-do and other doggie mysteries. And by the time that we got him back to his own home, he was quite exhausted, and fell fast asleep for the rest of the evening. His snoring shook the rafters.

Extract from my review of the guachinche/bodega in the hill village of Pinolere:

"Pig out in Pinolere!
If you are a lover of pork in its many differing Tenerife guises, do read on.

We are climbing up the steep hillside above La Orotava, in the direction of Aguamansa. Before we reach there, we are searching for a signpost to the village of Pinolere, the site of the Black Pig Fiesta. We are well into vineyard country. On a sharp right hand bend, we spot the sign, lopsidedly pointing off to the left, the road twisting along between the vines. Over the barranco *we go, through the village, dozing peacefully in the heat of the sun, and then before us is the Bodega Hermanos Polo, with tables on the terrace outside. Although there is a small thatched hut for indoor dining (and it does look rather quaint), this is essentially an outdoor venue.*

Perched on the side of the mountain, with stunning views over the vines down the valley back towards the sea, the whole place reminds me most of those quintessential rustic eateries to be found in the hills behind Cannes and Nice. Nothing like anything in the hotspots such as St Paul de Vence, you understand, more the rustic restaurants a little off the beaten track. That does take me back more years than I care to remember, and I also remember standing here last year, with my son and his family at my side, looking out over this beautiful valley. I feel immediately a warm and comfortable glow as the memories come flooding back.

There are some 20 trestle-type tables, covered with nicely sun-faded checked plastic tablecloths, and surrounded by the usual uncomfortable wooden benches. Would that I had brought my cushion! The courtyard terrace is dotted with shade trees, and when we arrive, a little after 1 p.m., some tables (and therefore trees) are already taken. I am glad that I booked ahead for a tree.

All in all, it is a rural heaven, everything that you might conjure up in your mind's eye. The open air kitchen area is hidden engagingly behind a dilapidated fence, the only clue to its existence being a galvanised chimney smoking upwards and wafting the tantalising scent of gently roasting pork into our nostrils.

The waitresses are all wearing smartly logo-ed polo shirts in white with red embroidery. They sport the title Guachinche. Almost as soon as we are seated, a large basket full of bread is plonked down onto the table, with a smile.

We ask about wine. With a nod by our waitress to the interior of the small chai (where wine is fermented or stored), we walk to the door and identify a row of large stainless steel vats and flagons of wine on the floor surrounding them. So, the wine really will be local, and we guess that the vineyard but a hands-breadth from the terrace may well be its origin. A litre of red is ordered, and, true to form, it arrives in two old used bottles, probably of medicinal origin. No matter, it is really well chilled, as is the way in Tenerife.

We smack our lips appreciatively, munch on the bread, and sip some water to help it all on its way. The young waitress is learning English, and is keen to try it out on us. With no menu, we learn that we can start with salad, cheese, ropa vieja *or* huevos estrellados *(loosely translatable as fried eggs with chips). After that, would we like the pork? Or the pork? In addition to the usual chops or steaks (*carnes a la brasa*), today being the weekend, there is a special offer of* cochinillo *(suckling pig). It is being offered sliced and marinated. I do not really approve, but, yes, please!*

First comes our salad. It is a generous plate, heaped with lettuce, onion, beefsteak tomato, grated fresh beetroot, olives and pickled carrot. Once again, the peppers have received an automatic deletion. Not only is it tasty, once dressed, but it has been presented nicely, sometimes a rarity.

Then, on to a plate of queso blanco with a centrepiece of olives, almost a staple dish in Tenerife.

The pork is now ready for us, so a large serving dish is borne aloft to our table, accompanied by a bowl of chips aplenty. Hot and crisp, just as they should be.

My wife takes a mouthful of the pork, and I swear she starts drooling with delight. There are mmm's and aah's around the table. Is this the most tender and flavoursome pork that we have eaten on this porcine island?

That little piglet did not go to its sty in the sky in vain.

We just sit under our shade tree and munch our way through it all, taking our time in the best Spanish tradition, admiring the stunning views down the valley, with the sheer mountain backdrop almost immediately behind us.

This is not a place where the food should be hurried, and it is popular with the locals. There is not a table free when we leave. No English or German voices are to be heard cutting through the force 10 gale of Spanish families talking through the serious business of the food before them, and yet we are less than half an hour from Puerto and the coast. Should I really be revealing this place to my reader?

As with the menu, there is no formal bill. There are six of us and we are asked for €25.20 for the salad, the cheese, suckling pig in abundance, chips, wine, two soft drinks, bread and bottled water. That has to be a result for the views alone, regardless of the singular economy of the bill."

A whisper had it that there was going to be a wine fair down in the town, with tents erected around the harbour walls. All the island's major wine producers would be there. How could we not go?

We walked down from home and in 15 minutes were overlooking the harbour and could see that eight open sided tents had been erected for the wine fair, billed as the *Gran Fiesta de los Vinos de Tenerife*.

We remembered the event from a couple of years ago, and so were looking forward to it. But it did look a lot smaller. Could it really be so? Popular events such as this tended to grow, did they not, rather than shrink? And it was so popular last time that you could hardly move. I think that more wine was spilt than drunk!

The first tent that we came to doubled up as the ticket office for payment of the entry fee. There were two levels of charge this time round. For 5 euros you got five tickets for five drinks, one marked for each tent, and a small *copita* glass, nicely engraved for memory of the occasion. For 2 euros, you just got a glass. It needed a bit of thinking to get your mind round just why you would opt for the latter.

Armed with our tickets, we did the rounds. At nearly 8 p.m., the place was already bustling, but not overly busy. There was a tent for each *Denominación de Origen* (DO) area of the island, and a couple of extra ones at the far end where nibbles were being prepared, such as Serrano ham. There didn't appear to be the full cooking experience as last time, when the queue for the (excellent) paella stretched into the adjoining parish.

No matter, glasses to the ready, we visited the first tent, where a number of wines were displayed. The requested *blanco seco* turned out to be a *blanco afrutado*. At the second tent, we opted for something which turned out to be rather forgettable. Two down and three to go. At the tent covering the DO area for Viñatigo, I spotted a bottle of their *Gual*. Something out of the ordinary, a little different, not cheap, but nevertheless a pleasure to taste for the first time.

We still had to make a visit to the Frontos vineyard, which is at the other end of the island. There were a number of Frontos labels on show, and I asked if there was a list, with explanations and prices. The young man was clearly taken aback by the query, and retreated for a consultation with his elders. He returned, saying that there was only a leaflet of the particular local area. He came back with it, and I ask him to point out which one was Frontos, and where it was exactly. He was nonplussed once more and retreated again for advice. We decided to save him from further embarrassment.

We had now come to the last tent on our circuit. It was the one for DO Tacaronte Acentejo. And there was a list! Our excellent though unusual choice was the Viña Norte Maceracion Carbonica, made by the old 18th-century single processing system whereby the whole grape clusters (as opposed to the more usual methods nowadays of crushing and de-stemming) are put into a tank, which is then CO_2-saturated to induce fermentation, producing a light and fruity wine with a soft palate that should be drunk young.

I had only found out the date of this wine fair a few days earlier and by word of mouth, not by publicity issued by the local tourism office. No wonder it was poorly attended, which is such a shame because Tenerife wines are generally outstandingly good, not well enough known, and are not done the justice that they deserve.

Pedro and I regularly swap addresses for places to go out to eat. I don't know exactly how it started, but I rather think it was Pedro trying to educate me away from eating down in the town when we first came over here. Whilst there are a number of excellent places to eat down there, and some at very reasonable prices, we have always tried to be a bit more adventurous and patronise the places that the locals eat in. And so we spend quite a bit of time up in the hills trying to find places off the beaten track that have been recommended to us.

Pedro would lean over our gate and tell me that he had eaten at so and so place at the weekend and that it was superb. Often he would not remember the exact name of the place, and so I would produce a paper napkin or something similar, with a flourish, and he would start to draw the directions. It would commence with a point somewhere that we were both supposedly familiar with, such as a roundabout or crossroads. Wiggly lines would then be scribbled, ending in a cross in a box to signify the destination.

When you are looking at it on the paper as he draws it, you feel reasonably confident that you will be able to track the place down. It is quite another matter when it is dark and you discover that Pedro has inconveniently forgotten a roundabout or two, or a couple of turnoffs. Ending up in an adjoining village and asking for a restaurant that does not exist there is not conducive to a pleasant evening out.

We have learned that there is a way around this conundrum. We are retired now, after all, so we look on it as a challenge, and sometimes do a daylight recce to plot the exact location. We have spent many a happy hour trundling along from village to village, cursing Pedro, but hopefully ending up at yet another gem of a place.

One such was in La Cruz Santa. Pedro told us that it was one of his favourites and that it specialised in fish, cod in particular, which featured on the menu on a Saturday evening. This was a while ago, before we had learned that most cod is of the salted variety, unless you are patronising a high end establishment.

Try as I might, I cannot get to grips with the Spanish love for salted fish. I have only eaten it in restaurants, where they should know what they are doing with it, but the texture of it just seems all wrong. It is sold everywhere, and has to be reconstituted by soaking overnight before cooking. It is all a hangover from the olden days when the fishing boats went over to Newfoundland and the men on board had to salt the catch before they could get it back to base. People swear by it, but I would rather swear at it.

We took Peter along with us and parked in the centre of the village. We had a glass of wine in the Bar Rallye and then walked along the road to the evening's venue, which we discovered lurking down a very steep side street, fronted by what looked for all the world like a domestic garage entrance. In we went, and the place opened up quite attractively, yellow ochre walls and dark wood tables.

We ordered bread and wine, and a starter that now eludes me, and for the main course, of course, the cod. Peter wisely had chosen something completely different. When the cod came, it was smothered in red *mojo* sauce, reeking of paprika, covering something less than a centimetre thick. We pushed it round our plates wishing that we could magic it away.

There was a gust of wind as the garage door opened, and in walked Pedro with a group of friends.

"Aha! I thought I might find you here this evening. And I see you are having the cod! Isn't it just wonderful? *Que aproveche!*"

He and his friends took a table nearby, and started a riotous evening, all in good humour. Sally and I stared at each other before we made the most of that slimy cod. I hope Pedro never noticed how much was taken away on our plates. Salt cod? Never again, but I would go back there for something different.

Another of Pedro's recommendations was to a country restaurant outside La Orotava, run by a family called Gomez. I could not make head nor tail of the napkin directions, so off we set and, for a change, spied a small hand written sign leading up a tiny tarmac lane. Hazarding that we had done enough of a recce, we left it at that.

Come the evening, we motored up the lane, vineyards on either side, until the land came to an end, with two places, seemingly both restaurants, one on each side of the road. There were no signs, but the one on the left seemed to be doing the better business, so we marched in there and thankfully saw the right name on the menu.

Plonking ourselves at a distance from the fiery brazier that was running at full throttle, we placed our orders. Looking around, we could see the USP of the place, which Pedro had been keen to point out as its identifying feature. All of the windows were of the double glazed variety, but none of them had actually been installed as such. Instead, they had just been left at a rickety angle against each embrasure, just fitting where they happened to touch, which was not a great deal. Sometimes the glazed unit was double the size of the window opening.

It was the strangest of places, but there were two upsides to it. Firstly the food was wonderful, and secondly the windows let in a lot of draught to keep us cool from that brazier.

And so, we voted it another resounding success from Pedro!

On the subject of recces, our friend Peter has also got into the habit of doing these for places that have been recommended to him. He was recently taken to a place that he reported as being quite superb, with excellent views down the valley to the sea.

"We must go there. The food was wonderful! How about one day next week?" He suggested.

Peter kindly picked us up and off we set. Up and up the valley, higher and higher, we went.

"Yes, I am sure that this is the right road. It must be very close by now. It will be on the left hand side."

Further and further we climbed, the car by now grinding along in second gear. We really were up in mountain goat country. Eventually we ran out of road by one of the reservoirs, and Peter admitted that he actually hadn't a clue either where we were, or where that darned restaurant might be. Even though he had done a recce that very morning!

Up in the hills above us, you will find yet another layer or type of restauration, a type much frequented by Pedro and now by ourselves. It is the rise and rise of the *guachinche*, much disliked by the official restaurants.

A *guachinche* is a temporary restaurant, often in a large commercial garage or outbuilding, which serves limited menus and offers only some soft drinks such as 7up! (the seven in the foregoing being pronounced over here with that "b" instead of the "v", and then with the final "p" being silent, so making the product completely unintelligible and incomprehensible when grunted to you by your waiter), and of course their own local wine. It is a system whereby they can legally sell their own village wine, and the family prepares and serves the food. You may eat, sitting on old barrels, at formica tables covered in plastic cloths. It's great fun.

In one of these places, in fact it was a garage of sorts, a large lorry was parked for the night, testimony to the other day jobs of the owners. One of the large wheels and half inflated rubber tyres were very conveniently placed to act as a backrest for me. I have been a lot less comfortable for a lot more money.

They are forbidden by law to serve other types of alcoholic drinks other than their own wine and must close when their wine supply is exhausted. This means that they may typically open in about June when the wine from the last harvest has been deemed to be ready to drink, and they will close about four or five months thereafter, when their wine has run out, depending on the size of their vintage.

They have ever co-existed uneasily with formal restaurants,

because they are seen to be taking business away from them. But customers will, as ever, vote with their feet, and *guachinches* are always busy, a testament to their prices and their quality and their so different atmosphere.

The food is nothing too fancy. The better ones will offer a starter of a mixed salad, or *garbanzas* (chick peas), *pimientos de padron,* or *fabada,* much loved by Sally and myself. This is a stew of butter beans with lumps of pork or other meat cooked in it. *Garbanzas* and *fabada* come in lots of different guises, some with peppers, some with chilli, others with sweet blood sausage. It is best to order one portion between two, otherwise you might not manage your main course.

I have taken a great liking to those little green peppers which are served everywhere and called *pimientos de padron*, and which are grown everywhere in huge clusters on bushes. Deep flash fried and covered with a sprinkling of olive oil and rock salt, they are unsurpassable. And if you get a particularly hot one in your pile, then it is supposed to bring you luck. I have had three so far, in two years' worth of munching through platefuls. Actually, two in one plate alone, which is unheard of. But on the other hand we know many people who have never received the bounty of a hot one in 20 years, so missing out on having the top of their head being blown off!

The main course usually will be either chicken or pork, or very occasionally beef. All will be cooked on a fiery brazier providing that perfect charcoal taste, and will be accompanied by a mountain of chips. The chicken is never less than half a bird and not a small one at that, and the pork will be either immense chops or a complete fillet. And all per person! We had never seen pork chops the size of a dinner plate before we came to Tenerife.

The father of the family oversees things generally and takes orders, mother will be at the chip pan, one daughter in charge of the salad, and yet another at the bar. The son or sons are the waiters, and a couple of cousins might be at the fire. It is all a family affair.

The local wine is usually red, although some do offer the other alternative, all served as cold as possible, with frost on the container. That container might be an old used wine bottle, but more often it will be an open carafe.

We cannot remember ever eating a bad meal in a *guachinche*, and so we are regular visitors, not least because it is virtually as cheap as cooking for oneself at home. There are about a hundred of them in our area alone, so presumably there are many hundreds on the island.

The views are unsurpassed, because they are up in wine country at an elevated level, and you can look back down away across the valley to the twinkling lights of the town. The only problem is the tortuous drive back down to the coast, but we always manage to blot that out from our minds until the very last moment.

Extract from my review of one of our favourite guachinches, above the hill town of Santa Ursula:

"We are going to one of our favourite stamping grounds, which I generally refer to as "Guachincheland", that area above Sta. Ursula, La Matanza and La Victoria, in the north of Tenerife, that seems to have an unbounded number of guachinches.

Anyway, we are going to a favourite, high above Sta. Ursula, well into vineyard country. Up and up we motor, occasionally needing to drop to first gear when delayed by an agricultural vehicle on its way home for the evening. But, on arrival, it is closed! I know it's good, but surely they cannot have gone through all their wine already, can they? It seems, from an old gentleman perched on his front step, that indeed they have.

We motor on, dropping down the hill towards a roadside sign that we saw earlier. We will try there. When we arrive, welcoming lights are beginning to twinkle. We park in the road and march up to the entrance. It looks great, and we are hopeful of yet another "find".

This is clearly going to be an upmarket guachinche: we can see that from outside. It appears to be the best part of a complete house, not just, for example, a cleared out commercial garage. The approach is appealing, and we pass up some steps, leading across the garden which has vegetables growing in abundance. A man and a young girl are busy on the stoop, peeling a vast bowl of potatoes. Our noses are pulled by a seemingly irresistible force through the front door and towards the large open brazier, next to which hot, smiling people are at work, grilling vast pieces of meat. It is like Dante's inferno by that brazier.

We go into the main room, which doubles as the front lounge, as it has a balcony and sliding patio doors. There are two tables out on the balcony. In the main room are set up two tables for six and three tables for four. I wander off for a bit of a look-see and discover two other rooms (presumably bedrooms) set up with a table for six or eight in each, for private dining or overflow. One such room is already occupied.

We are early, but this place is already humming.

We park ourselves whilst there is still space. There is no menu, and it is left to the very friendly and piratical looking server to list the available offerings. The beef has already sold out, he tells us, and there is no goat tonight. Everything else is available. We order the fabada, followed by a large mixed salad (no peppers!) and then pork chops.

Half a litre of red village wine is brought, together with a large bottle of water. Bread comes too, with an excellent garlic dip.

I think that this is going to turn out to be one of the poshest guachinches that we have been to, and it makes a change to be sitting on old leather chairs and not on upturned barrels.

The fabada is excellent, with a pleasant kick of chilli, and the bowl is soon wiped clean with the remains of the crusty bread. The pork chops, well-seasoned, are so large that we have difficulty in imagining the animal from which they came. Just where do they breed pigs that big? The bowl of piping hot chips, hand cut, defeats us. We can eat no more. A plastic bag is brought to do duty as a doggy bag, and so our faithful old friend at home will have a treat for his breakfast tomorrow in return for his penance in being left behind tonight.

By now, there is not a table, or indeed a chair left free in the place. The decibel level has increased to fever pitch, and about 40 people, many with small and well behaved children, are having a really great night out. It is wonderful to be part of it.

On my way to the loo, I have to pass by the kitchen. Seeing that I am discreetly carrying my camera, I am invited into the kitchen where the cooks happily invite me to take their photograph before they rush back to their brazier. I march onward to the loo further down the hall. It is spotless. It looks newly tiled, and everything works. My wife reports the same for her visit.

Although there was no written menu, we did get a written bill. We paid a total of €11.50 a head for a lovely night out. The whole place was spotless, the service (although a tad slow because of the numbers) was excellent, and the food determined that we shall visit again. Very soon."

23

Roussillon

The phone rang one evening.

"Hi! It's me. How are you both doing in Tenerife?"

No name, just picking up where we had left off last time we spoke.

"When are you coming to see us? You do keep promising..."

"I know, Dick, but we had the business to sell first, and then the upheaval of the move over here to Tenerife. We are only just catching our breath!"

"So, what's stopping you now?"

Dick is a very old friend. I have known him since my skiing days, and that was a very long time ago. I first met him on a skiing holiday in the French Alps. He was living in Brussels where he had some highfalutin' job with the EU.

Dick was a high flyer. He and his first wife also had an apartment in Italy (naturally near a ski resort) and we would drive down there with him at a furious pace (why are all my friends frenetic drivers?) and ski all day and drink all night. But we were all much younger then and life seemed so much cheaper.

Evenings were often passed at Beppe's tiny eponymous restaurant in Morgex, a few kilometres out of Courmayeur, where Beppe himself would serve us memorable food in his small underground cellar restaurant. I still remember it so well.

Our friendship has continued in an amiable way over the years. We phone when the mood takes us, and meet up when it is convenient. He came over from France for our wedding at Bolton Abbey, bringing as his gift some antique brass spigots. However, he forgot to leave them with us, and they travelled backwards and forwards between England and France, visiting England every so often but not quite reaching what should have been their final destination until very recently.

Once we were settled here in Tenerife, his invitation flew in to go and visit him.

"No more excuses. You can fly to Barcelona cheaply, and I will pick you up."

How could we refuse? Not only had it been a while since we had seen him, but he had acquired yet another new wife in the meantime. We had also made a point that retirement to Tenerife would accelerate, not hinder, the pleasures of travel elsewhere. On this occasion, the widening of our horizons would be to an area of France that neither of us had visited before. So we booked, and flew with Ryanair into Girona, north of Barcelona, that much nearer to his mountain lair in the foothills approaching Andorra.

Ryanair seems to receive a disproportionate amount of flak, but not only have we found them to provide an impressive service, but we are delighted that they offer a discount from their fares for legitimate Canary Islanders such as ourselves.

As promised, Dick was waiting for us in the arrivals hall. It was already lunch time, and he wanted us to visit a restaurant that he knew.

"Come on, let's hurry. We can get there in time for some late lunch. I want you to see the place."

So without further ado, we piled everything into the car and swept off for all of a kilometre, if that. Then we dived down a side street and came out into a large lorry park. In front of us was quite a presentable looking restaurant, obviously a place where the locals would eat, and equally obviously completely unknown to any passing tourist.

There were smartly laid tables, and the inevitable television blaring out from close to the ceiling, as is the norm in Spain everywhere. It is usually a football match that is on, and also usually either Real Madrid or Barcelona, or beloved "*Barca*" as it is known in these parts.

We found a table, and enjoyed the three course set menu with wine. Everything seemed to be home made, and came from a large kitchen where a number of people were toiling over huge steaming cauldrons.

Dick decided that I should drive afterwards. "Well, I had a couple of beers while I was waiting for you, and what with the wine as well… Anyway, you like driving more than I do."

And so, an hour or so later, we came to his village, back over the border into France, and lying on the road as it starts its climb towards Andorra. At first sight, it was very picturesque, with peach trees in blossom along the valley floor and flowers in window boxes everywhere.

Dick has two houses in the village. One was for himself, and the other one was for the animal menagerie of his American wife. Only in France could you find such an amicable and adult arrangement.

The village was medieval, and so was Dick's house, in all senses of the word. It was a continual work in progress. Goodness knows how long this work had been going on, but the plumbing arrangements still came under the heading of "French antique".

"Welcome to my humble home," said Dick as we crossed the threshold. "Here at last. Your bedroom is down below. Let me raise this trap door and you will see the stairs. Hang on to the rope to steady yourselves. I think that there will be everything that you need, but if not, just give me a shout. I'll see you back up here in the lounge when you've unpacked."

Our large room was reached down an extremely steep and

narrow loft-type staircase, and in view of the necessity to hold on to the rope attachment to steady one's progress, I decided on the spot to be almost teetotal that evening.

When we reached floor level, the room opened out attractively to reveal its original purpose, that of a sty or byre for the animals of yore. However, it was spacious and had a pretty window, a doorway with a racing bicycle parked across it to deter intruders, and, heaven for Sally, an en suite bathroom.

It had been a while since the restaurant was left behind, so Sally was first to engage these facilities. But when the plumbing was cranked into life, the earth moved for her.

"My God, what's all that noise?" I shouted through the closed door. "What's going on in there? What have you done?"

Her wailing told me that something had gone seriously wrong.

"Come in, come in." said Sally, by now in floods of tears.

The entire toilet had shuddered across the floor of the bathroom, with water cascading out from underneath. I entered to see a sea of water. We had only been here some ten minutes, and she was already wrecking the place.

"Never mind, it's not your fault. It must have been like that beforehand. But we had better go upstairs and tell Dick, because it will need repairing pronto."

"You go back up there and tell him." she cried.

"We had better do a bit of mopping up first," said I, "and let's see if we can turn off the water somehow."

After some clearing up, we also inspected the bath, and noted that it was one of those tub-like things that either you sit in or squat in, with an overhead shower that, at that time of day, emitted only a dribble. So a funny bath it would have to be for her. I opted for the dribble, and it was not at all bad. I've had much worse in my time.

We changed and went upstairs to see our host. Wine was on the table, and so we chatted for a while, catching up on our respective gossip. There was clearly no urgency about the problems down below.

Later, we set off in search of Gaston, the plumber, whom Dick had already phoned but who was yet to answer his summons.

A pleasant enough chap was Gaston, and he had a story. Plumber *extraordinaire* to the locals and ex-pats alike, he drove a rickety old *Deux Chevaux* in original Citroen battleship grey, and lived, so we were told, in the garage of his rather nice village house. Later on it was confided to us that he was only living in the garage so as to avert a potentially embarrassing domestic situation better avoided here.

Gaston was finally run to earth in the local bar, promising to come first thing on the morrow after he had surfaced from his usual long evening propping up the bar counter. It was a nice enough village bar, one might say typical, and we were brought nibbles to go with our drinks. People passed by, and everyone knew Dick. Soon, the entire village seemed to know us too, for we were introduced around like a couple of prize ponies.

It had been a lovely day, although a bit too eventful for Sally.

Dawn broke crisp and clear. The air was fresh up in the hills and after breakfast we decided to explore and go on a village walkabout. Dick offered to stay behind to meet Gaston. The village was full of lovely old houses, dilapidated in that genteel style that only the French can achieve. Narrow streets, cars parked haphazardly, and the smell of bread wafting from the nearby *boulangerie*. And as soon as we turned a corner, we realised that it was market day.

The square had overnight filled with covered stalls, keeping off the sun which was already becoming quite warm. There were so many things of interest, but we couldn't afford to dabble much, because of the weight of our suitcases on the plane home. Typically French, the market had stalls laden with wonderfully fresh vegetables, cheeses galore, and fresh meats and salamis, all available to touch, smell and squeeze, so frowned on back in England. It was all a riot of colour and a hubbub of noise as stout matrons competed to sell their wares and other stout matrons competed to buy the best on offer, using elbows where necessary to ensure that they kept their place at the forefront of the queue. Looking down on it all was the Canigou, one of the highest mountains in the Pyrenees. It was still heavily capped with snow, and, of course, it could not fail to remind us of El Teide, back at home.

As in Tenerife, lunch time is important in Roussillon. It would not be complete for us without a visit to a bistro. Dick walked us along the outer walls of the village and we came upon what seemed to us the quintessential little French bistro, painted French blue (of course) and dozing in the sunshine, just waiting for us, the first customers of the day.

Dick knew the patron (again, of course) and so in we went.

We were treated to a coarse country game pate with chopped gherkins in it, the like of which one does not find in Tenerife. This was followed by some fillets of John Dory, lightly pan-fried, with boiled potatoes and a large mixed salad. Dick was yet another friend who was not keen on salad, trotting out the usual, "It's rabbit food, you know," so we tucked in. It was all delicious, particularly the walnut dressing. The wine was a good local one from the Pays d'Oc, and we were given a little taster of a local dessert wine to send us on our way.

In the evening there was to be a picnic on the beach. Dick would say no more, and we were intrigued. What a great idea, we thought, but slightly confusing because we were at least 30 kilometres inland. Was Dick going to be doing something really special in our honour? Were we going back to the coast for one of those dreamy moonlit barbeques on the beach that you see in films, where fresh crab and lobster are lovingly prepared in large skillets over a fire of driftwood, as the reflection of the moon glitters on a placid silken ocean?

Not so, not at all. Nothing could have been more different.

On the edge of the village is a river. It makes a jink as it passes by the end of the village, and lo! there is a small beach thrown up by its meandering over thousands of years.

Friends congregated at Dick's house, but for some reason that we never quite understood, we all decamped to someone's house and not to the beach after all. Lydia, whose house it was, had obviously been called upon to do the food, and oddly provided us with hard boiled eggs, cold tomatoes, mass-manufactured pate that no self-respecting Frenchman would have been seen dead near, some supermarket cheeses still in their plastic wrapping, and then, as the *"pièce de résistance"*, she finally bore aloft a vast platter of chips, almost stone cold! The house itself was in a major state of disrepair whilst upstairs in the living room there was a baby grand piano, heavily covered with dust.

Yet strangely, something potentially so utterly dreadful was thoroughly enjoyable. Thank heavens the wines were good! We all had a really fabulous time, and most of us met the next day for morning coffee, and remembered the evening with true pleasure.

After three days with our old friend and his new wife, we had come to terms with the quaint plumbing issues, and the lavatory had at last been anchored to terra firma. We had enjoyed ourselves immensely, but next morning it would be time to say goodbye.

We decided to take Dick and his wife out to dinner in a town about ten kilometres away. The restaurant boasted a Michelin star, and we dined outside in the little courtyard of an old *bourgeois* house, sitting under the stars and with candles flickering and guttering all around us in the warm evening breeze. Surprisingly, and most pleasing to my pocket, the cost was less than I had expected.

We went back to Dick's house, abseiled down the staircase, and slept the sleep of the just.

All in all it had been a superb break, much better for being able to just up-sticks and go, without too much planning other than to arrange for Freddie to go off on his own short break holiday with the poodles. And therein lay one of the great advantages of being retired, and having good friends, we were learning.

Now, we must await a return match here in Tenerife. Hopefully, it will be soon.

24

Fiesta!

Almost any day in Tenerife can be a good reason for the holding of a *fiesta*, formal or informal, and it can take many different forms. There are too many *fiestas* in our part of Tenerife to name them all individually, but a number of them have some impact on our lives, if only because they make a legal excuse for a day off, and the shops close for the day.

There is the *fiesta* for a small local village, where everyone turns out and lines the streets, watching a parade of carts bedecked with anything that can easily be brought to hand, such as palm fronds, flowers and indeed vegetables. Bunting is draped between street lights to give a festive air to the proceedings. Special meals are prepared, old men sit in the shade playing cards and smoking, children run around everywhere, and the *mamas* look on and smile benignly. There is normally a religious significance to each *fiesta*, but it does sometimes get a bit blurred into the background, with jollity taking over.

A larger town will have a more formalised event, known as a *romaria*. Originally the word *romaria* translated as a pilgrimage. Each year we go to the one at Los Realejos, a country town clinging to a steep hillside about four kilometres away from where we live. There, the sides of the main street are set out with plain wooden chairs for the event, and everyone is charged €1 for the privilege of being seated to watch the procession. Since it all lasts for a number of hours, it is good value, and indeed necessary for our aging bones.

Freddie is not allocated a chair, and sits at my feet. I swear that he can remember it from last year, because he is on edge and awaiting the arrival of food. The nose is a-twitching!

The procession starts, as ever, with a march past by the local town band. You can hear them warming up their various instruments from far away at the other end of the high street. When they come into view, you can see that a huge effort has been made. Everyone is in full regional dress uniform, and they play for all they are worth. The crowds cheer and wave flags at them.

Then come the horse-drawn carts. The horses are magnificent beasts, the carts huge, and bedecked with flowers, vines and the like. Freddie looks at the horses and cows with great respect, and keeps close quarters with me.

Everyone in the parade is wearing local traditional costume, bright and colourful, with the women in head dresses, and the men in half trousers and long striped socks, and sporting jaunty felt hats, almost Tyrolean in style.

The woman seated next to me consumes a huge packet of sunflower seeds. She cracks them between her front teeth, and spits the husks out into the road in front of her. Soon, the patch of roadway is almost covered. I glare at her, keeping Freddie on a short leash so that he can't hoover up the husks, but she is indifferent to all around her. To her a dog is just a dog and her seeds are a Spanish custom.

A funny little hand-driven tractorette is next along. It usually does daily duty as a rotovator, turning over the stony earth on the narrow terraces higher up the valley. It putt-putts along, sounding as though it will breathe its last gasp at any moment, and it's also towing a trailer, laden down with produce.

Then another shout goes up and the masses press forward.

There are huge cows with massive horns, two or four at a time, clad in antique wooden yokes, pulling vast carts or drays like the floats we had back in Blighty at the local gala in days gone by.

And then yet another shout goes up, and people start to move forward again.

What's happening? Freddie already seems to know. His memory bank has kicked in, and I suppose with his doggy nose, he can smell things so much further away.

A lorry appears round the corner, almost covered with garlands. The driver's vision must be almost obscured by the waving fronds around the windscreen. On the back is perched, none too securely, a huge barbeque! The men are grilling sausages and pieces of pork. Outstretched hands are raised in unison, and hot sausages fly through the air, closely followed by the pieces of pork.

Luckily, we grab one large sausage to share between the three of us. It is heavenly, direct from the griddle and flavoured by the wood smoke. But hard to handle, it's so hot. Not that it seems to bother our asbestos-throated pooch.

More food is on the way, and Freddie remembers more than we.

The distribution of hard boiled eggs at events such as this is an old Canarian custom. This time, it is children on the back of a lorry that are bombarding everyone with the eggs. We can hardly see them for the decoration, but those eggs are shot out from the sides as though from a mortar in a never ending stream, and all are nimbly caught by young and old alike. The sunflower seed-chewing woman keeps sneaking back up to the children and ends up with at least half a dozen hard boiled eggs in her pinafore. It would be an eggy dinner for her family later, and an eggy treat for Freddie this afternoon.

He will no doubt be egg-bound tomorrow morning.

There are then a team of dancing girls in costume, and yet another band, a brass one this time, playing some melody unknown to us. But it gets the crowd going once again, and everyone breaks into a plaintive Canarian song.

All this goes on for more than a couple of hours, the entire cavalcade doing two laps of the town.

It has been yet another afternoon to remember, with our canine companion having received more than his fair share of the food being tossed out from those floats: he has, if I counted aright, polished off two hard boiled eggs, two sausages, one pork chop and a number of large scraps of *chorizo*. No wonder he remembers it from last year.

Puerto has bigger and better *fiestas*, held throughout the year. For most of them, bunting lines the streets everywhere and the town is dressed up to the nines.

Just as in Santa Cruz, the biggest and the best of all the *fiestas* is Carnival. It takes all of a fortnight, and it's huge, as famous in Spain as that of Rio in Brazil. There are parades, art and book activities, gastronomic events, wine events and music, always music, everywhere.

We go to the main parade on the last Saturday. It winds its way all along the main promenade, and the floats are breath-taking works of art, having cost significant sums of money to create, each sponsored by a town business. We grab comfy seats in a café wherever we can, and pay for them in the purchase of cold drinks.

In the evening there will be a race like no other, one of the star events of Carnival and only open to the town's male waiters. As of old, most of them dress up in frocks and high heels and lots of make-up, and are flagged off by the Town Hall, finishing the race in the main square. First prize goes to he who has dressed the best and most outlandishly. This year we see that one entrant is dressed as El Teide, one as the entire island, and yet another as an ambulance! Most appropriate, considering that there is always a sprained ankle or two along the way. Thousands come to watch, and there is dancing to a live band afterwards in the square until the early hours.

Then there is the Festival of the Sardine.

This is a religious festival, and the whole town takes part. The clergy from the different churches of the town lead a parade, with a group of hefty chaps bearing on a plinth an immense sardine, some eight feet long, and presumably made of papier maché, painted in fishy colours but bizarrely sporting bright red pouting ruby lips, representing the bounty of the ocean for the local fishing community. At the end of the parade, the sardine is ceremoniously immersed in the sea, flowers are strewn in the waters of the harbour, and prayers are said by the presiding clergy, before the fireworks that have been strategically placed within the sardine are ignited, blowing the entire effigy to kingdom come in the outer harbour. The whole parade then reforms and the process (*sans* sardine) is then repeated in reverse.

The largest religious festival in Tenerife each year is the one at the town of Candelaria, home of the Black Madonna, on the other side of the island from us and about 12 kilometres south of the capital, Santa Cruz.

For the event, which takes place in August each year, thousands of pilgrims (I have heard the number of 30,000 used quite authoritatively) make the journey from all over the island. It used to be that they would all walk to Candelaria, with the most devout doing the journey on their hands and knees. As Tenerife is rather a hilly place, the walk would in most cases take a day or two, requiring a camp for the night quite high up in the hills. And it can get cold up there, high in the hills, even in August. Nowadays, a huge number of those going will still walk, and the *autopista* which bypasses the town will be black with those moving along it on foot. It has become such a problem that the local police have announced that they will make an instant 200 euro fine against anyone found walking on the *autopista*.

In my opinion, they will not be carrying saddle bags big enough to fine thousands of people.

But wait! My local paper has now reported that a "Pilgrim Path" is to be built along the hard shoulder of the *autopista* in time for the next annual pilgrim walk. One lane of the road is to be closed so that this path can be built alongside the hard shoulder. There is uproar in the press since that stretch of the *autopista* had only recently been widened anyway, and this new path will cost an extra million euros or two.

Just imagine the dangers inherent in allowing pedestrians so close to speeding motorway traffic. Where else in the world would you see a motorway partially closed for a couple of months in order to build a hard shoulder specifically for people to walk on?

A really unusual cause for a celebration, if not a full blown *fiesta*, is the cochineal beetle.

"The what?" I hear you ask.

In the old days, cochineal – a colorant or dye used, for example in cake decoration and cooking, and for the staining of fabrics – was made by the grinding up of cochineal beetles. The beetles were bred onto, and lived their lives on, prickly pear bushes. The locals would come together and dress themselves in protective gear, padding their legs and arms with straw or brown paper to protect themselves from the spines of the bushes. Then they would scrape the beetles from the bushes, and take them away to be processed.

This tradition died out when an artificial dye substitute was created to satisfy the market much more cheaply. The loss of the cochineal trade and the changeover to artificial dyes produced one of the largest economic collapses and forced emigration that the Canaries had ever experienced.

The market is now returning due to the scares that have been reported in the use of artificial dyes. Cochineal beetles are once again in favour, and are on the way back to being big business. Fortunately, there are still a few long-retired beetle collectors who can explain the process of beetle breeding to the young people on the island. This year the festival has been scheduled for the beginning of October, a perfect example of an old tradition being renewed, both for tourism purposes and also for local commercial reasons.

So, we shall go and have a look at it all, but I think that we may decline any invitation to actually participate. Sally has never been too keen on beetles!

Also of interest to us are the two almond festivals held in Vilaflor and other small towns and villages. In February official walks are organised through the hillsides to admire the almond blossom, which cascades like puffy candyfloss creating an airborne carpet of colour for miles around. Later in the year, it is time to go back there again, around early October, depending on the weather, to help to bring the harvest in. In Aripe, the locals dress in traditional attire and re-enact the age old custom of beating the branches of the almond trees with sticks to dislodge the ripened nuts. The harvest is then loaded into panniers on donkeys and brought back to the main square in front of the church, where the harvest is blessed. There is food, drink, music and merriment all day, culminating in dancing under the stars when night has fallen. Sheer magic!

Extract from my review of the Canarian Black Pig Fiesta:

"High on a hill… no, not 'stands a lonely goatherd'… is the annual Canarian Black Pig Fiesta at Pinolere. Although it's not promoted, I have received a late tip-off, and so I motor up into the hills above La Orotava to reach the small isolated village of Pinolere. I have no idea what to expect.

I am directed to the ethnographic park (and no, I don't know exactly what that is either) within which various stands have been erected, each one taken either by an individual restaurant or winery. There is a two euro entrance fee to pay and a further stand, curiously sited well to the rear of the assembly, is selling tickets at 1.5 euros each, to be exchanged for a beer, a small glass of wine, or a tapa.

These restaurant stands, perhaps just over a dozen, are taking it very seriously, and excellent ranges of tapas are on offer. One such is for the Hotel Victoria in La Orotava. Their warm blini with rocket (actually it was baby spinach) and smoked salmon is to die for. Another stand, which had better remain nameless, has but two tapas on show, presumably hopeful that the throng of passers-by will place an order for something more freshly prepared. Whilst sitting opposite to them, taking a cold beer, I saw no takers, but the friend that we were with entertained us greatly by falling backwards from his plastic chair, completing the tumble in perfect slow motion.

The Canarian Black Pig stand is doing a roaring trade. Their offer is a little tapa of pork with grilled banana on a skewer, topped with a spicy dollop of mojo sauce. These tapas are selling like, well, hot pork and bananas. But they must be losing quite a bit of trade to the freeloaders (myself included) who take advantage of the never ending plates of free crackling and shredded warm pork that they keep putting down on the table in front of the stand.

Talking of pigs, for that is the name of today's game, that was the only stand that seems to be doing anything porcine, other than the inevitable Serrano ham. No black pigs are actually in evidence although, to be fair, having live pigs in the vicinity of their recently roasted brethren might make them slightly uncomfortable. They have, however, sent a picture of themselves, in lieu.

If I must single out one stand in particular, it is the one that is clearly making the greatest effort. And that is for a restaurant this is not yet open! Trays of scrumptious tapas are laid out on their stand, and a chef is working away at a pan on a hot ring. I ask what it is. I am told that it is to be a mushroom risotto. I do like a good risotto. The problem is that most restaurants fail miserably, usually due to the fact that they part cook in advance and hope that it can be finished off at the later time of order. It always fails. As this is almost ready, I hand over my last 1.5 euro voucher and am soon presented with a sublime risotto, redolent of mushroom flavour, loaded with chunks of mushroom, and topped with a swirl of decent olive oil. I am in heaven.

The restaurant, set to open in the middle of September, will be called El Ayanto and situated in Calle San Agustin 7, La Orotava.

So, a really worthwhile four hours are spent high on that hillside. In all that time, I do not hear another English voice (or German, come to that). It gets me out into the beautiful unspoiled Canarian countryside, there are stunning views back down to the coast, and I enjoy some special food, all washed down with quality La Orotava valley wines.

25

Vet Visits

As Freddie continues to age, the more it seems that he needs the services of the local vet. Very much like us, really.

When we first came over here with him, we immediately got him registered at a veterinary practice in La Orotava that had been recommended. The boss, Alejandro, was welcoming, friendly, caring, and spoke some English. We have been with him ever since.

We had never heard of heartworm. It seems that it is some insidious worm that attaches itself and wriggles its way into the heart, and so eventually would cause the death of your dog. Freddie immediately was put on a course to boost him up. At the same time, he was registered onto the Canary Islands electronic tracking system, Zoocan, so that, should he be lost (heaven forbid, because of his limited Spanish!), then he could be recovered through the microchip that had been inserted in his neck as a youngster.

Freddie just loves his regular visits to the vet for his booster jabs each six months. Some dogs have to be dragged in to the vet's surgery, kicking and screaming, their claws digging into the linoleum leaving white lines as witness of their tortured passing. Not so our Freddie. In he will rush, giving a bark to Cristina the receptionist to announce his arrival.

"*Hola,* Freddie! *Qué tal, hoy*?" She leans over the counter and smiles broadly at him.

"Very well, thank you," he barks back.

"Alejandro will see you in a minute. Do you want to wait outside as usual?"

"Yes," says Freddie. "Just give me a call. In the meantime I shall go and cock my leg in those bushes and terrorise that small spaniel cowering behind that hibiscus!"

"*Qué*? What, me?" whines the spaniel, trying to melt into invisibility behind the bush. He really need not bother, Freddie is really only interested in passing the time of day with large dogs. Anything spaniel sized or smaller is ignored.

Freddie cocks his leg for the third time, and settles down with us to wait for his name to be called, no doubt with half his mind on the free biscuit that is always offered at the end of his visit.

One time we made an appointment to take Freddie along because he had a small open wound on the side of his ribcage. It had suddenly appeared as from nowhere.

"Ah!" muttered Alejandro after doing a bit of prodding and poking. "This is a common problem in hot climates. It looks to me like the foongoose."

We looked at each other blankly.

"Sorry, Alex, what did you say?"

"It is the foongoose. It is common at this time of the year, but we must treat it straight away before it gets deeper under his skin and affects him in other ways."

"This foongoose, can you explain it a bit more?" We were still stumped.

At that stage, Freddie chipped in.

"Come on Alex, spit it out. What's all this nonsense about foongoose, and how are you going to get rid of it? Oh, an ointment? Well that's OK then. And by the way, have a go at my dew claws would you whilst you've got me standing on this high table. I'm beginning to catch them on my master's trousers."

In the end, between us all, we finally translated his Spanglish to mean "fungus"; a fungal infection that Freddie had picked up, but which could be quickly treated. Within a couple of weeks all signs had disappeared, though we continued the course until the ointment ran out.

Alejandro was always very thorough, and even photographed Freddie as well as weighing him and feeling him all over. It seemed that he was slightly overweight, despite enjoying four walks a day, and we put it down to his age and build. We had also brought along his x-rays from England, and they clearly showed that our old chap was catching up with the two of us in seeing the onset of old age. Arthritis had set in to his front elbows and one of his shoulders. The latest Tenerife x-ray showed us all too clearly that the bone in the off side shoulder was beginning to break down and splinter in the joint. He has a regular pill to ease the aches and pains but I think that the dosage is soon going to have to be increased. It's such a shame, because he is still determined to be so active.

So sadly, such is life.

Another time, the reason for a hasty visit was for the emptying of his anal glands. Some owners do this job themselves, but the stench is so overpowering that I have always preferred to entrust that particular pleasure to my vet.

One evening, as were sitting watching TV, I looked down and watched Freddie treating us to his virtuoso performance of "scooting" along across the lounge carpet. He was looking up at me rather apologetically whilst sitting on his haunches and dragging his bottom along using his front paws for traction. It was hilarious to look at, but I knew immediately what that was about. Those glands were full and needed squeezing out.

So, early next evening we went to La Orotava and the nice veterinary nurse, without uttering a word of complaint, squeezed around his backside for all she was worth. We stood well back and went outside as quickly as possible. Freddie had a beatific grin on his face, and that would be that for about another year. Aaaaah!

But the car stank terribly, all the way home.

To cheer ourselves up, we reminded ourselves that we were about to go away for a few nights for our anniversary. The previous year we had finally been to stay at the Iberostar 5-star Grand Hotel Mencey in Santa Cruz, the subject of a multi-million euro refurbishment. A lovely building, it overlooked some less than lovely other buildings to one side, and an exceedingly cramped bedroom did little to endear itself to us. This year we were going to the Hotel Jardines de Nivaria on Costa Adeje in the south of Tenerife. It turned out to be so good that we actually extended our visit and we had a wonderful time. I took the chance of writing a review of their flagship restaurant, La Cúpula, an extract from which appears below:

"The Hotel Jardines de Nivaria is situated in the south of our fair isle of Tenerife, hard by the beach of Playa de Fañabé. Set in exquisite mature gardens, with two swimming pools, it was almost a pleasure to part with our hard earned money in exchange for the delights it had to offer.

One such was La Cúpula, one of three restaurants within the hotel, and clearly their most prestigious, the kitchen brigade being led by chef Ruben Cabrera. It is open to the general public, and recently has won the award for Best Hotel Restaurant in a well-known Canary Islands publication.

It really does hide its light under a bushel. No signage betrays its presence within the main part of the hotel until you literally arrive at its portals. Broaching them, one is transported to another dimension. There is a lot of dark wood, tall pillars, and a semi-circular bar area at one end. I thought that it was the epitome of a dining room in an old traditional London club, whilst my better half went for the restaurant of a 1930s transatlantic liner. If you combine the two, you will get the picture. A relaxing, quality place to spend an evening. Would the food live up to it?

Ushered to our table by Toni, the head waiter, we were handed a menu and a wine list. Staff shimmered about, seemingly anticipating our every need.

We placed our orders, including a bottle of white Martin Codax from the eponymous Bodega in DO Rias Baixas in northern Spain (€29.75). At

100% Albarino, it was well worth the money in these surroundings, delicately crafted and with a nice long finish.

An amuse bouche was laid before us; it was presented in a large bowl and turned out to be a small rectangle of seared tuna (yes, still very pink in the middle) with a topping of tiny chopped slivers of green tomato, the whole surrounded by a pool of clear mushroom broth, intensely reduced to provide a heady flavour.

My starter was a dish of four fresh scallops flown in, we were told, from the Peninsula. They came with a side jug of spicy barbecue sauce, and the dish was flamed at our table as a piece of elegant theatre (€20.50). My wife chose the ceviche of very fresh turbot topped with three avocado bombs, a couple of tiny erect deep-fried banana spears, and a scattering of redcurrants (at €15.50). The turbot was just perfect and the avocado bombs, looking for all the world like green grapes, defied description. Truly a triumph both of artistry and substance.

The waitresses continued to shimmer about and the head waiter gave a perfect imitation of Jeeves, appearing to my shoulder as if materialising from the ether, always a second before being needed. A rare talent, indeed.

See, already too many superlatives, and we had yet to reach the main course.

These were to be a duck dish (€20.50) and a steak dish (€24.50). The duck was wild, set on a bed of leek and potatoes and accompanied by a delicious almond and garlic jelly. Wild duck is notoriously smaller than the cultivated variety, but the chef had managed to instil both succulence and flavour. My small steak (which gave a nod to an old bugbear of mine, nouvelle cuisine) had been sourced from the Esla Valley in northern Spain.

A pause then led to dessert which for my wife was a sorbet of Grand Marnier and mandarin accompanied by mint ice chips (€7.00) and for me, the much trumpeted "Bonsai of my Dreams". I had no idea what I would be getting, but it turned out to be a small dark chocolate tree decorated with fresh mint leaves. Its base was secured in a shallow bowl and surrounded, as though by a verdant pasture, with green mint granita garnished with tiny edible fresh flowers. By its side was a bowl of dry ice spreading its clouds to imitate my *bonsai tree being in a magical garden. This cost an extremely reasonable €9.50 for something that one will remember and dine out on for a long time to come.*

Such levels of quality of ingredients and execution of dishes are a clear marker for targeting a Michelin star.

My wife was brought a golden bowl of dessert chocolates, scattered on edible soil with yet more tiny flower petals. A long stemmed red rose was delivered. And finally, as Trevor Macdonald used to say on News at Ten, I came to my own personal nirvana, a glass of Humboldt Tinto Dulce 2001. I savoured it. I was transported. I have already emailed to Bodegas Insulares, enquiring where I can buy it.

And so to coffee, taken out on the terrace, watching a glittering moon arcing through a dark and silken sky. What an evening for an anniversary"!

Life can play some cruel tricks, can it not?

Just when things are all running smoothly, fate determines that one is going to be in for a seismic upheaval. Indeed, today our world has been turned upside down, as though El Teide himself had rumbled in the night.

Freddie came in from the garden this morning looking mystified and unsure of his surroundings. Looking at him closely, we could see immediately that he had had what we believed to be a stroke. One side of his face had dropped, and he did not seem to be in control of his facial functions. It had left him with his jowl on that side flapping a bit loosely compare to the other. We then noticed that one of his ears, that on the same side, was a bit skew-whiff.

We were out of the house and into the car in an instant, headlights blazing as I carved past other cars on the way up the hill into La Orotava, pulling up at the vet's without a thought for proper parking. I rushed in to alert them whilst Sally and Freddie followed more slowly.

Alex was fortunately on duty and examined Freddie minutely,

doing a whole barrage of tests, and also pointed out that his eye on the same side was not closing properly. Was it a stroke, or was it a tumour in his head? Without a brain scan there was not going to be a definitive answer. We were bombarded with information, too much to take in, in the midst of our, and his, distress.

What it boiled down to was that our beloved Freddie was seriously ill with a condition from which he could not recover, although, with medication, it could be controlled.

He could not understand what had happened to him, and we could not tell him.

The pills are doing something positive for him, because they have stopped the rot. He is slowly coming to terms with how he must live his life by adapting to what he can and now cannot do, and we are doing the same. There will be no recovery to where he was before, only a new way of life from henceforth, provided it can be stabilised. I can see in his eyes as he looks so mournfully at me that he cannot understand this sudden change in circumstances. But we do firmly believe that he is not in pain.

He could, of course, have another stroke, and that would be that. If it is a tumour, then it will only get larger as time goes by, and that will also be that.

Should it be the tumour, we deem that at 11 years he is too old to have major head surgery. Before he could be operated on, he would need to have a full head scan. For all of the wonderful medical equipment on this island for humans, there is no specialist veterinary scanner here. The nearest is on Gran Canaria, the next island. The trip would be fraught with distress for Freddie because firstly there would be an uncomfortable car journey, followed by a trip on the fast ferry caged in a box, then a journey of nearly an hour to the veterinary hospital, then a full anaesthetic before the scan, all to be followed by the same process in reverse to come back home.

If the scan was to reveal that an operation was a necessity, then that would involve major surgery, a difficult decision to take for any age of dog, let alone one in the autumn of his years. When it comes to something like this, then money can be no object, but the question has to be asked as to whether it would be right to subject him to all that could be involved.

We continue to adapt from day to day. At present, Freddie is back on good form with the aid of the magic pills, and all three of us are coming to terms with the changes that we are making in our lives. The magic pills are continuing to work their wonder, and Freddie continues to enjoy his life, only slightly inhibited in his day to day activities.

If there is any funny side to all of this (and it is so difficult at the moment to find one), it is watching him eat his dinner, when half of his food falls out on one side as he chews, because that jowl does not hold it in, so everything takes twice as long!

26

Bavaria

After Georg and Eta had stayed with us in Tenerife, we had a standing invitation to go back to Oberammergau, and they were now pressing for the return match.

After a flying visit to Sally's parents back in Lancashire, we booked an easyJet flight out of Manchester, direct to Munich. It was something that we would not have been able to do before we retired. Diaries would have had to have been consulted and synchronised, appointments put off and clients alienated.

At the airport, we sat quietly in the lounge area, killing time, waiting to be called for our flight. Next to us came a group of a dozen or so young Scotsmen whose main object in life appeared to be to try to sink as many pints of lager as possible before their flight was announced. Idly, we wondered where they might be going.

Lo and behold, later, there we were, sitting in our seats on the plane, when they all struggled aboard. Clearly, some of them had a bit of difficulty in staggering along the aisle to get to a spare seat. Shouting and waving bottles, they made their way towards the rear of the plane.

A few would not be quiet or sit down, and eventually the head steward decided to wade in and make his presence felt. He looked a bit insipid, and finally the captain was called and a couple of the miscreants were hauled off the plane for what we assumed to be a stern chat. The captain eventually reappeared with them, and made an announcement over the tannoy.

"Ladies and gentlemen, I am sorry for the delay in getting away from Manchester. Some of you may have noticed that we have a group on board that have consumed a large quantity of alcohol. In the interests of passenger safety I am therefore taking the decision that this will be an alcohol free flight. None will be served during our flight to Munich."

And this is where it all went wrong. In hindsight, which is all very easy as we all know, he should have offloaded them there and then. We were no sooner up in the air than they restarted the mayhem by drinking from their own bottles of spirits that they had secreted on board. The head steward eventually plucked up the courage to move to the rear of the plane. Quick as a flash, he snatched a bottle from one of them, together with a plastic glass that had been brought on board.

"The captain announced that there was to be no drinking on this flight," he said with only the faintest of tremors in his voice betraying his nervousness. There were, after all, a number of hulking great lads involved, most of them at least three sheets to the wind.

"Gerroff! It's our own." The words were more than a little slurred.

"That doesn't matter. The rules of the company state quite clearly that you may not consume drinks that have not been purchased from the crew on board. This bottle and plastic glass will be evidence for when we land."

We were glad when we landed in Munich, though confined to our seats while a squad of German police pushed their way through the plane, pistols strapped to their waists, all young men with regulation buzz cuts. They looked the sort of people that you would not wish to argue with, drunk or not. Quite a number of passengers cheered when the inebriates were led away to the cooler, to be followed by a hefty fine of 400 euros a head the next day.

Georg, who in his younger days had been a competitive driver in club races and rallies, still drove his car, currently a hot BMW, as thought he was in a race. It was early evening as we pushed our way through the rush hour traffic out of Munich. Soon we hit the *autobahn*, the right foot was firmly planted to the floor, and the speedometer wound round until it seemed to get stuck on the 260 k.p.h. mark. That's quite fast enough for us. Fortunately, we had been through all this before, but we were really pleased when the end of the autobahn came into sight, and we turned off up into the hills towards his picturesque alpine valley.

Yellow speed signs flashing irately at us, we hurtled through Ettal, where the monks make the world famous *digestif*, and soon we were approaching Oberammergau, and their wonderful hotel. Eta and their daughter Carola were there to meet us.

"Welcome, welcome, it is so good to see you again. Have you had a good journey?"

"Quite eventful, really!"

We desperately need the bar, and cold Bavarian beer was quickly before us.

A plate of snacks shimmied in, and soon we had recovered enough to start to take an interest in our surroundings. They told us that they had been making serious alterations, as they moved to retirement, and Carola had now agreed to take over the running of the business. Our hosts were itching to point out their refurbishments to us. This new bar had been immaculately constructed and furnished, as had the entire refurbishment of the ground floor of the hotel.

They had spent an awful lot of money on all of this, and it really did show. Glass lamp shades were from Murano, the original home of Italian glass blowing near to Venice. The new exercise rooms were the last word in up-to-the-minute machines. All of this had been done to turn their superior traditional Bavarian hotel into a 21st-century vehicle suitable for Carola to take the helm.

Oberammergau is world famous for the Passion Play that takes place in an especially constructed outdoor auditorium every ten years. During the Thirty Years War, the whole region had been hit by the plague. In 1633 the villagers of Oberammergau prayed to be spared, saying that they would put on this special event every decade should the plague pass them by. Indeed it did pass their valley by, and they were all saved, and so the Passion Play was born and the first event took place the following year in 1634.

It is an extravaganza. It runs from May to October, and most of the locals participate. Georg was in it for most years until this last one, and one year played the pivotal role of Pontius Pilate. Carola too was a regular. The play lasts for nearly eight hours each day, with a break for lunch in between. It sounds as though it could be all rather heavy going. But people come from all over the world to see it.

After a reacquainting stroll round the village the following morning, we were driven off to Georg and Eta's new home. They had moved out of the top floor of the hotel to make way for Carola, and bought an apartment in a small exclusive development on the edge of the village. On the way there, all the fields were bright yellow with a thick carpet of dandelions. They had only been in residence for just over a week, so nothing was as it should be, but it had all the makings of a lovely home, and we knew it would be furnished with great taste.

It was nice to start to relax and unwind, but Georg was having none of it. A countryside tour had been planned, covering an area that we had not visited before. We piled into the car and headed generally south, in the direction of Austria. Not far out of Oberammergau, we flashed past the splendour of Linderhof, one of the many fairy-tale palaces built by (mad) King Ludwig. Soon we arrived at a lovely lake, perfect for a coffee stop. Instead, we zoomed on past.

Further on, in the forest that spans the border between Germany and Austria, we started to notice a higher than usual concentration of BMWs, all of the latest model, driving along in either direction. I had to mention it.

"Georg, have you noticed all these BMWs all of a sudden?"

"Ha! Yes! BMW bought an old hotel near here and have totally rebuilt it in the modern style. They use it for business seminars and weekends away for executives."

And round the next corner, there indeed it was. A vast edifice of glass and concrete, totally out of all harmony with its forest surroundings. And it was surrounded by what seemed like half a day's factory production of the latest models, all parked together.

It seemed that everyone in southern Bavaria makes the trip into Austria to buy petrol. It is so much cheaper over there. Huge queues form as everyone tanks up before turning their vehicles back homeward.

We came to Neuschwanstein (new-swan-stone), that fabulous castle perched on the cliff like something out of a Disney fairy tale, yet another creation of King Ludwig when Bavaria was a kingdom in its own right. Huge horses were pulling covered wagons full of chattering Japanese tourists up the hill to visit the castle.

"Are we going to be joining them?"

"No, certainly not, not enough time today."

Back into the car once again after the coffee stop, and the rain was falling quite heavily now. That didn't in any way inhibit our driver or his trusty steed. Not one kilometre per hour was sacrificed to the sodden surface, and we were treated to a master class in car control.

An orange light on the instrument panel was flickering almost constantly as the traction control system took the strain and kept us pointing mostly in the chosen direction. Our seatbelts were surreptitiously taken up another notch. I was mildly concerned at those tiny rubber contact patches and wished I had inspected the tyres better. Surely the brute forces of inertia would eventually overcome the controlling hand of the electronic safety systems? It would seem not on this occasion, and we breathed a collective sigh of relief.

The way back was through minor roads and farming villages, with farmers hastening their tractors back to cover, and herds of cows returning home to be milked. I can only suppose that none of them saw the momentary flash of metallic blue as we hurtled past them all, the car taking up its full suspension travel as it dug deep into the tighter corners.

Miraculously, the clear skies reappeared as we pulled into Oberammergau and drew up in front of the hotel.

Next day, it was Motor Club day. As members, we were invited.

The motor sport club in Schongau was celebrating its 60th year since inauguration, and all local motor clubs were invited to send delegations to the event. The party was also to include the ceremony of the raising of the maypole.

Maypole?

At lunchtime, a number of local chaps sidled into the hotel, all dressed in yellow polo shirts embroidered with the name and logo of Oberammergau Motor Sport Club, ADAC affiliation badges stitched into them too, as well as Georg's hotel logo on the sleeve.

As you may have guessed, Georg was the Club President.

One poor chap by the name of Willi arrived without the correct shirt. Georg instructed him immediately to go home and find it. He slunk away, suitably chastened.

We were introduced around, and then Georg took the driver's seat of a small bus that had pulled up outside, and we bowled along about 30 kilometres, turning off just before Schongau into a grand park.

Steins of beer were being hefted by those already present, and the large kegs were being rapidly drained. Many were dressed in traditional lederhosen, so there was much slapping of thighs.

In the big car park was a long pole, fashioned from just one tree, and nearly 20 metres long. We were to witness the ceremony of the raising of the pole. A mechanical digger trundled into the car park, with a grabbing attachment bolted on the front. Straps were manhandled around the bole of the tree, and away we went.

It took half an hour of careful measurement to get it erected in exactly the right position so that it could slot in between the metal supports dug into the ground. When it was in place, more beers had to be drunk to celebrate, and that pole would stay in position for the next four years, until the ceremony was repeated. The pole had been painted with the blue and white chequered colours of Bavaria, and it had little shields sticking out at intervals to represent the local towns of the area.

Then it was finally time for dinner at the restaurant in the park. Over a hundred of us were seated at long trestle tables, with our Oberammergau mob being all together in their yellow tops. There were speeches of welcome, speeches of achievements in the past, speeches by other motor club presidents, and a fine speech by a leading light in ADAC (naturally a close friend of Georg) who had come along to praise our efforts. Cups and shields were presented.

As this all drew to a close, immense dishes of pork and dumplings were laid before us and were attacked with gusto. Even after all that beer, one had an appetite from being out in the fresh air for so long.

Then it was time for dancing and singing, as only Bavarians can do. Georg was still putting away the beers, and my thoughts were turning to the drive back afterwards.

Fortunately, Georg's old rally co-driver had been detailed to take the helm for the way back. It took a lot longer, but the time was passed by choruses of local refrains. Curiously, one much loved one was 'Always Look on the Bright Side of Life' in German, with much whistled accompaniment for the choruses.

I was very proud to have been elected a member of the club, and I now wear my yellow emblazoned polo shirt in Tenerife, much to the puzzlement of the local German population.

I wanted Sally to see Lindau, that wonderful old medieval town on Lake Constance. Ever since I first went there some 20 years previously, I had always thought that the lakeside promenade had to be one of the most beautiful places to spend some time.

Off we set, Georg attacking the bends with customary brio. By gum, but that car could shift. We were glued into the overtaking lane, with the indicator winking permanently to let those in front know that we were coming through. As usual, we were the fastest car on the road. Georg liked to have a bit of fun with Porsches, knowing that I have owned a few in my time. They reach their electronic engine limiters before his hot BMW does, and he enjoyed seeing the surprised expressions on their faces as he cruised past them on the *autobahn*.

Just over an hour later, we got to the old part of Lindau and looked for a parking space near the lake.

We walked down to the waterside, and ambled along the stunning promenade. Sally was entranced, it was all so beautiful. The statue and the lighthouse guarding the entrance to the harbour were immense and impressive, and so large that they could be clearly seen from an aeroplane when flying overhead. It is from here that the old paddle steamers plied their trade across the lake to Konstanz in Switzerland. Nowadays, the boats look just as lovely, but have more modern power.

The lake shimmered in the watery sunlight and we chose one of the terraces on the front to take our tea and coffee. Georg did not surprise us by ordering a cake. The café was part of the lovely old Hotel Reutemann, perfectly modernised and refurbished, and an old haunt of mine. That hotel is idyllic, and could not be better placed. The loos are perfection too and would get 11/10 in one of my newspaper reviews!

Then we strolled around, going back along the waterfront, taking in the warmth of the day and the clarity of the air.

"Are you hungry yet?" asked Georg. He was, as ever, always ready to ruminate.

"Do you have anywhere particular in mind? Is there a better choice than the place that we have just left?" I asked.

"Let's wander into the oldest part of the town and see what we can find. I have eaten there very well in the past."

We ended up standing outside the local Best Western Hotel and my heart sank. However, the restaurant, opening out onto the side of the street, looked immaculate, and there was a menu in a brass holder to tempt us. Interestingly, all of the staff were seated in the restaurant enjoying a meal.

In we went, and the head waiter jumped up from the communal table. Like everyone in the place, he was formally attired in black and white. It all looked very professional.

"How may I help you?"

"Well, it looks as though lunchtime service may be over, as you are all eating. I suppose that we are too late?"

"No sir, not at all. Please come in and be seated. I will bring you menus in just a moment."

We went on to enjoy an excellent meal of fish from Lake Constance, boiled potatoes, green beans and a salad, together with a bottle of local white wine that we were told had been grown from grapes less than three kilometres away. All of the staff were smiling and happy to be of service, even though the hour was late.

And as we later pulled out of Lindau, back towards the main road, Sally agreed with me that it had been just the most perfect place to visit.

Afterwards, we went to the Zeppelin Museum in the next town,

Friedrichshafen, where the original Zeppelins had been constructed. In the museum was a full size partial reconstruction. Nothing could prepare one for seeing just how enormous they were in reality. The engines were colossal.

Just as we were coming to the end of our tour, Georg's mobile phone trilled. He took the call and his face dropped. It was Eta. It seemed that Georg had been having such a good time with us that he had entirely forgotten that he was meant to be hosting a tourism meeting at his hotel that evening. Away we went, this time really with Georg's foot to the floor. It was a good thing that German *autobahnen* were de-restricted. The headlights were on for the duration, and mostly so was the offside indicator. Vehicles scattered in front of us to ease our progress. There was no aggression, other drivers accepting that they should move out of the way for a very rapid car closing on them at a high rate of knots.

We just hung on tight and got back to the hotel just as the first delegates were walking in.

All too soon it was time to strap ourselves in for the repeat experience of the *autobahn* run back to Munich airport, and bid "*Auf wiedersehen*" to our friends in Oberammergau.

Two weeks later, we had a phone call from Georg.

"I'm just going to send you an email with an attachment – I hope you don't mind!"

The email arrived, and the attachment was of a photograph clearly showing someone with an uncanny resemblance to Georg in his sunglasses, passing rapidly by a speed camera. The email informed me that I had been done for speeding! I really could not think why, but the Italian police seemed to be under the impression that it might have been me at the wheel, despite the fact that I was nowhere near Italy on the date in question.

Two more weeks later, another email arrived from Georg. It informed me, as a paid up member of the Oberammergau Motor Sport Club, that the annual jamboree next year would be held in Venice. A luxury coach had already been reserved to take everyone from Oberammergau via Innsbruck and the Brenner Pass down to Venice. In all, it would take a week with visits to Padua, Lake Garda, as well as Venice and other interesting excursions.

I called Georg back straight away.

"We would really love to come along. Count us in."

La Serenissima would be at her best in April, before the heat started to make its presence felt through the city drains.

In my original introduction to the readership of *Island Connections*, I had been labelled as a *critico gastronomico*, but in addition to restaurants, they had also used the word "events" and so occasionally I try to broaden my appeal to the readership. The weekend after we had got home from Bavaria, I saw a poster in the local supermarket for a forthcoming Classic Car Exhibition by a motor club based in La Orotava. It was to take place that very weekend.

Extract from my review of a local classic car rally:

"On the day, and at the appointed hour of 4 p.m., we stood by a small roped off area of the vast car park, and waited, and waited. An hour and a half later, a scarlet Alfa 1750 arrived on the back of a low loader. The Alfa was in full race trim, complete with ballooned and riveted arches, slicks and roll cage. It was gingerly lowered on to the tarmac before being coaxed into life. I assumed that the slicks made it non road legal. An ear shattering roar brought some more bystanders along, but we all had to wait another half an hour before a proper flurry of classic cars descended on us.

There were about 15 of them, some in race trim, such as a variety of hot

Simcas, an NSU TT which had clearly been breathed on quite extensively, a couple of Renault 8s (one sporting reverse Gordini paintwork), a 2002, a Beetle, and the usual SEAT 124 bevy of 1800/2000s in various stages of tune. One of the 124s had an all lady crew on board.

There was a lovely French Alpine A110 in bright (dare one say Canary?) yellow, a change from the more usual and almost standard Alpine blue. Nice condition and its original builders back in Dieppe would have still been proud of it, as was its owner, standing alongside. A heavily modified version took the honours in, I think, 1971 on the Monte Carlo Rally. It was a rally car that swept all before it for a number of years. Some 50 years after it was born, the new pre-production A110-50 was thrown round the GP circuit at Monaco to much acclaim.

Despite the thunder of the Alfa, I chose two stars of the show. One was a Fraser Imp, actually badged as a Sunbeam, in blue and white with a "Tenerife" roof. Much modified, I did like the fact that all of its lines had been brought inboard in very professional fashion. Interestingly, it was also sporting HSCC insignia. The other star was an E9 BMW 3.0 CSL, the clue being in that last "L". Not in A1 condition, it nevertheless was in the correct colour of Chamonix white, with also correct narrow Martini side flashes, and being an "L" for lightweight (as for Leicht in German) it was nevertheless worth more than a bob or two. As there was no front dam it was probably an early model from the '68 to '75 model run. The final incarnation of that car, the famous Batmobile racer, would nowadays command at least six figures, particularly so with any provenance.

The poster had advertised that there was to be something less static taking place the next morning, Sunday. Back we went, to see that more classic cars had been parked nearby in some sort of automotive sympathy. A blue and white Capri gave nothing away, but a lovely Integrale, otherwise de-badged, and sporting a large rear wing and a battery of Cibies on the front, attracted my attention. The wheel arches here had not been ballooned, but were nevertheless extended, just as they had left the factory nearly 30 years ago. Pity about one of the front seats, though, the padding chewed away as though by some crazed canine. In addition, half a dozen SEAT 124s in varying colours were lined up alongside.

Ears were shattered once again, and the earth seemed to move as the racing Alfa fired up all her cylinders. A line formed up and the cars were led in convoy across the main car park and down to a roped off area comprising a circuit round the factory units of the poligono, including a chicane. It took some time to get them all going for a sighting lap, and then they were off.

Even in the heat of the day in Tenerife, racing slicks (a good half a dozen cars were on them) need time and effort to achieve track temperature and work to their optimum. I wondered if that fact had escaped one or two of the participants.

The Alfa roared round, but did not overly excite. The 124s hardly wagged their tails. The lady crew just cruised, but no matter, it was nice to see a well maintained car, which, from the exhaust note, was probably unmodified. One of the R8s decided not to apply sufficient opposite lock on the corner below us and as a result it did a slo-mo 180 and became stuck right on the apex. Much flag waving alerted the approaching convoy while remedial action was oh so slowly taken. I think that the preposterously wide rims on some of the entrants resulted in a conversely diminished turning circle. Later on, the same R8 completed another unheralded 180, much to the delight of the crowd, just before crossing the finishing line around the next corner.

The Fraser Imp never exercised its rear end, as far as I saw. I can't say I blamed the driver, because it was always notoriously difficult to catch when you lost it, the engine hanging over the back, with no suspension geometry to assist you, like that of even an old Porsche.

For me there were two stars. The first was a very quick Simca, white with a red roof and blue arch extensions. Very noisy, too, and with a lovely rasp on the over-run, it was driven with much brio, and I reckon with a quick rack fitted by the way it attacked the turn-ins. The other was the CSL. It seemed so effortless in the way that it cruised around at the same speed as a lot of the racers, and on road tyres at that, occasionally stepping out before being deftly brought back into line.

A great morning out, clearly enjoyed by everyone there, participants and onlookers alike. Such a pity that it suffered from the Tenerife bugbear that seems to dog our tracks: the lack of promotion to the tourists who would have been delighted to attend (especially Dad and his sons) and who would, no doubt, have spent some of their hard earned holiday money into the bargain.

Come on Club de Vehiculos Clasicos Tenerife and the various sponsors involved! Have you fixed the date yet for next year? Tell us about it all, well in advance. Get it into our diaries."

Perhaps I shall soon be promoted to Motoring Correspondent?

27

Poodlemania

We were invited on a free holiday.

The poodles were being temporarily deserted by Peter, who was going back to Devon for a family reunion. He would be away for two weeks, but before he booked his ticket, he wanted to ask us if we could look after the dogs in his absence.

"How are you fixed for a few nights, staying in my house to look after the girls?"

We both adore Peter's dogs. They are great fun, even though they're not the brightest of buttons. Best of all, Freddie will be in seventh heaven. Peter gets the nod straight away.

When the day came, our packing filled three suitcases. We can no longer travel light as we did in our youth. Freddie was going frantic. He knew not what was afoot, but he knew that something special was happening, because his bed was going with him, as well as his magic pills. He sensed an adventure with a capital A.

Peter never can resist leaving us notes of what to do and where to find things. We opened the fridge to put our stuff away.

"Do please use up the spread and finish up the eggs," was written on the first post-it note.

Thank you, Peter. Search as we may, we could find but one egg.

"I have made a lemon jelly for John," was written on the second note.

Why? But I am not an ingrate and it will doubtless slip down easily after dinner.

We put our things into the store cupboard. Here there were yet more notes:

"Use the onions and potatoes, they will only go off."

The potatoes actually had already gone off, and so we threw them away.

"Finish off the chocolate biscuits."

There were only two!

In the freezer there was a little note to tell us to finish off the half used packet of frozen peas.

On the dining room table, there were yet further instructions.

"Please water the new tomato plants every day. Please feed the birds with the bag of seeds left out on the terrace window sill. There are two new palm trees, so could you give them a big drink every day to get them established? The gardener will be coming tomorrow, but I will pay him when I get back."

The lists went on and on. Bless him.

He texted us before he got on the plane, ostensibly to check that we had settled in all right, but we reckoned that he was really checking on how his dogs were. The first telephone call came in the next morning, bright and early whilst we were out with the dogs for their walk to the park. We did not connect, so he left another message.

Later, we texted him back to tell him to push off and have a good holiday. He would hear from us soon enough should something go wrong. And, inevitably, it would.

We could not make the ice maker push out the cubes for our gin and tonics at sundown. An investigation showed that the system was clogged up with cubes, probably because it had not been used for a day or two. The cubes had all fused together. No matter, the judicious use of a sharp knife (one of ours that we brought with us; Peter, like Sally's mother, does not seem to have sharp knives) and there was a clatter of cubes into the receptacle. The situation was retrieved. We made a note to keep it working on a regular basis at sundown each night!

We had brought dinner with us. I had made a chicken casserole, and it would be just the thing for our first night away from home. I could just pop some potatoes into it to finish it off.

But before that, it was time for walkies.

We let the poodles haul us up the hill to the little park, where they could mooch around for a while. Freddie was allowed off the lead, because he had been well trained and would come back to us on command, though we kept our eyes sharply peeled for anything untoward. The poodles could not be let off the lead, even by Peter, because they would just bolt for the horizon, not even fleeing in tandem, should they see anything of interest.

I cast my mind back to one afternoon before Freddie had had his stroke, when we had invited the poodles to join Freddie in Parque Taoro, the big park adjacent to us. Peter slipped their leads, thinking that all would be well in such a large area. One of the poodles spied a cat, which was sitting on a wall at least 100 metres away, and they were both gone in the blink of an eye. Peter shrieked and yelled, and it took us ages to find them, by then well outside the park, and happily grazing a roadside verge.

Most afternoons, our walk would be along the Calle Santiago. A lovely road, quiet, with immaculately kept bungalows on the one side, and rather more majestic houses, mostly owned by Germans, on the other. Those bigger houses would all be worth well over a million euros, probably not less than two million. Fully grown palm trees lined one side of the road. There is an awful lot of old German money on this island.

Half way down the street, as we passed one of the bungalows, the curtains twitched aside and a gentleman, stark naked, stood in the window. He was elderly and, we suspected, lacking some of his marbles as well as his clothing. Unfortunately, he stood well forward in full view as well as full frontal. We had seen him a number of times before, and so simply waved and then looked the other way. Peter had been very put off by this apparition some weeks earlier, and had forsworn to walk past again. It did not bother us, but we did hope that he stayed indoors.

Back at base, it was time for all the dogs to take their evening repast. A disorderly queue formed and bowls were put out on to the back terrace. Freddie attacked his (much smaller) bowl of dried food with gusto as usual, as though there was never going to be another meal during his lifetime. All was gone within a few seconds. The poodles received a combination of wet and dried food, and ate as they walked, slowly and in stately fashion. Some of their food was consumed, and then they turned aside in unison. The procedure, we had been told in one of the numerous notes, was for us to lift their bowls and then hand the food back down to them later on.

No, no, sorry, Peter, that is not our way.

I have always been of the mind that you put down the food, the dog eats it, then the empty bowl is picked up and washed, ready for the next time. It had worked very handily through a number of my dogs, the only exception to the rule being if a dog was feeling unwell. Then they were excused and all routine went out of the window.

It was a rude awakening for them to find that they were stood over and cajoled into eating up most of the contents of their bowls. When they left it, the food went, never to reappear until the next meal. It took but two meals for them to understand the deal, and all was harmonious thereafter.

When we went into the village to do our daily shopping, the dogs came too. It was a pleasure hitching them all up like horses in the Wild West to a convenient post on the pavement. The poodles, being very large, were admired, albeit from afar. Freddie, on the other hand, always seemed to attract a small knot of children who wanted to pet him and ask questions. We told them that he was born back in England, had flown over to the island all by himself (gasps of astonishment!) and spoke perfect English (squeals of surprise!).

The children rushed to tell their mothers all about it. Soon there was a little throng standing still and staring, watching the dogs sitting quietly as we took our morning cuppa. It turned out that unfortunately we had tied their leashes to a bicycle rack, preventing a number of people from getting to work. They were too frightened to approach!

The dogs stayed where they were as we went into the greengrocer's shop. We came out, laden with different fruits and a small bag of potatoes. The poodles started to dance around, and it took a moment or two before we realised that this was part of a ritual and that they were expecting a treat from us, as Peter would have given them. We knew not what, and we didn't want upset tummies, so they had to do without.

Then on we went to the paper shop. One of us held the dogs, and the other disappeared inside to get the local daily Spanish rag. Although we couldn't read every single word, we do read the paper nearly every day to improve our vocabulary, and our understanding of what people were saying. It also gives us a handle on world news, but, since that seems to be uniformly unattractive nowadays, we often pass over it fairly quickly.

That done, we meandered home, exercising the dogs by walking round a couple of extra streets. The flowers on this island never cease to amaze us, and each garden has *bougainvillea* or other similar climbing and flowering shrubs poking over the high walls and through the garden gates. Everywhere was a riot of colour, and we regularly stopped to admire another unknown plant that we discovered.

For the most part, these were long lazy days at Peter's, looking after the dogs. I did a bit of gardening for him, and watered some of the thirstier plants each evening when the sun went down. In the afternoons, we always took a little time out and went home for our swim. Our little foundling usually opted to stay with the poodles.

The next day dawned gloomy, and so we decided to leave the dogs, after they had their walk, and take a trip to the lighting emporium. This was a vast shop situated on the edge of a village further along the coast, just before Icod de los Vinos. We needed two new bedside lights, as ours were really too small and were bought six or so years ago when we were furnishing our place just as a holiday home. Or perhaps it might be nearer to the truth to admit that as we get older, we needed bigger and more powerful lights to read by in bed?

Despite the overhanging clouds, the *"panza de burro"*, it was a pleasant drive. As usual, our coffee stop was at the Texaco garage, *El Mirador*. We sat in the window of the *cafetería* which overhung a huge drop down to the land below, and thence to the sea, which today had white horses prancing about in the bay.

Munching on the shared Danish, Sally spotted a family of pigs way down on the land, running free through the scrub, searching for whatever pigs search for. They were Canarian black pigs, much prized for their ham, and with them was a gorgeous litter of piglets, running hither and thither, their snouts into everything. A huge sow was resting quietly in some shade, presumably having just provided them with their latest liquid meal.

The lighting shop beckoned, so we motored on. As usual, the car park was busy. It did not take long to find a number of lights that would suit us. We were looking for something a bit Spanish. Not too ornate, but something out of the ordinary. We were lucky enough to pick up a matching pair very suitable for our bedroom, with painted wrought iron flowers wound around the stand. A couple of weeks later, Peter called in for tea and Sally proudly showed him our new lights.

"Huh. Dust traps," was all he said. I could have brained him.

On the way home from the lighting emporium, we could not resist stopping at one of the roadside shanties where local fruit and vegetable produce was being sold. There were always, but always, sacks of oranges on sale for very little money. Prickly pears must be in season, but I had never got round to trying them because, frankly, I do not know what to do with them. Also, once, in Corsica, in my youth, I got a tender part of my anatomy rather too close to a prickly pear bush, and I have never forgotten it.

On our return, the poodles leapt about like things possessed to welcome us back. Freddie offered his usual barks of welcome, and hoped to be rewarded with a slice of carrot, his favourite. Back in England he was a sucker for a stick of celery, but he would not touch it over here. Neither of us has ever been able to explain this conundrum.

One night we decided to walk into the village to a newish *tapas* bar that we had recently heard about. The bar was in a quite upmarket restaurant that we had been to a few times before, but, with the recession, everyone was looking for new opportunities to make money. So a *tapas* bar had been created within. We got a cheery nod when we went in, and sat down. We said that we had come for the new *tapas* menu, and a faint cloud passed across the face of the proprietor.

Just why is it that when you ask for something less than the full Monty, you are taken to be a second class citizen? I recall that it happened to us at one particular restaurant in town, and we shall never return there. Rather posh it was, with a high end reputation. We took some people there for lunch to try the menu of the day that we had seen advertised in the local paper. When we asked for that menu, which had not been brought to us, we were almost ignored for the rest of our meal. Just why are many people in the restaurant trade so blinkered?

Anyway, we chose our *tapas*, and had cold German beers to go with them. All was well, and we congratulated the owners on their successful transition to the world of the *tapa*. They looked pleased at last, and so they should, because, in the end, we were paying nearly as much as a "proper" meal would have cost.

Our route back along the main street took us past a little bar owned and run by two gay friends. We got on well with them, and were only sorry that we did not patronise them as much as we would have liked because they were only open in the evenings, and we live in the next town. But there we were, so we could not walk past. There was much jollity and kisses all round as we stood in the entrance to the bar.

We ordered a couple of beers. If we hadn't come from dinner, normally we might have one of their cocktails. The place was packed as usual, with a small party of Scandinavians in residence, as well as the usual locals. I suppose that news travels fast anywhere where there is somewhere good to go.

The dogs had been on their own now for nearly three hours, and it was time to get back to them. They must have their night-time walk down the Calle Santiago, hopefully without the cabaret.

During the night, however, it seemed that we were invaded by a regiment of shock troops all wearing hob-nailed boots. We sat bolt upright in bed, clutching each other, petrified.

Was it burglars?

It would not have surprised us, because one of the ground floor doors had to be left open all night for the poodles. They had never been house trained to hold on all night. This seemed so crazy as to be almost unbelievable, and it had taken us some time to get used to the fact that we were to sleep in a house where just about anybody could call in whilst we were asleep. Only Freddie gave us some confidence, as his bark would raise the dead.

But there had been no bark.

And no, there were no shock troops out there. We deduced that the poodles had decided to go up on to the flat roof in the middle of the night. Not only was this roof immediately above us, so that we could hear their hideous games, but the metal staircase up the side of the building was straight outside our room as well. When all is silent in the middle of the night, those poodles' toe nails on a metal staircase could make one hell of a noise.

I resolved to block off the staircase first thing in the morning.

And so, one day merged into another. The sun shone, the dogs were walked, and we pottered about here and there. The two weeks had flown by, and soon it was time to go home. The poodles hung around, staring morosely at us as we packed, knowing that something was going on. Peter had just texted. His plane had landed a few minutes early, and he would be back in time for lunch. We sloped off, our work complete, and left the poodles to enjoy their ecstasy to come.

As we left, I think that it might have been Freddie that thought of the grand idea to celebrate our homecoming by enjoying a celebratory lunchtime of our own. And so it came to pass...

Extract from my review of a northern coastal restaurant called Mint Jelly:

"A tip-off from Spanish friends led us to the pretty village of El Sauzal in northern Tenerife, to visit a restaurant named Jalea de Menta.

Turning off the TF5 and slaloming down the myriad corners into the town, teetering on the top of the cliffs, we ended up parking opposite the Ayuntamiento. In the little square, more of a triangle really, there was a pleasant terrace on which were six or so tables shaded by their attendant parasols. This was a really attractive spot to while away some time. The Ayuntamiento was a lovely old building, whilst the steps up to it were akin to some vast stairway to heaven in a film set. A fountain tinkled nearby to add to the atmosphere.

We sat in the shade of the restaurant terrace, and ordered a couple of cañas from the friendly waitress. The drinks arrived accompanied by a bowl of olives.

Would we like a table later, asked our waitress?

Well, yes we would, that's the whole idea of it, but she was not to know that I was there with a view to a review. I wandered inside on the pretence of visiting the conveniences. And that is where I came up against a few unexpected shocks. Their loos were very good, even down to small branches of fresh leaves draped over the hand basins.

And the room at the rear, where the restaurant was housed, was a revelation. So prettily laid out, split into various areas, each with their own function. You might choose from comfy seating on settees with low tables for an early evening aperitif before dinner, green plastic chairs for drinks in the bar area, white tables and chairs around the panoramic windows for snacks and coffees throughout the day, or dine on comfy upholstered chairs with smartly dressed tables. It sounds an odd set up, but works very well, as we saw.

From the menu presented in both Spanish and English, we ordered the Potage, a thick homemade soup of verduras (squash, peas, onion, calabacin and potato) with a couple of chunks of chicken breast nestling therein, followed by an Arroz Caldoso de Pescado y Mariscos and Huevos Estrellados con Jamon Iberico. These might translate as a Fish and Shellfish Rice Stew, and a very upmarket breakfast of Double Egg and Chips with Iberico Ham and lots of trimmings.

With our wine, a dry and nicely perfumed Bodega Tajinaste from La Perdoma in the La Orotava valley, we had warm bread accompanied by heart shaped pats of butter and a little pot of tomato pulp with olive oil and herbs. The butter had been infused with caraway and garlic, but both so delicately that they were a delight; a far cry from that usual offering of garlic butter or dip that can be strong enough to strip your tonsils away and leave you craving isolation from any other human being for the following 24 hours.

The arroz caldoso, a little like a moist paella, came complete with a small crab, a large chunk of hake, a handful of tasty prawns and a scattering of lapas (limpets). It was splendid, with the exception of those lapas, which had the constituency of school erasers of old that one might discover in later years languishing deep in your old pencil box; and so earning the plate only 9/10. The huevos estrellados on the other hand scored a perfect 10 for their crunchy chips, generous amount of Iberico ham and brace of runny fried eggs. Was this the perfect breakfast or lunch?

As usual, there was the fractured translation service, and, quoting that, we could have ordered "Studs with vinaigrette and Iberican jam" which turned out to be Asparagus with Iberico ham at €8.50, "Spine of Pollack with prawns" at €12.50 (spine meaning back, saddle or loin) or even "Reed black octopus with pope and king prawns" at €12.50 (layers of octopus with black potatoes and langoustines). I nearly chose the tempting "Watercress salad with cheese in aspic palm jelly" for €7.60 but would have preferred it as Ensalada de Berros con queso en aliño de miel de Palma. *That sounded much more attractive!*

Too full for the offered postres, *of which samples were displayed in a cool cabinet (and great they looked, too), we tottered to the loos whilst the bill was being prepared. Meeting afterwards, we both exclaimed how nice it was to have seen those fronds of fresh leaves draped around the wash basins.*

Someone here clearly cares.

The view from the restaurant was all that you could ask for. Ahead was an uninterrupted view of the ocean, with La Palma just visible in the distance. To the left was El Teide and the Orotava valley, and to the right, a view down the coast to El Pris and the cliff head beyond. You really could not ask for better.

We paid €13.50 for the wine, €4.20 for the Potage, *€10.20 and €12.50 for the two main courses, and very attentive service. And so, some €41 lighter, we bade goodbye and made our way home.*

Here is a place that will cater for your every whim, be it just a coffee on the terrace, an up-market pastry, a beer whilst standing at the bar, aperitifs with friends, a light lunch, or the full works; the choice is yours. Indeed, something for everyone."

I think that Freddie, however, had been rather pleased to get back to his own bed at home at last. He likes to sleep a bit more nowadays, and we are so pleased that he can now shut his eye after we have bathed it and gently rubbed on some soothing ointment. It has become our nightly ritual.

28

Goings and Comings

Sally's mother and father, back in perfidious Albion, were getting on in years; both were in their early nineties. They had led full and interesting lives.

Joan had been a nurse in WW2, and looked after hundreds if not thousands of wounded airmen who were billeted at Lytham Hall in Lancashire. Since then she had been an absolute paragon of a housewife, always putting her husband first, as many of that generation always did.

John had been the owner of a well-known and prestigious motor dealership in the Blackpool area, inherited from his father before him. He was an avid golfer most of his life, continuing to play until well into his eighties, aided by having a friendly "spotter" to mark the destination of each shot on the course. He was a long-time member at Royal Lytham, being Seniors' Captain one year. He had long been registered blind, but had always, since I had known him, retained a bit of peripheral vision and been able to spot a sixpence that someone had dropped on the floor!

He had been visibly ageing these last months, and had a number of falls. His weight was falling away, and realistically, the end would soon be nigh. After yet another of those falls, later bringing on a heart attack, John was taken into Victoria Hospital in Blackpool, and it was pretty clear that he would not be leaving there until he had passed away. Too much care was needed for him to be looked after at home, with Joan almost unable to get up the stairs now through her own infirmity.

Naturally, his children wanted to be there before the end came. And so an open ended plane ticket was purchased, and, sadly, Freddie and I waved Sally off from the airport. She was gone for a while, and then the long expected call came for me too to buy my ticket.

Freddie, understanding none of all this, went off to stay with Peter and the poodles, who themselves were only just back from their latest escapade. How they had got out, nobody knew, but much later the in same day they were found walking the main street of the village, about a mile distant from Peter's house, perfectly happy, and were brought back home by the Chief of Police, no less.

It was a good funeral, as funerals go. Sally's brother delivered a memorable eulogy, and the place was packed. I remember being at a previous funeral where he was chosen to give the eulogy, and where, in his nervousness, he launched into it before the coffin had even arrived. We all sat there looking at our boots until someone had the gumption to stop him in mid flow. I think that it took him a year or two to see the funny side afterwards.

After the funeral service, yours truly was delegated to be in charge of cones and coats, getting back to the house pronto to move the no parking cones, then taking coats from people on arrival. This inevitably made me the primary meeter-and-greeter. In my dark blue suit, crisp shirt and black silk tie, I am quite sure I was taken for the hired help, but no matter.

The outside caterers delivered veritable mountains of food, and the trusty attendees scoffed the lot, including the best little fairy cakes that I have ever eaten. Oh, how Freddie would have liked those cakes. When we were still living in Lytham, John and Joan would come to us or we would pop over to Poulton for tea with them, and Joan would always have a batch of home-made currant buns at the ready. Freddie loved them, recognising the tin when it was brought out, and always barked in the hope of receiving a second helping. He knew her as "Granny with the buns" and he knew exactly what that meant when it was time to go there. There was much anticipatory drooling on the back seat on the way over!

The sad day drew to a close and as always in Lancashire, it ended with a good cup of strong tea, John's favourite, and we all raised our cups to him, in quiet tribute.

He would have appreciated that.

It has been some three months since Sally's father left us, and her mother has just surprised us by accepting our long standing invitation to come to stay for a couple of weeks.

That invitation had long been on the table for both of them, but John could never have made it because of his eyesight and frailness, and Joan would never have left him by himself. One evening the phone rang, the bombshell dropped, and the planning had to start.

Joan's legs are a trouble to her nowadays, so this is going to involve a wheelchair. She can walk a hundred yards or so, on a hard surface, much further on carpet or the like, but then the pain gets too much.

Fortunately, there is an airline that flies out of Blackpool direct to Tenerife at this time of year.

Blackpool International Airport, as it styles itself nowadays, is little more than an extended Nissen hut on an old aerodrome, with Jet2.com, the aforesaid airline, being accommodated in a temporary marquee on the side. It is a rotten place. Parking is crazy, check-in horrible, facilities almost non-existent, and the loos…!

But Jet2.com could not have been more helpful on the phone, offering a service of wheelchair supply, and delivery of Joan to the food service entrance to the plane, so she will be hoisted aloft on a hydraulic ramp, surrounded by piles of sandwiches and bottles of pop.

Would that I could be there with my camera!

She will take it all in her stride, we know, and so all is now ready. A wheelchair has been hired at both ends. Lists have been written of places to go, things to do, where to eat and what to see, whilst she is with us. We will not achieve a quarter of it while she is here for her fortnight in The Fortunate Islands, but we are determined that she will have the best time ever.

And so the waiting is over. All is in place, and the three of us are ready to set off to the airport to collect her. Of course, Freddie must be part of the welcoming committee, expecting her when he sees her, without a shadow of a doubt, to remember his old chum "Granny with the buns" to hand them out to him on arrival, likely scattering pieces of cake around the arrivals hall. There will be gales of laughter all round, and an elderly black and white dog giving a fine impression of a whirling Dervish whilst simultaneously hoovering up that cake.

And now my diary reminds me that on this date, three years ago, we achieved the impossible by moving lock stock and barrel to our hidden corner of this island in the sun.

What have we made of it all? Have our expectations been met? Have we been happy? Have our lives changed? If we could scroll back those three years, would we do it all over again? With a few caveats, I can honestly say a resounding yes.

Of course, there have been highs and lows, as there would have been had we stayed back in England, but certainly there have been so many more highs than lows that they pale into insignificance. We have hit all of the "pros" on my list at the beginning of this book, and the "cons" have, for the most part, evaporated into thin air.

In no particular order, as the saying goes (and yes, we do enjoy Strictly Come Dancing over here!)…

We have laid to rest the problem of the weather that everyone told us made the north of Tenerife a no-go area. Of course, there is a little more rain than in the south of the island, but that is a benefit rather than the other way around. Here everything is green, even during the prolonged dry spell which this year lasted some months.

Being retired here and with excellent air connections, particularly because we can fly back to mainland Spain at half price, we have travelled more than has been recorded here, even though, because of rising aviation fuel costs, our flight tickets have doubled in price.

The local people of Tenerife are a joy, ever kind and helpful in so many ways. And the levels of service are almost beyond our understanding.

We have sought out wonderful restaurants in out of the way places, at prices inconceivable back in England.

We have learned to speak sufficient Spanish to be comfortable in most areas of conversation. We are greatly indebted to Eva. She and her family have become treasured friends.

Spanish administration systems, at first seemingly impenetrable, have fallen into line as our command of the language improved. They just do everything differently in Spain!

As to costs, it is cheaper to live here than in England. Prices do go up, as they do everywhere, but we need no central heating, we live a healthy outdoor life, and it is as cheap to eat out as to eat in, and fuel is half the price. The dreaded VAT, or its equivalent in the duty free Canary Islands, IGIC, is only 7%.

Last but not least, we have fallen in love with this part of the island, our hidden Tenerife. It is indeed a green and pleasant land.

Our original budget has been shot through with holes. We had planned our moving costs and integration in Spain down to the last euro, or so we had thought. Our contingency planning costs were similarly eaten up. Moving abroad is an expensive and serious business, and like others who have told us similar tales, the rapacious financial demons have nibbled away at our assets. But again, overall, has it been worth it? Oh, yes, indeed it has!

So, should you, the reader, dare to dream the impossible dream, then I hope that the pleasure that this book has given me in the writing of it will spur you to take, with a certain confidence, the life changing decision to make your own move, whether on a permanent basis or not. It does not have to be to our hidden Tenerife – perhaps I should even hope that you choose elsewhere, so that we can keep it to ourselves!

But forgive me now; I must away. A cold nose is insistently pressing against my leg. Freddie is demanding his morning constitutional. Like two old codgers, bent and warped with age, we will take a turn or two around the park together. The sun is shining, the air is crystal clear, and, as usual, it is going to be another perfect Canary day.

Adiós y hasta luego!

Restaurant Review List

Here are contact details for a few of the places that have been the subjects of my newspaper reviews. All are just that bit out of the ordinary. Some may have a wonderful view, some may have an inventive chef, some may be in out of the way places, and some may combine all three. Please do offer them your patronage should you visit the island, but do bear in mind that ownership, chefs, quality and opening hours may have changed since this list was compiled.

Asadores La Villa
Calle Molinos de Gofio, Edf. San Jeronimo, Local 11, Poligono
San Jeronimo, La Orotava, Tenerife
Tel: 922 336 173
Open: Daily
Loo Score: 8/10

Bodegón Campestre
Ctra. General Las Cañadas, Km7 La Esperanza, El Rosario,
Tenerife
Tel: 922 297 112
Open: 1200 to 1200. Closed Monday
Loo Score: 6/10

Bodega El Raspon
Camino Tafuriaste 30, Las Candias, La Orotava, Tenerife
Tel: 922 326 757
Closed: Monday and Tuesday
Loo Score: 5/10

Bodegón Matias
Calle Guanche 2, Los Pinos, La Orotava, Tenerife
Tel: 922 320 259
Closed: Mondays
Loo Score: 6/10

Bodeguita Tito
Camino del Durazno 1, Puerto de la Cruz, Tenerife
Tel: 647 933 433.
Open: daily from 12.30 to 23.00 except Sundays

El Acueducto
Avenida de Canarias 23, Los Realejos, Tenerife
Tel: 922 353 792
Closed: Sunday
Loo Score: 6/10

El Ayanto

Calle San Agustin 7, La Orotava, Tenerife
Tel: 922 326 592
Open: Daily
Loo Score: 9/10

El Caldero

Calle El Cabezo 8, Paseo Maritimo, La Caleta, Costa Adeje,
Tenerife
Tel: 922 168 099
Open: Daily to 11 p.m.
Loo Score: 7/10

El Mercado del Agricultor

TF5, Km 49, La Guancha, Icod de los Vinos, Tenerife
Open: Saturday and Sunday throughout the year
until about 2 p.m.
Loo Score: 7/10

El Mundial 82

Calle La Marina 18, La Caleta de Interian, Los Silos, Tenerife
Tel: 922 840 969
Open: 12 noon to 10.30 p.m. every day except Wednesdays
(closure)
Loo score: 5/10

El Padrino
Calle El Lomo 17, 38400 Puerto de la Cruz, Tenerife
Tel: 922 382 937
Open: Evenings and Sunday lunch. Closed Mondays
Loo Score: 7/10

El Tenderete
Los Afligidos 11, La Montañeta, 38419 Los Realejos, Tenerife
Tel: 922 342 594
Open: 1900 to 2300. Closed Monday
Loo Score: 5/10

Guachinche El Moral
Calle Nueva 73 a/a, La Corujera, Sta. Ursula. Tenerife
Tel: 647 540 594
Open: Thursday to Saturday 12.30 to 23.00. Sundays from 12.30
to 17.00
Loo Score: 7/10

Guachinche Polo (Bodega Hermanos Polo)
Calle Alzados Guanche, Pinolere 38310, La Orotava, Tenerife
Tel: 661 065 506 and 606 581 778
Open: Wednesday to Sunday, from 1 p.m.
Loo Score: 2/10

Jalea de Menta
Av. Inmaculada s/n, 38360 El Sauzal, Tenerife
Tel: 922 571 775
Closed: Mondays
Loo Score: 9/10

La Cocina Di Dona Rosa
Av. Maritima 23, Playa San Marcos, Icod de los Vinos, Tenerife
Tel: 92 81 34 65
Open: Daily
Loo Score: 4/10

La Cúpula
Hotel Jardines de Nivaria,
Calle Paris, Playa Fañabé, 38660 Costa Adeje, Tenerife.
Tel: 922 713 333
Open: 7 p.m. to 11 p.m. daily. Closed Sunday.
Loo Score: 10/10

La Solera
Calle Laurel 2, La Montaña, 38410 Los Realejos, Tenerife
Tel: 922 354 535
Open: 12 noon to 4.30 p.m. and 7 p.m. to 11.30 p.m. Closed
Wednesdays
Loo Score: 7/10

Mirador de Humboldt

Ctra. Pinito s/n, 38300 La Orotava, Tenerife

Tel: 681 092 267

Open: Daily until dusk

Loo Score: 6/10

Terraza Taoro

Ctra. El Taoro 9, 38400 Puerto de la Cruz. Tenerife

Tel: 922 388 868

Open: Daily

Loo Score: 5/10

And finally, should you ever find yourself in Bavaria, I can thoroughly recommend a typical Bavarian hotel in a picture perfect village, home to the world famous Passion Play:

Hotel Turmwirt

Ettalerstrasse 2, D – 82487 Oberammergau, Bavaria, Germany

Tel: 00 49 88 22 92 600

Open: All year

www.turmwirt.de